PRAISE FOR *THE CONTEMPORARY CFO*

'Brilliant! An insightful and highly relevant view into the ongoing evolution of the CFO role and the transformation of the finance function and companies more generally.'
Tony Latham, Chief Financial Officer, Bacardi

'Business are changing, evolving and adapting at a pace never seen before. CFOs are expected to play multi-dimensional roles, drive the transformation, foster capabilities and deliver performance. By framing the role through the lenses of a digital engineer, entrepreneur and economist, Michael Haupt has brought to life the impact a strong CFO can create, for winning both today and tomorrow. This book is a treatise on many highly relevant topics with key insights and practical implementation actions. A must-read for all professionals.'
Srinivas Phatak, Executive Vice President Finance, Unilever

'An essential read for CFOs, and an asset for the wider executive team. By dividing the content into three parts, the book explores the central role of the CFO but also addresses relationships to peers on the board, the need for contemporary finance leaders to integrate across functions and the necessary tools for modern corporate governance in changing times.'
Christian Langer, Chief Digital Officer, HHLA Hamburger Hafen und Logistic AG, and former Chief Digital Officer, Lufthansa AG

'Spot-on! Michael Haupt superbly describes how technology is as essential to finance today as double entry accounting has been for centuries. He provides concrete clues to help a CFO navigate through a digital finance transformation, keeping in mind that data is its Alpha and Omega'
Christophe Lambinet, Global Head of Finance, Legal and Compliance Technology, Nestlé

'This book is a super-interesting read and details how CFOs should be a driver of change rather than be driven by it. Creating an inspiring work environment and developing psychological safety within the team is, I believe, key to successful transformation, along with choosing the right people for

the team with the right mindset and allowing them the space to come up with bold new ideas, work on projects, develop an intrapreneurial spirit and establish a culture that embraces mistakes as learning opportunities.'
Sonja Simon, Chief Financial Officer, SAP Latin America

'An excellent, actionable guide for current and future finance leaders seeking to drive sustainable growth and value creation in an increasingly complex and interconnected business environment.'
Mark Shadrack, Chief Operating Officer, Hope and Homes for Children, and former Vice President Finance, Unilever

'A powerful insight into the changing landscape and role of CFOs in this dynamic environment – reminding me of many inspiring conversations with Michael Haupt and our Finance Leader Round Table.'
Anoop Aggarwal, Chief Financial Officer, Mars Pet Nutrition, and former Vice President Finance, Digital and Staff Officer, Mars Incorporated

'Talking about the future is always hypothetical and speculative. *The Contemporary CFO* brings it to the point: future is happening now. This makes the book unique: a clear blueprint and call for action for finance executives, supported by extensive original research at academic standards, combined with exclusive insights from in-depth interviews with top management and hands-on experiences from delivering transformational change in leading global organizations.'
Ulrich Kloubert, board member, TechFunder, and former academic director, GEM Global E-Management, University of Cologne

'A must-read for leaders keen to understand and apply the principles underpinning successful digital transformation. Packed with timely yet timeless insights about business performance and growth in a connected world, this is an essential guide for finance, business and technology executives.'
Mark Waller, Chief Digital Strategist, TechShifts Media

'Michael Haupt has written a must-read for CFOs and their teams who really want to make the digital finance leap. This book helps finance leaders not to go after all the bells and whistles but focus on what really matters to drive transformational change.'
Mohamed Bouker, Partner at Deloitte, and co-author of *The CFO in Pole Position*

The Contemporary CFO

*How finance leaders can drive
business transformation, performance
and growth in a connected world*

Michael Haupt

KoganPage

First published in Great Britain and the United States in 2022 by Kogan Page Limited

2nd Floor, 45 Gee Street
London
EC1V 3RS
United Kingdom

8 W 38th Street, Suite 902
New York, NY 10018
USA

4737/23 Ansari Road
Daryaganj
New Delhi 110002
India

www.koganpage.com

Kogan Page books are printed on paper from sustainable forests.

ISBNs

Hardback   978 1 3986 0293 9
Paperback 978 1 3986 0290 8
Ebook   978 1 3986 0291 5

British Library Cataloguing-in-Publication Data
A CIP record for this book is available from the British Library.

Library of Congress Cataloging-in-Publication Data
Names: Haupt, Michael (Leader of finance), author.
Title: The contemporary CFO: how finance leaders can drive business
   transformation, performance and growth in a connected world / Michael
   Haupt.
Description: New York, NY: Kogan Page Inc, 2021. | Includes
   bibliographical references and index.
Identifiers: LCCN 2021035993 (print) | LCCN 2021035994 (ebook) | ISBN
   9781398602908 (paperback) | ISBN 9781398602939 (hardback) | ISBN
   9781398602915 (ebook)
Subjects: LCSH: Chief financial officers. | Leadership. | Organizational
   change. | Strategic planning.
Classification: LCC HG4027.35 .H38 2021 (print) | LCC HG4027.35 (ebook) |
   DDC 658.15–dc23
LC record available at https://lccn.loc.gov/2021035993
LC ebook record available at https://lccn.loc.gov/2021035994

Typeset by Integra Software Services, Pondicherry
Print production managed by Jellyfish
Printed and bound by CPI Group (UK) Ltd, Croydon, CR0 4YY

CONTENTS

LIST OF FIGURES

ABOUT THE AUTHOR

Michael Haupt is a Partner in Deloitte Consulting, based in London, UK. He is a senior business and thought leader of Deloitte's Finance, Performance Management and Technology practice in Europe. Michael works very closely with many senior finance, business and technology executives of leading global companies. He has written *The Contemporary CFO* to help current and future finance leaders drive business transformation and performance with a focus on sustainable growth and long-term, multistakeholder value creation. He donates the royalties of this book to charities dedicated to helping children in need.

PREFACE

As I write this, our global economy is going through a profound transformational change, which is forcing us to rethink how our companies work and create value. Indeed, it causes us to question what 'work' and 'value' actually mean. Everyone talks about the Digital Revolution, and no company is immune to it. The good news is that the majority of companies, big or small, can benefit from it – if they transform accordingly. The transformation of our economy and our companies is enabled by extraordinary technology innovation but shouldn't be limited by it. Rather, it is an opportunity to harness multiple converging trends to create a more human-centred, inclusive and sustainable contribution to society.

Covid-19 has significantly accelerated and amplified these trends. While some business leaders can't wait to 'get back to normal', others have begun to recognize the opportunity to leave the past behind and to reimagine how their organizations operate – not just to survive the next wave of turbulences but to thrive in our increasingly fast-changing, connected world. This book is written for the latter, specifically for the current and next generation of CFOs and finance leaders in large, established corporations – a group of leaders that I have had the privilege to work with for many years, and that I believe can make a meaningful contribution, not just in finance but in business and society overall. That said, this book is equally relevant for the wider group of corporate leaders in business, operations and technology, who have taken on strategic roles and responsibilities for driving digital business transformation, performance and growth in their organizations.

Writing a book in times of turbulent change and uncertainty is challenging. There are no best practices, no benchmarks and no quick fixes to be shared. However, dealing with turbulences and uncertainty is not new; significant key learnings, combined with the new realities of the connected world, can provide finance leaders with valuable new perspectives and insights on how to shape the way forward. My goal is to explore these key learnings, new realities and perspectives – drawing on my own experiences in delivering transformational change in leading global organizations, countless conversations with senior leaders in finance, business and technology, and an extensive review of the latest research and relevant literature.

It is not my intention to provide a detailed, easy-to-follow playbook on how to deliver business transformation, performance and growth successfully. Any attempt to do so is likely to fail – the situation of each company is different, and there is simply too much change at present. Instead, the aim of this book is to help leaders ask the right questions in shaping an individual journey for their companies.

While there is great insight to be gained by exploring the Digital Revolution at a principle level, the book is not a philosophical study, but a call to action. It focuses on what leaders can and should do, *today*, to help prepare their organization for *tomorrow*. Looking ahead, times are very likely to remain turbulent; and yet, as Peter Drucker reminded us in his 1980 book *Managing in Turbulent Times*, 'the greatest danger in times of turbulence is not the turbulence itself, but to act with *yesterday's* logic'.

Writing this book has been a rewarding journey, which significantly enriched my thinking and enlivened my conversations and work with my clients and teams. I hope that by sharing my own discoveries, others may also feel encouraged to ask new questions, and create new ideas, insights and inspirations that will help them lead the necessary transformational changes ahead.

ACKNOWLEDGEMENTS

Like every book, this one is the result of many direct and indirect contributions, and the kind support of many people to whom I am grateful, and who I like to acknowledge here.

I should begin by thanking Dr Ulrich Kloubert and Mark Waller for their continuous encouragement, constructive challenge and inspiration.

One of the most valuable gifts that you can receive as an author is feedback from your target audience. Many experienced finance and business leaders have shared valuable insights that have helped shape this book, be it through focused interviews, work-related dialogue or personal conversations. I am particularly grateful for the input from the members of my 'Finance Leader Round Table', in particular Mark Shadrack, Sara Heuer and Anoop Aggarwal.

Deloitte is, in many ways, a remarkable organization and it would not be possible to mention all the people who, directly or indirectly, have contributed to the development of this book. Yet, there are some individuals who deserve particular mention.

First, I am very fortunate to work with a very talented team, who contributed directly through their inputs and feedbacks on the manuscript, but even more so indirectly through their work across our many clients. Being a partner is a rather intensive role, and it would simply not be possible to find the extra capacity and energy needed to write a book without a strong team – so, my gratitude and special thanks go to Alice Stephen, Srini Raghunathan, Tim Leung, Payal Shah, Mateus Begossi, Matt Stallard, Andre Jansen, Nabanita Gosh, Katherine Goodes, Stephen Flavahan, Chris Rees, Jeevi Paramanathan, Ed Demirciler and Boyka Komsulova for all their outstanding work and support over the last years.

Second, there are my fellow partners Simon Kerton-Johnson, Neil Jones, Simon Barnes, Rob Cullen, David Anderson, Jonathan Calascione and Nigel Wixcey, as well as my global colleagues and finance consulting leaders Jason Dess, Dean Hobbs, Matthew Pieroni, Mohamed Bouker and many others, who provided valuable insights, guidance and perspectives.

Third, there are Stephen Marshall and Sam Axten, who were incredibly helpful in navigating Deloitte internal compliance and legal requirements, and in shaping our formal partnership with Kogan Page.

Finally, I would also like to acknowledge two former Deloitte partners. First, Stephen Ehrenhalt, for his sponsorship in shaping my/our early thinking about 'Finance in a Digital World', as well as for supporting me and my team in key moments that mattered. Second, Jonathan Copulsky, whom I met during a climbing expedition at Kilimanjaro in 2016. Jonathan introduced himself to me as a senior partner of our US firm, when he saw me sitting in front of a mountain ranger hut with a Deloitte-branded pen – preparing my partner case for the next round of panels due to take place in London just one day after returning from Tanzania. Not only did we talk about the physical mountain in front of us (which both of us managed to summit a few days later), and the professional mountain in front of me (which I managed to 'summit' that year), but also the intellectual mountain and satisfaction of writing a book (Jonathan had published a book, *Brand Resilience,* as a Deloitte partner in 2011). Since our initial encounter in Tanzania in 2016, Jonathan kindly provided further encouragement and guidance on how to approach the development and publication of a book, as well as on how to balance the demands of becoming a partner and author – all of which was invaluable to me. It is perhaps also worth mentioning that Jonathan went on to co-author and publish his second book, *The Technology Fallacy,* in 2019 – a research-based exploration of *digital maturity* and *digital business transformation*, and a source of inspiration and insight that has been referenced multiple times throughout this book.

Furthermore, I would like to acknowledge the outstanding guidance and support that I have received by my copy development and publishing team. This includes Emma Murray and Philip Whiteley, who – very patiently – introduced me to the world of writing and publishing; as well as Amy Minshull and Adam Cox and the highly professional, collegial and supportive team at Kogan Page – with all of whom I am looking forward to collaborate again in future.

The greatest thanks go to my wonderful wife Juliane – my greatest inspiration, biggest support and best friend. This book is dedicated to her, and to our children, with my deepest love, joy and gratitude.

DONATIONS OF ROYALTIES AND DISCLAIMER

Donations of royalties

All royalties from this book will be donated to support children in need. As intended at the time of writing in March 2021, the donations will benefit the following two charitable organizations.

Deloitte 5 Million Futures (5MF)

Deloitte 5 Million Futures (5MF) is the Deloitte North South Europe (NSE) social impact strategy, aiming to help five million people get to where they want to be through access to education and employment. 5MF seeks to address inequality by overcoming barriers to education and employment, empowering individuals with the skills needed to succeed in the economy. Focused on inclusion and aligned to the UN's Sustainable Development Goals, 5MF is part of Deloitte's Global WorldClass commitment to empower 50 million people by 2030 – one of the ways Deloitte is aiming to bring the firm's purpose to life by making an impact that matters.

Hope and Homes for Children

Hope and Homes for Children is driven by a vision of a world in which children no longer suffer institutional care, and in which every child grows up in a loving family. Contrary to what many people believe, orphanages and other forms of institutional care do not protect children. They have devastating consequences, exposing them to abuse, neglect, bullying and loneliness, harming their development and denying them a voice. They are also unnecessary. Some 80 per cent of children in orphanages have at least one living parent who, with the right support, can better protect and care for them. By closing institutions, reuniting families, building new families and working with governments to provide family-based support and services, Hope and Homes for Children is working towards a day when every child can grow up in a loving family. More information can be found at www.hopeandhomes.org.

Disclaimer

This book has been written in general terms and while the key authors and contributors are working for Deloitte, it is recommended that you obtain professional advice before acting or refraining from action on any of the contents of this book. Deloitte LLP accepts no liability for any loss occasioned to any person acting or refraining from action as a result of any material in this book. Deloitte LLP is a limited liability partnership registered in England and Wales with registered number OC303675 and its registered office at 1 New Street Square, London EC4A 3HQ, United Kingdom. Deloitte LLP is the United Kingdom affiliate of Deloitte NSE LLP, a member firm of Deloitte Touche Tohmatsu Limited, a UK private company limited by guarantee (DTTL). DTTL and each of its member firms are legally separate and independent entities. DTTL and Deloitte NSE LLP do not provide services to clients.

Introduction

The connected world

We are living in the middle of a digital revolution, and no industry is safe from its influence. The emergence of new technology has a profound effect on the way we do things – both personally and professionally. By 2030 an additional five billion people are predicted to join the digital world, meaning that most of the projected eight and a half billion people aged six years and older will be connected via the world wide web.[1] Most of us will own and use many highly connected devices in parallel, which will add to the exponentially growing ecosystem of 'smart' machines. Both humans and machines will interact in radical new and expanding ways, benefiting from a rapidly growing global network infrastructure that is expected to run at least a hundred times faster than it does now.

What was once science fiction is fast becoming reality. In 2002, the science fiction movie *Minority Report* (set in 2045) gave us some seemingly outlandish futuristic concepts,[2] yet most of them have already started to become part of our everyday lives: driverless cars, voice-controlled homes, facial and optical recognition and multi-touch interfaces, to name a few, reminding us of the deeply human weakness of thinking exponentially. According to Google director Ray Kurzweil, people intuitively gravitate to think in a linear way, and thus – against better judgement – significantly underestimate the speed and extent of future expansion and development. 'Today everyone expects continuous, linear development in technical advances, but the future will surprise us far more dramatically than most observers believe', Kurzweil says. 'Very few understand what it will mean for the pace of change to accelerate even faster.'[3]

Indeed, it seems almost unfathomable that the size of the 'digital universe' was predicted in 2017 to begin doubling at least every two years, leading to an explosion of data – the 'raw material' and 'fuel' which supports accelerated growth through innovation, global collaboration and knowledge-sharing.[4]

Only organizations that fully embrace the digital revolution will be able to benefit from the boundless opportunities presented by the connected world.

A need for transformational change

Indeed, the connected world is already reshaping our economic landscape to such a degree that most businesses are forced to change fundamentally now, or accept the reality of being left behind. Companies that have become the leaders in their industry by delivering continuous, sustainable growth and profits will suddenly be at risk of losing their customers, as new, fast-growing and digitally-enabled businesses will enter and reshape their industry sectors and markets.

We have already witnessed the fates of companies that turn a blind eye to this reality. Video and game rental service company Blockbuster, photography specialists Kodak and Polaroid, bookstore chain Borders are just a few common examples of companies that experienced the disruptive impact of digital innovation. But the media and book industries are not the only ones affected: industries across all sectors face disruption. Anyone who hopes that one's own industry sector and organization may not be affected and chooses to continue along as before is likely to make a risky call. Every company is likely to be affected – it's just a question of time and severity until the old business model is being challenged, and in many cases at risk of being rendered obsolete. This does not necessarily mean that every company must change their business model overnight, but that most organizations will need to evolve much faster in order to keep pace with our rapidly evolving connected world, and that the majority of companies may find that they need to do business in very different ways. And, as the rate of economic change and evolution accelerates further, it is not entirely unrealistic that the average lifespan of S&P (Standard & Poor's) 500 listed companies is expected to shrink to less than 12 years by 2030.[5]

Organizations must learn to thrive in this era of accelerated and often unexpected change and defend themselves against the risk of being left behind. They must be prepared to capitalize on new and often unexpected growth opportunities; to rise to ever-present and unseen risks and challenges by reinventing themselves and the way they do business proactively, fundamentally and continuously; to take a much greater responsibility to resolve the major societal and environmental challenges of our time. To do all this, organizations need, perhaps most of all, strong leadership. And while changes on this level will need the support of a wide range of corporate leaders and stakeholders alike, the Chief Financial Officer (CFO) may have a particularly important role to play in preparing for the change to come – not only in relation to their own finance teams, but in the business as a whole.

The expanding role and remit of the CFO

While CFOs continue to be responsible for managing the finance function, the level of reach and influence of their role extends far beyond functional and indeed organizational boundaries. The old stereotype of a mere 'book-keeper' is long outdated. In most companies, only the Chief Executive Officer (CEO) wields as much influence as the CFO. Most other executives who operate at board level play an important role, of course, but their remit tends to be focused on driving a specific business unit or function, which limits their ability to drive end-to-end transformational change across the company.

The growing number of CFOs appointed to take on company-wide responsibilities for driving digital business transformation, as observed in CFO surveys, indicates the expanding role and influence of the CFO.[6] Armed with extensive experience of operating across business functions, and supported by a highly influential leadership team – which in most corporations not only includes a wide network of finance leaders operating at corporate, business unit and market level, but often also the Chief Information Officer (CIO), the Chief Data Officer and the Head of Global Business Services – it is obvious that CFOs are uniquely well-positioned to lead or co-lead technology-enabled and enterprise-wide transformation.

In some companies, the CFO has taken on key responsibilities of the Chief Operating Officer (COO) – in fact, studies indicate that the trend to create a combined CFO/COO role began growing considerably in the 2010s and 2020s.[7] In companies with a separate role structure, CFOs have to collaborate more closely with COOs and other executives to drive transformational business change. Finally, considering the need to take a wide range of external stakeholders, such as investors, board directors and regulators along on this journey, CFOs will need to be at the centre of shaping the long-term, multi-stakeholder value-creation strategy for the connected world – a powerful but also challenging prospect in these ever-fluctuating times.

While the future of work in finance may need further clarification and refinement within the context of an increasingly digitized, cross-functionally operating organization (a topic that we will explore further throughout the book), the remit of the CFO and their direct leadership team continues to grow rapidly – as do the expectations on the CFO. Study after study confirms that the expectations of CEOs on the CFO have increased significantly. According to Charles Holley, former CFO of Walmart, CEOs seek CFOs who, over and above all traditional responsibilities, can help their peers make the right decisions and understand the implications of those decisions for the whole company.[8] These CFOs are tireless change agents and strong communicators who can interact effectively with a wide range of stakeholders.

At times, CFOs appear to be held to a higher standard than anyone else in the company, largely because of the responsibility they hold in protecting the company while driving transformational change to meet uncertain needs in the connected world. But how are current and ongoing CFOs coping with these rising expectations?

From a CFO perspective

During Deloitte's UK CFO Vision Conference in 2020, CFOs of leading global corporations indicated that, on average, they are already spending more than 50 per cent of their time on driving business transformation – a trend that the majority of finance leaders expect to increase even further.[9] Asked about the main focus areas of their transformational activities, they stated that – in addition to a continued focus on enterprise-wide cost reduction and ongoing business portfolio changes – the digital transformation of the core business had become a top priority. In interviews and conversations with CFOs about their evolving roles and responsibilities in driving digital business transformation, CFOs specifically called out the need to transform their core business processes and operations (especially the standardization and digitization of core processes, data and systems platforms), the development of new management practices to enhance performance and growth within an increasingly fast-changing and uncertain business environment (especially the adoption of new, more dynamic approaches to resource allocation, planning and performance management), the integration of new digital business models (especially the management of new revenue and profit models), the management of risks (especially cyber security and new risks associated with new business and profit models), and sustainability (especially the requirements related to environmental, social and corporate governance (ESG), and 'the race to net-zero').

And while the majority of CFOs seem to embrace and thrive on these new responsibilities, most finance leaders also highlighted a number of challenges to progress at pace and at scale, especially the limitations created by old and fragmented operational infrastructure, as well as a lack of capabilities and capacity to deliver a complex, technology-enabled business transformation, at the same time as navigating an increasingly unpredictable and often turbulent business environment. That said, CFOs also recognized the evolving dilemma related to this: while it is accepted that these commonly raised challenges can create significant barriers to change, they can often only be resolved through transformational change itself – and as such, would have to be addressed upfront.

From a business perspective

When Deloitte asked about 150 senior business leaders (outside finance) in leading global organizations about the fast-evolving role of the CFO, nearly 80 per cent agreed or strongly agreed that their finance leaders have an important critical role to play in shaping and driving the wider digital transformation of the business;[10] however, less than 50 per cent felt that their finance leaders and teams have yet to develop the necessary capabilities to meet these expectations. Among other aspects, the business leaders indicated a lack of support from finance in shaping the overall transformation strategy and business case (56 per cent), the investment planning and execution (50 per cent), as well as the measurement and the communications of the return on investment (52 per cent) from their digital strategy.

In a series of follow-up interviews with senior business leaders, in particular those in charge of driving key aspects of digital business transformation, it was further highlighted that in order to deliver wider transformational change on behalf, or in direct support, of the business, current and future finance leaders would have to shift their focus away from driving short-term cost reduction and profit maximization towards generating long-term business performance improvement and growth. Also, while risk management was acknowledged as an increasingly important and business critical capability, most business leaders indicated that CFOs would have to move away from an attempt to avoid risks through rigid controls towards a more entrepreneurial approach that embraces risk taking as a key prerequisite and driver of value creation, and that creates more space for experimentation-driven learning and innovation. Most business leaders are generally confident that their CFOs are able to lead key aspects of digital transformation on behalf of the business, yet also indicated that they would expect their current and future finance leaders to dedicate more time to the development of people capabilities and leadership skills, and cultural change, as well as to the adaptation of core business and financial management processes to help enhance the speed, agility and resilience of the business overall.

In essence, most finance and business leaders recognize the urgent need for transformational change, and the critical role CFOs and their teams can and have to play in driving key aspects of it. Yet, while most finance leaders are used to managing transformational change, both sides acknowledge that the digital revolution represents a range of new challenges that they have not seen before – and that not only require a modernized infrastructure, but potentially also a fundamentally new approach to business strategy, new (performance) management practices, new people and leadership capabilities, as well as cultural change. Within this context, most business and finance leaders highlighted that the level of (ongoing) business change required is creating significant pressure on themselves, their organizations and their people, especially in times of economic and social turbulences, yet any attempt to 'play safe' may result in significant long-term risks for their business. Simply 'doing nothing', or even just 'doing something', or 'just doing finance only' are not options for the majority of organizations. As one CFO of a leading Fortune 100 company puts it: 'As senior leaders, we simply need to understand that the world will continue to move even faster. We need to prepare ourselves to meet the demands for a business we haven't even seen yet.'[11]

Developing digital maturity (and how this book can help)

The goal of this book is to help CFOs address the key drivers of a wider transformational business change and, more specifically, to explore and specify the role that current and future finance leaders can play in driving *digital maturity*.

Digital maturity, as defined and applied in this book, is not just about technology and it is not just about what technology enables. Digitally maturing organizations are able to adapt and align their strategy, structures, capabilities and culture to a business environment that is increasingly defined by technology. As research shows (see following box), companies with high digital maturity tend to derive greater business benefits from ongoing digital technology innovations, as well as from their investments in delivering technology-enabled business transformation.

With this in mind, the focus of this book is less about the implementation and the mastery of specific digital technologies, and more about the role that finance leaders can and should play in driving sustainable business transformation, growth and performance in a connected world.

DIGITAL MATURITY AS A KEY DRIVER FOR LONG-TERM BUSINESS PERFORMANCE AND GROWTH

The proposed definition of *digital maturity* draws on established organizational theory that was originally developed by David Nadler and Michael Tuschman in 1980,[12] and that has been adopted in a series of relevant research projects and reports, including an annual global executive study that has been conducted by *MIT Sloan Management Review* in collaboration with Deloitte Digital since 2015, as well as a range of related executive surveys and studies conducted by Deloitte in the late 2010s and early 2020s[13] and which emphasize the importance of *organizational congruence* as the primary driver for business performance.[14]

Organizational congruence means that a company can only succeed when the strategy, the work to deliver the strategy, the people who do the work, and the enabling organizational structure, capabilities and culture, have been sufficiently developed and aligned. This applies not just within the context of the organization itself but – perhaps even more importantly – also within the context of a fast-evolving economy. Within this context, digital maturity is not a fixed target, but rather describes the organizational agility and ability to adapt to, and benefit from, a continuously changing and largely technology-driven business environment.

While the strategy and approach to *digital business transformation* is unique to each company, digitally maturing organizations tend to share some common traits. In search of these traits and the pivotal factors that can lead to digital maturity, *MIT Sloan Management Review* and Deloitte carried out a range of comprehensive research studies, including a global survey of over 16,000 business leaders over a period of four years.[15] In addition, individual member firms within the Deloitte network carried out a number of related regional surveys.

The key findings from this research, coupled with insight from practical experience in delivering digital transformation, as well as ongoing conversations with business, finance and technology leaders, has resulted in a crystallized set of core traits and pivotal factors that appear to help organizations derive greater business impact and benefit from their digital transformational efforts – or in other words, become a digitally maturing company:

- **Tangible factors:** There are several tangible traits and pivotal factors that are characteristic for digitally maturing companies. Some of these factors are foundational, which means that they are necessary to develop other factors, and therefore should be prioritized in developing a digital transformation strategy. These include *intelligent process automation*, *data mastery*, *people and organization development*, as well as a scalable and secure *technology infrastructure*. Once in place, these foundational factors can enable a company to accelerate the development of enhanced traits and factors of digital maturity, including a *unified customer experience*, the development of *digital business models* and the participation in *digital business ecosystems*.

- **Intangible factors:** While developing these tangible traits is essential, organizations need to do more to achieve higher-level digital maturity. According to the Deloitte research, only about 60 per cent of organizations that have developed most of their tangible traits were able to reach a median level of digital maturity.[16] This indicates that there are other 'intangible' factors that play an important role, including the development of new *digital leadership skills*, the adoption of alternative approaches to *planning and performance management*, and *cultural and behavioural changes* needed to promote *entrepreneurship, cross-functional collaboration and continuous learning*.

To summarize, companies that want to achieve a high level of digital maturity will have to adopt a transformation strategy that balances the development of both tangible and intangible traits and factors. CFOs should feel encouraged to sponsor and support this path: the research conducted by Deloitte clearly associates high-level digital maturity with superior financial performance results. In fact, about half of the surveyed higher-maturity organizations reported that their net profit margin and their revenues were significantly above the industry average.

That said, the Deloitte research also highlights that in order to achieve high-level digital maturity, most organizations and their leaders – and especially also their finance leaders – will have to adopt a new mindset, which encourages the habit of looking at old problems with new eyes. Executives play an important role in cultivating this mindset by adopting new perspectives and new ways of thinking – key aspects that have influenced the structure of this book.

New perspectives for CFOs (and how this book is structured)

Not every CFO will need to become an accomplished digital leader to deliver a digital business transformation; however, there are new perspectives, learnings and insights that finance leaders and their teams may find useful to help them develop the digital maturity of their company. The exploration of these perspectives, learnings and insights form the foundations for this book.

In Part One, we will discuss what a CFO can do to build the foundations of a digitally maturing organization. By applying the perspective of a *digital engineer* – with a particular focus on customer-centricity and *the art of design thinking* – we will explore the need to reimagine and transform core business *processes* (Chapter 2), *data* (Chapter 3) and *people* capabilities (Chapter 4).

In Part Two, we will focus on the role that CFOs can play in driving enterprise-wide business growth and performance, considering the new demands of an increasingly complex, and unpredictable, connected world. By taking on the perspective of a *digital entrepreneur*, and by introducing *the art of systems thinking*, we will explore how today's finance leaders can create a more human-centric, holistic and systemic approach to performance management, while enabling their companies to operate with greater agility. We will discuss the key levers available to CFOs to drive an enterprise-wide transformation by making changes to the *strategic and operational performance dialogue* (Chapters 7 and 8), and by establishing a growth- and learning-oriented *performance culture* (Chapter 9).

In Part Three, we will look beyond the boundaries of a single organization. By applying the lens of a *digital economist*, and looking at *the art of network thinking*, we will uncover new forces and emerging digital business models that are rapidly reshaping our economies and society in the connected world. Within this context, we will discuss the role of finance in managing *digital business platforms and ecosystems* (Chapters 12 and 13).

We will conclude the book by reflecting on the needs and opportunities for companies to make a greater economic and societal impact through long-term, multi-stakeholder value creation – and discuss the important role that CFOs can play in creating *multi-stakeholder value* (Chapter 14) for their business, the economy and society overall.

Figure 0.1 is a visual representation of the outlined structure of the book, illustrating how the key themes and building blocks covered in each of the following three parts of the book will build on each other to form a holistic and integrated view on how finance leaders can think ahead and drive business

FIGURE 0.1   How the book is structured: the connected world

The Connected World

Part One The engineer perspective (and the art of design thinking)

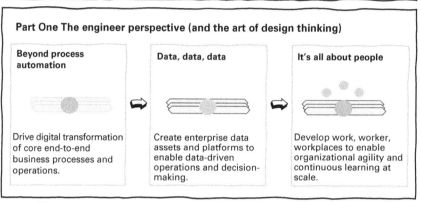

Beyond process automation

Drive digital transformation of core end-to-end business processes and operations.

Data, data, data

Create enterprise data assets and platforms to enable data-driven operations and decision-making.

It's all about people

Develop work, worker, workplaces to enable organizational agility and continuous learning at scale.

Part Two The entrepreneur perspective (and the art of systems thinking)

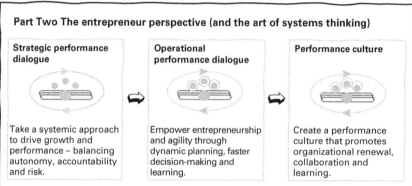

Strategic performance dialogue

Take a systemic approach to drive growth and performance – balancing autonomy, accountability and risk.

Operational performance dialogue

Empower entrepreneurship and agility through dynamic planning, faster decision-making and learning.

Performance culture

Create a performance culture that promotes organizational renewal, collaboration and learning.

Part Three The economist perspective (and the art of network thinking)

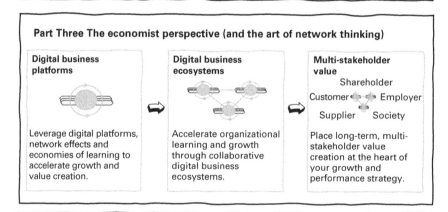

Digital business platforms

Leverage digital platforms, network effects and economies of learning to accelerate growth and value creation.

Digital business ecosystems

Accelerate organizational learning and growth through collaborative digital business ecosystems.

Multi-stakeholder value

Shareholder
Customer — Employer
Supplier   Society

Place long-term, multi-stakeholder value creation at the heart of your growth and performance strategy.

Sustainable Economic Growth

transformation, growth and performance in a connected world. At the end of each part of the book is a summary of key takeaways and guiding questions for practical application and further research, as well as a recommendation on how to get started.

To gain the full benefit of the book, I would recommend first reading through all three Parts (especially Chapters 2–4, 7–9 and 12–14) at least once to understand the key dependencies between them, and then going back and working through the topics of greatest relevance for your company.

Notes

1 United Nations Department of Economic and Social Affairs (2017) World population projected to reach 9.8 billion in 2050, and 11.2 billion in 2100, UN, New York, www.un.org/development/desa/en/news/population/world-population-prospects-2017.html (archived at https://perma.cc/8M7B-CZ7Y)

2 Loughrey, C (2017) Minority Report: 6 predictions that came true, 15 years on, *The Independent*, 25 June, www.independent.co.uk/arts-entertainment/films/features/minority-report-15th-anniversary-predictive-policing-gesture-based-computing-facial-and-optical-a7807666.html (archived at https://perma.cc/SN2G-4FJS)

3 Kurzweil, R (2001) The law of accelerating returns, Kurzweil Accelerating Intelligence, 7 March, www.kurzweilai.net/the-law-of-accelerating-returns (archived at https://perma.cc/V5NN-QFG8)

4 Inside Big Data (2017) The exponential growth of data, Inside Big Data, 16 February, insidebigdata.com/2017/02/16/the-exponential-growth-of-data/ (archived at https://perma.cc/FE35-MQLX)

5 Anthony, SD, Viguerie, SP, Schwartz, EI and van Landeghem, J (2018) 2018 Corporate longevity forecast: Creative destruction is accelerating, *Innosight*, February, www.innosight.com/wp-content/uploads/2017/11/Innosight-Corporate-Longevity-2018.pdf (archived at https://perma.cc/SQ5N-GMYC)

6 Deloitte (2018) Special Edition: European CFO Survey, Spring, www2.deloitte.com/content/dam/Deloitte/pt/Documents/finance/180615_CFO-Survey-Report_Digital-Chapter_Interactive.pdf (archived at https://perma.cc/GAN6-JPKT)

7 Thier, J (2020) 2020 Trends: Rise of the CFO-COO, *CFO Dive*, 26 January, www.cfodive.com/news/2020-trend-cfo-coo/571060/ (archived at https://perma.cc/W7TV-656B)

8 Holley, C (nd) What CEOs want – and need – from their CFOs, Deloitte, www2.deloitte.com /us/en/pages/finance/articles/what-ceos-want-and-need-from-their-cfos.html (archived at https://perma.cc/WD9D-8W4X)

9 Deloitte (nd) The CFO Program: Step ahead, www2.deloitte.com/global/en/pages/finance/articles/step-ahead.html (archived at https://perma.cc/BGZ4-UC2X)

10 The data related to these statistics was collected in 2018/2019 as part of the annually conducted UK Digital Disruption Index Survey. See also: Deloitte (nd) Digital Disruption Index: Aligning strategy, workforce and technology, www2.deloitte.com/content/campaigns/uk/digital-disruption/digital-disruption/digital-disruption-index.html (archived at https://perma.cc/58DY-6DEH)

11 Ehrenhalt, S (2016) Crunch time: Finance in a digital world, Deloitte, www2.deloitte.com/content/dam/Deloitte/uk/Documents/strategy/deloitte-uk-so-crunch-time.pdf (archived at https://perma.cc/F3PL-CVS2)

12 Nadler, D and Tushman, M (1980) A model for diagnosing organizational behavior, *Organizational Dynamics*, **9** (2), Autumn, pp 35–51

13 Including a series of Deloitte UK Digital Disruption Index Executive Surveys conducted since 2017. Deloitte (2019) Digital Disruption Index: Aligning strategy, workforce and technology, www2.deloitte.com/content/dam/Deloitte/uk/Documents/consultancy/deloitte-uk-digital-disruption-index-2019.pdf (archived at https://perma.cc/B8AW-CYBP)

14 Kane, GC, Phillips, AN, Copulsky, JR and Andrus, GR (2019) *The Technology Fallacy: How people are the real key to digital transformation,* p 40, MIT Press, Cambridge, MA

15 Gurumurthy, R and Schatsky, D (2019) Pivoting to digital maturity: Seven capabilities central to digital transformation, *Deloitte Insights*, www2.deloitte.com/content/dam/Deloitte/br/Documents/financial-services/DI_Pivoting-to-digital-maturity.pdf (archived at https://perma.cc/Q23Y-WC4G)

16 Gurumurthy, R and Schatsky, D (2019) Pivoting to Digital Maturity: Seven capabilities central to digital transformation, *Deloitte Insights*, www2.deloitte.com/content/dam/Deloitte/br/Documents/financial-services/DI_Pivoting-to-digital-maturity.pdf (archived at https://perma.cc/Q23Y-WC4G)

PART ONE

The engineer perspective (and the art of design thinking)

01

Introduction

Learning from history

History provides us with several examples of what happens when long-standing business models are called into question by revolutionary technology innovations. One of the most illustrative examples is the introduction of electricity in the 19th century. At the time, most factories were powered by big steam engines positioned in the basement to supply power to all machines. When electricity arrived, the majority of companies decided to buy electric motors, only to simply place them where the steam engines used to be. Unsurprisingly, the new motors did not result in significant productivity improvements. In fact, the opportunity to save energy costs was offset by the investments needed to embed the new electrical motors.

It took most companies 20 to 30 years, or about one generation of management and engineers, to realize that electricity was much more than just an efficient source of energy. It was an opportunity to remove long-standing constraints in how a factory was organized; for instance, moving from a single common source to multiple, independent and distributed sources of power – a concept that triggered a major revolution at the time.

The electrification of factories allowed pioneering companies to adopt a new business model: efficient mass production. This was the dominating business model in most industries throughout the 20th century, and has remained so until well into the 21st century. Henry Ford, arguably history's greatest pioneer of efficient mass production, initiated this breakthrough by introducing highly specialized, moving assembly lines for producing the famous Ford Model T in 1913. In the early days, Ford built cars the same way as everybody else – one at a time. By introducing automation, in combination with a re-engineered production process, Ford and his engineers introduced the assembly line. Applying Adam's Smith principle of labour division, Ford placed workers at appointed stations and the chassis was hauled along between them using strong rope.[1] The chassis stopped at each station, where parts were fitted, until it was finally complete. Each department in the manufacturing process was broken down into sub-processes and assembly lines. As Ford was heard to remark, 'everything in the plant moved'.[2] As a result, production speeds increased – sometimes they were up to four times faster.

Producing cars more quickly than paint could dry, at less than half the cost, immensely influenced our economic thinking and management theory throughout the 20th century. In fact, most of the leading companies in successive decades became large and successful because they leveraged the same principles that Ford used to achieve efficient production and delivery of standardized products and services at scale.

History not only reminds us of the business model that most of the large established companies were once designed for, and that remained the model during the first decades of the 21st century, but also raises three important points of caution as businesses enter an unpredictable future.

First, in times of disruptive change, many leading established businesses can be slow to adapt. The introduction of electricity may have produced big winners, such as Ford, but there were plenty of losers too – primarily large and well-established businesses that failed to act quickly and decisively enough. In a short period, it drove the highest rate of business failure for incumbent companies in the 20th century outside of the Great Depression. But these big companies did not fail because they were not aware of what was happening, or because they did not have access to the best engineers; they failed because they had become so proficient and successful that many suffered from so-called 'status quo bias'. Held back by their own size and blinded by their own success, they did not anticipate the huge impact of technology innovation and, therefore, subsequently missed opportunities to transform their businesses early enough to survive.[3]

Second, history also shows us that although the implementation of new technology is necessary, many companies are insufficiently prepared to cope with a major economic shift. Transformational change requires established companies to have the courage to reimagine and re-engineer their core business and operating models. These models will be enabled by technology, but also require a clear focus on new customer needs, products and services, together with the core business processes and organizational capabilities to deliver them. This was Henry Ford's vision: to completely re-engineer production processes and redesign his factories from top to bottom so that his workers, no longer dependent on one centralized power source, could employ their skills and tools in the most efficient way possible.

Third, the winning businesses during the Industrial Revolution were those that focused on exploring how electricity could enable them to become more efficient, rather than those companies that made generating electricity their business. Companies that built on-site generators for electricity made the mistake of identifying energy production as a source of competitive advantage, rather than using it to drive innovation and competitive advantage within their own area of expertise.

Keeping these historical learnings in mind, we can turn our view towards the ongoing digital transformation of businesses. Based on the principles of scalable efficiencies that were applied by Henry Ford and other pioneers of the previous Industrial Revolution, many leading companies have achieved significant growth and productivity. For a long time, these organizations were able to maintain and extend their competitive edge through continuous, but incremental, improvements to their operating models. In these traditional operating models, however, scale inevitably reaches a point of diminishing returns, which creates a limitation that digital business models are designed to overcome. Granted, it may take several attempts and some time for a new digital business model to generate profits comparable to those of incumbents (which is why they may remain undetected and underestimated at first), but once they are operating successfully they can accelerate growth at exponential levels, thereby rapidly disrupting established markets and companies.

Collisions between traditional and emerging digital operating models are taking place across all industries. In fact, it is difficult to think of any established business that is not facing an urgent need to fundamentally transform its business and operating model. Digital technology innovations, from cloud computing to 3D printing, offer exciting new opportunities for companies to reimagine how to operate across all areas of the business. From a finance perspective, for example, these technological innovations have given rise to a 'new digital toolkit for CFOs', which includes new platform technologies such as cloud computing, blockchain and in-memory computing, advanced data analytics and visualization technologies, and new cognitive technologies including robotics process automation (RPA), machine learning and artificial intelligence (AI), as well as collaboration and crowdsourcing platforms (see box).[4]

THE NEW DIGITAL TOOLKIT FOR CFOs

The following seven digital technologies should be embedded in the CFO's toolkit. These technologies can, individually or in combination with each other, be used to enable the digital transformation and modernization of finance-owned and finance-supported business capabilities and activities. Some of these technologies are foundational (especially cloud computing, in-memory computing, cognitive computing, blockchain and collaboration), which means that they can be used as a platform on their own, often to enable the use of other technologies and applications (such as data visualization, data analytics, machine learning, artificial intelligence and crowdsourcing):

- **cloud computing**: a method of data storage using the internet, allowing finance to use key solutions and services 'as-a-service' without making large investments in building internal technology;

- **in-memory computing**: a way of storing information in main memory to achieve faster response times and the ability to process significantly greater volumes of data;

- **cognitive computing**: a portfolio of technologies, including AI, that can be used to mimic (RPA) or to simulate human skills such as speech recognition, natural language processing or learning;

- **collaboration platforms**: technologies used to support collaboration across employees, be it to share knowledge or gain insights, for example also through crowdsourcing;

- **blockchain**: a platform for digital assets where transactions are verified, and securely stored on a digital distributed ledger, without a governing central authority;

- **visualization**: technologies that use innovative visualization techniques and enhanced user interfaces to help humans explore and present large and complex sets of data;

- **advanced analytics**: the continued development of enhanced methods of analysing large data sets (big data) using new techniques and tools.

Thinking differently about digital transformation

One of the key challenges of digital transformation is that both the problem and the expected outcome are often difficult to define upfront. Most of us, especially those working in finance, however, are used to spending a lot of time analysing a problem in detail, assuming that a thorough upfront assessment of a particular situation and potential solutions, together with a detailed plan, can lower the risks that come with change.

There are several problems with this approach – not least that defining a problem in conventional ways tends to lead to unimaginative incremental solutions rather than more transformational change. In these situations, the *Art of Design Thinking* can help as it uses a more fluid and human-centric approach. Design thinking is not about shaping a prettier solution, but is more to do with developing technology-enabled solutions to address new customer and employee needs. This might sound simple, but in practice it sets a high bar for most companies that often struggle to design a solution that simultaneously achieves functional utility, ease of use and efficient and effective use of resources and technology, while creating impactful customer experiences.

Put simply, design thinking means finding new solutions by focusing on the human. At its core, working as a designer involves studying people at work, and developing 'personas' to understand their perspectives, unmet needs, challenges and expectations. Thinking like a designer can transform the way organizations develop products, services, processes and strategy by bringing together what is desirable from a human point of view with what is technologically feasible and economically viable, often using rapid prototyping as a way to imagine, develop, validate and evolve new innovative products and solutions in an iterative way. Design thinking also assumes that people may have difficulties in communicating their problems, let alone creating solutions. In many ways, Henry Ford may have, knowingly or unknowingly, illustrated one of the core principles of design thinking with the quote he is widely attributed as saying, 'If I had asked people what they wanted, they would have said faster horses.'[5]

Design thinking is not new: it has been around since the late 1960s. Multiple studies show that companies that have adopted design thinking successfully in their product, service or operations design tend to experience a remarkable positive impact on their performance. According to a study from the Design Management Institute released in 2014, the S&P 500 companies that invested most in design thinking processes, capabilities and leadership have outperformed the rest of the Index by an astounding 211 per cent.[6]

A year later, in 2015, the Hasso Plattner Institute (HPI), a close partner of Stanford University, published a study of 181 companies that have implemented key principles of design thinking across the whole organization.[7]

Approximately 70 per cent of companies stated that the new approach had both improved the working culture of their teams and made innovation processes significantly more efficient. Of the for-profit companies surveyed, 29 per cent reported a significant increase in sales. McKinsey research monitored the correlation between financial performance and investments in design thinking-related initiatives over a five-year period and across 300 listed companies, and found that the revenue growth of top design performers was almost double that of their industry peers.[8] The shareholder return growth of top design performers was 70 per cent higher than their industry peers. And finally, a Deloitte study published in 2016 found that out of 7,000 executive respondents, a staggering 79 per cent felt that human-centric design was 'very important'.[9] Furthermore, those companies that self-identified as 'high performing' were three to four times more likely than their competitors to be using design thinking internally.

The results of these studies are impressive and hint at a few additional, important principles for digital transformation that executives today should be adding to historical lessons learned:

- First, independent of the technology, the sector or the economic situation (all of which differ significantly across all studies and experiences), the key starting point for designing technology-enabled solutions is a deep understanding and relentless focus on people's needs. Understanding where the friction points are from a customer or employee perspective, rather than from a technology perspective, for example, is critical but often neglected.

- Second, transformational change in a connected world, although focused on finance-related aspects, cannot be delivered in functional silos but requires a cross-functionally integrated approach and team.

- Third, digital transformation may be triggered and enabled by technology innovation, but will need to focus on bringing together all the core elements of the design of an operating model, especially all process-, data- and people-related aspects of the transformation. Ultimately, technology innovation will have truly made an impact when it becomes so woven into our business operations and ways of working that they are indistinguishable from it – much in the same way as electricity.

Based on these principles and learnings, we will continue to explore how CFOs and finance can help redesign the company's core end-to-end processes and operations (Chapter 2), data flows and platforms (Chapter 3) and people

FIGURE 1.1   Introduction to Part One

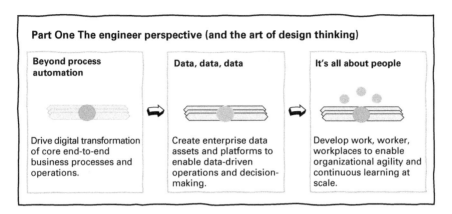

Part One The engineer perspective (and the art of design thinking)

Beyond process automation	Data, data, data	It's all about people
Drive digital transformation of core end-to-end business processes and operations.	Create enterprise data assets and platforms to enable data-driven operations and decision-making.	Develop work, worker, workplaces to enable organizational agility and continuous learning at scale.

capabilities (Chapter 4) (see Figure 1.1). While we will remain focused on the implications of all this for finance leaders and their teams, our discussions will also embrace a broader and cross-functional business context.

Notes

1   Munger, M (nd) *Division of Labor*, The Library of Economics and Liberty, www. econlib.org /library/Enc/DivisionofLabor.html (archived at https://perma.cc/ U6FM-V666)

2   Experience Ford (nd) homepage, www.ford.co.uk/experience-ford/history-and-heritage#assemblyline (archived at https://perma.cc/N3CM-N7NJ)

3   McAfee, A and Brynjolfsson, E (2018) *Machine, Platform, Crowd: Harnessing our digital future*, pp 19–21, WW Norton & Company, New York, NY

4   Ehrenhalt, S (2016) Crunch time: Finance in a digital world, Deloitte, www2. deloitte.com/content/dam/Deloitte/uk/Documents/strategy/deloitte-uk-so-crunch-time.pdf (archived at https://perma.cc/B8RQ-JBZP)

5   Vlaskovits, P (2011) Henry Ford, innovation, and that 'faster horse' quote, *Harvard Business Review*, hbr.org/2011/08/henry-ford-never-said-the-fast (archived at https://perma.cc/HD8U-U85X)

6   Rae, J (2015) 2014 Design Value Index Results and Commentary: Good design drives shareholder value, Design Management Institute, May, www.dmi.org/ page/DesignDrivesValue (archived at https://perma.cc/CJ7L-3PR2)

7   Schmiedgen, J, Rhinow, H, Köppen, E and Meinel, C (2015) Parts without a whole? The current state of design thinking practice in organizations, Study Report No 97, p 144, Hasso-Plattner-Institut für Softwaresystemtechnik an der

Universität Potsdam, Potsdam, thisisdesignthinking.net/why-this-site/the-study/ (archived at https://perma.cc/XF76-6Z9C)

8 Sheppard, B, London, S and Yeon, H (2018) Tapping into the business value of design, *McKinsey Quarterly*, 21 December (podcast), www.mckinsey.com/ business-functions/mckinsey-design/our-insights/tapping-into-the-business-value-of-design# (archived at https://perma.cc/P2QJ-DKNC)

9 Deloitte (2016) Business meets design: Creative changes starts here, Deloitte, June, www2.deloitte.com/content/dam/Deloitte/de/Documents/technology/ Whitepaper-business-meets-design-english-long-version.PDF (archived at https:// perma.cc/Z59E-WCYT)

02

Beyond process automation

New needs and expectations

In many ways, we have already become dependent on the connected world and the enormous value it creates for us. The mobile device in our pockets has more processing power than the computer modules used to guide Apollo 11 to the moon and back in 1969, and a stronger calculation engine than the Deep Blue supercomputer that beat the chess master Gary Kasparov in 1997.[1] Moreover, it allows us to connect with and use an exponentially growing range of services designed to support every aspect of our daily lives.

Many leading digital pioneers anticipated our evolving dependencies and emerging needs many years ago and are currently spoiling us with a seamless user experience that we have come to expect everywhere. We expect to design and buy customized products without extra cost; we expect to see real-time updates and analytics of our financials when we log into our bank account, or use an app to make financial transactions on the fly; we want to complete loan applications within seconds. We expect our service providers to be connected with automated access to data that we have provided before, and we become instantly annoyed if we cannot instantly locate information that we need to access for any kind of ad hoc query.

Without realizing it, we have started to expect every company – especially the ones we buy from, interact with and work for – to provide us with seamless user experiences: highly digital user interfaces, real-time access to information, around-the-clock services with personalized treatment, and global consistency of service quality with zero errors. This is the world to which we have become accustomed, and the world that our children take for granted. Some of us may stay loyal to a few traditional brands and organizations that we have valued in the past, but if they cannot provide the same value and experience, we have no qualms in walking away.

To meet our fast-evolving needs and expectations, established companies not only need to reinvent their products and services, but also the entirety of their underlying business processes. Reinventing core processes and customer interfaces goes far beyond the automation of existing activities; it requires the transformation of core business processes and the operating models surrounding them, using cutting-edge digital technology. Successful reimagination and re-engineering requires new perspectives and capabilities – challenging existing mental models, assumptions and structures at the most fundamental level with a relentless focus on evolving customer and employee needs, along with a deep understanding of the newest technology innovations.

The benefits that these transformational efforts can create for companies are not only significant, but necessary: enhanced customer service and experience, significant cost reductions, improved turnaround times and improved quality and controls, and the ability to interact with digital business ecosystems of the connected world, to name just a few. Augmenting or replacing analogue interactions and processes with digital software allows organizations to collect data that can be used to anticipate customer needs and experiences, improve process performance, enhance decision-making, prevent and mitigate business risks and accelerate learning and improvement processes. For most companies, the needs and benefits of a fundamental process transformation are obvious. Many have already made significant progress with impressive results. Too many, however, are lagging behind in delivering the transformational change at the speed and scale required to keep pace with the connected world.

Most businesses start their digital transformation by focusing on their front-office operations, which cover key areas such as core consumer and customer interfaces, and related business processes in sales and marketing, supply-chain, e-commerce and omnichannel experiences. However, efforts to transform the front office will not go very far unless they are fully supported by core business processes and operations in the back office. For most companies, therefore, a digital transformation covers fundamental changes to the core business model, ie the way in which a company creates and captures value (and which we will explore further in Part Three), as well as the core operating model, ie the way a company delivers value, specifically the core end-to-end business processes across the front and back office.

Enhanced process automation as a starting point

Technology-enabled transformations of the core business processes and operating model are not new. The vast majority of leading global companies have invested significantly in the deployment of large-scale enterprise resource planning (ERP) or customer relationship management (CRM) systems and the related creation of business services centres and process outsourcing – often with mixed results. While some of these investments have delivered important structural changes and measurable efficiency improvements, many large, established companies have been left to deal with rigid processes, highly complex and customized systems solutions, limited data quality and access, and poor user experience. The memories and scars of past process transformations are still very much present at the time of writing and, indeed, have left many finance leaders more sceptical and cautious about the real cost and benefits potential of technology-enabled process transformation.

It is no surprise that many CFOs and corporate leaders have been cautious in adopting the next generation of digital technologies to drive further process improvement. In fact, many finance leaders have deliberately limited their efforts to identify discrete opportunities for simplification and automation of operational process activities in shared services centres, particularly when it comes to using robotic process automation (RPA). RPA technology aims to reduce human error in tasks such as collecting, inputting, reconciling and consuming data from multiple IT systems, and as such offers a relatively fast and simple way to automate what, traditionally, were manual activities. According to Deloitte's 2017 State of Cognitive Survey,[2] and a research study of 152 cognitive projects published in 2018,[3] in some organizations RPA projects have yielded promising, rapid results based on limited investment and effort required. The US space agency NASA, for instance, piloted RPA to drive efficiency in their shared services centre. In selected process areas, the first wave of implementation resulted in significantly improved automation levels – well above 80 per cent – creating an attractive case for a broader deployment and roll-out of RPA and other cognitive technologies. As the project leader stated, 'So far, it's not rocket science.'[4]

Despite the simplicity of deploying RPA and the promising progress made by companies, research indicates that many companies, after making some initial progress, are struggling to drive process automation at pace and scale. An annual study run by Deloitte in 2018, involving senior representatives from over 500 leading global companies, found that nearly 80 per cent of the companies that had begun to pilot RPA were expected to see increased investments in driving process automation in the coming years, yet only about 4 per cent were able to deploy RPA at scale – a rather negligible increase from 3 per cent in 2017.[5] The majority of respondents cited process fragmentation, lack of IT readiness, data quality issues and other operational aspects as key barriers to progress.

While operational reasons are valid, and certainly to be considered, retrospective analysis revealed that the underlying rationale for lack of progress was in many cases related to a lack of a clear long-term vision and strategy to scale. Excited about early successes of experimental working, combined with an ongoing pressure to demonstrate quick results, it appeared that many organizations may have remained too focused on achieving initial, incremental improvements without taking the time to reflect on the underlying structural changes and capabilities required to drive transformational change. Not surprisingly, these organizations can find it difficult to move beyond the piloting stage. The long-term business benefits tend to be limited to small-scale 'one arm here, one leg there' savings that are difficult to realize. As a study by HFS Research stated in 2019, the 'piecemeal approach to intelligent automation is contributing to scale challenges and results that are decidedly linear rather than the hoped for and planned-for exponential benefits'.[6] According to its survey of 590 business leaders, only 11 per cent are using solutions that combine technologies in a way that connects people, process and technology across functional areas and that can be scaled to deliver lasting change.

Similar concerns have surfaced in instalments of the previously mentioned annual study conducted by Deloitte. While the number of companies that were investing in intelligent automation had increased quite significantly in 2019 and 2020, less than 40 per cent had developed a long-term automation strategy that describes the transformational scope, approach and efforts required to reach scale.[7] Not surprisingly, there are many noticeable differences to be found between companies aiming for incremental efficiency improvements, and aiming for transformational change. According to the 2020 survey report, the latter are much more likely to start their transformational journey by reimagining their core processes and operations across functional boundaries, whereas those that remain at a piloting stage are more likely to automate existing process activities. This does not mean that an incremental approach to process automation would be, per se, not sensible and useful (for instance, for those companies that already have solid processes in place, and/or that focus on processes that do not require a more fundamental redesign), but it does mean that executives looking to achieve transformational business change will need to adopt a different strategy to achieve digital maturity.

Creating a new digital core

In response to these challenges, organizations have started to develop and explore new strategies to transform their core business processes and operations. They are often referring to these strategies as the 'creation of a new digital core', which indicates a more structural transformational approach that is not only considering a broader use of digital technologies but also the need to look at the core operating model as a whole.

Key characteristics of core business processes: a reminder

Organizations intending to transform core business processes and operations will most likely impact the core mechanism by which they create value. Of course, processes come in different formats, and with different purposes, but what we tend to call a *core* business process is typically representing a series of recurring and inter-linked activities that are essential to run the operational engine of an organization. Processes, by their very nature, have been designed, or evolved, to perform these recurring activities in a consistent way, time and time again, and as efficiently as possible.[8] This, however, also means that the very mechanism that companies use to serve customers and to create value (ie their core business processes and operations) is intrinsically obstructive and thus very difficult to change. Moreover, companies have designed their core operating model around these processes,[9] which in turn also means that in order to transform these processes, companies will need to redesign the core operating model as whole.

A new benchmark for operating model transformation

The core operating model of a large company can be complex, often involving a wide range of interconnected workflows, people, partners and systems. That said, the main objective of a core operating model and its core underlying processes is relatively simple: the conversion of resources into products or services of higher value, with an intention to maximize economies of scale, scope and learning.[10] From Ford to Amazon, there is a long history of companies that have achieved significant business growth and performance by adopting the latest technologies to design and implement superior operating models and processes that can realize economies of scale, scope and learning at a scale that others cannot. Fuelled by the ongoing introduction of digital technology innovations, this history is going to continue – most likely, in ever-accelerating intervals. In fact, many large established companies encounter significant constraints and complexities that limit their abilities to accelerate growth – a competitive weakness that digitally maturing businesses are trying to target and overcome.

Perhaps more than any other company, Amazon has demonstrated how a highly digitally-enabled operating model can transform not only a business but a whole sector.[11] While most companies have continued to use digital technologies to automate existing core processes and operations to save costs, Amazon has reimagined how their core operating model, business processes and operations can be run, scaled and improved exponentially by leveraging the latest technological innovation, including cloud-based data and process platforms, advanced analytics and artificial intelligence. From demand sensing and forecasting, to order intake and fulfilment, to financial planning and performance management, self-learning machines are running Amazon's core processes and operations with almost unlimited potential to scale.

The key design principles that digitally-enabled operating models are based on is neither new, nor very difficult to understand: once a core business process has been digitized, it creates data that can then be used to feed machines and algorithms that will monitor and improve the execution of the process on an ongoing basis. Processes that are designed to cover the end-to-end customer journey will also be able to use the data to continuously enhance the customer experience. Moreover, advanced algorithms and artificial intelligence (AI) can use the data to improve themselves, and as such their ability to generate better forecasts, identify exceptions and sense risks, or support other forms of predictive analytics and data-driven decision-making. Removing human bottlenecks not only reduces the costs but also enables a company to scale faster, while minimizing the need for administrative and supporting activities. Companies like Amazon still employ many people, but most of them operate on the edges of their core business processes and operations: they focus on the design and supervision of machines, handle tasks that machines are not able to do, deal with exceptions, or analyse unexpected peaks and exceptions in forecasting.[12] In other words, humans still play an important role but the human–machine relationship has been inverted.

Digitally-enabled businesses are increasingly disrupting and reshaping almost all sectors, often leaving little room for traditional businesses to compete and grow. They are able to realize a range of very significant business benefits that many established companies with traditional operating models cannot: the reorientation of workflows towards the customer to enhance customer experiences and value creation, the creation of end-to-end processes that overcome functional barriers, the elimination of non-essential activities to reduce costs and complexity, the removal of (mostly human) bottlenecks to increase speed and scalability, the use of data analytics and increasingly also AI to enable continuous learning and improvement, and – perhaps most interestingly – the creation of 'process agility' which is made possible by modularizing and converting processes into multi-sided platforms that can then be connected or outsourced to an external network of specialized suppliers or partners. In many sectors, established companies will have no other choice but to benchmark themselves against their most digitally matured peers, as well as the digital newcomers that may enter and disrupt their markets. In doing so, many companies are likely to realize that they will need to consider and conduct a much deeper digital transformation of their core business processes and operations than they may have followed to date. But how can they get started?

Approaching the transformation of core business processes and operations

What might still sound like a new frontier to most has started to become the new normal for others, who are resetting the benchmarks for digital business transformation – one of the new realities of our highly connected world. That said, the creation of a 'new digital core' can be a significant and complex challenge for established companies. 'Best practices' have not yet crystallized (if they ever will, or indeed should), but there are some principles that organizations may want to consider in shaping their transformation strategy – many of which have been influenced by design thinking.

FOCUSING ON CUSTOMERS AND EMPLOYEES

People often approach digital transformation from a technology perspective. From the outset, they seem to have strong ideas about what the right technology solution should be. But in order to arrive at a new, more human-centric design, they must start from a user perspective – for example, by mapping out the user journeys for customers and employees. This approach will help them to reimagine and design processes that can significantly enhance user experiences and thus, value creation. It can also help them overcome constraining perspectives and mental models that have been shaped by existing organizational, technical or structural limitations.

FOCUSING ON CORE VALUE CREATION

Companies aiming to transform their core operating model should centre their transformational strategy and approach around the *most value-adding* core business process and user journeys, rather than the multitude of peripheral, supporting activities and services (as incremental approaches to process automation may do). This approach forces companies to take a step back and critically reassess which business processes and activities are truly value-adding, and therefore 'core'.

In an attempt to redesign the new digital core, companies have mapped out and rearranged the entire spectrum of cross-functional activities. A leading global manufacturing company, for instance, has developed an integrated, cross-functional 'edge-to-edge' customer and operations journey that spans across and connects the 'edges' of front- and back-office operations (eg from digital consumer to supplier interfaces). A new operating model has been redesigned to support this new journey, and to enable new levels of customer experience and operational excellence by removing functional silos and barriers, especially those that had existed at the intersection between sales and marketing, manufacturing and distribution, procurement and product development. As a result, the company is creating significant additional opportunities for growth, margin improvement, tax savings, and enhanced operational agility and scalability.

KEEP THE CORE LEAN

Most established companies have developed a wide range of additional operational processes, activities and capabilities that are not essential, nor differentiating for the (customer) value creation. Depending on the company and sector, these may range from facility management to financial accounting. Companies should take time upfront to evaluate whether these capabilities should form part of the future operating model, or whether there may be opportunities to reduce the complexity of a new digital core, and indeed the digital transformation leading to it.[13] Companies can leverage different models to deal with these non-core processes and capabilities, ranging from in-house and on-demand services to outsourcing.

USE A COMBINATION OF DIGITAL TECHNOLOGY SOLUTIONS

The starting point for most established organizations is characterized by a highly fragmented legacy data and systems landscape that may create significant barriers to the creation of a new digital core. According to the 2019 findings of a biennial survey run by Deloitte, only about a quarter of companies are currently leveraging a combination of digital solutions to enhance and digitize their core processes and operations.[14]

While many companies are in the process of planning and preparing to move their core data and systems platforms to the cloud, most are not yet at a stage that would allow them to make use of a fully developed technology infrastructure, including the next generation of ERP systems, advanced analytics and AI to run core end-to-end operational processes. To accelerate the transformation of core business processes and operations, companies are increasingly making use of modern workflow or orchestration solutions that are designed to create an enhanced user experience platform by integrating a new middle layer across their fragmented functional data silos. These platforms can offer attractive short-term benefits, not only by enabling and accelerating the core process transformation, but also by clarifying the exact user requirements and expectations. That said, leaders should not use these approaches as an excuse to fail to tackle their underlying core process, data and systems issues.

In the broadest sense, and in order to realize the long-term benefits of a new digital core, businesses will need to leverage predominately data-generating technology platforms (which, for example, may include a next-generation ERP system (see following box), but not necessarily RPA). This is because the data generated by a digitally-enabled process can then be processed and used for process optimization, insight generation and decision-making, as illustrated before.

USING NEXT-GENERATION ERP SYSTEMS TO DRIVE OPERATIONAL PROCESS TRANSFORMATION

As the leading global enterprise software providers are phasing out their product development and standard support services for older versions of their enterprise resource planning (ERP) suites over the next years, established companies should assess the opportunities to leverage the replacements of their current ERP systems to enable and potentially accelerate the transformation of their core processes and operations.

Most executives will recognize the limitations that their current ERP systems impose on the company in terms of agility and speed – often a result of monolithic systems that have been extensively customized but could not keep pace with business and portfolio changes. In most established companies, these systems are absolutely essential to run core business processes and operations ranging from material management, manufacturing, sales and distribution to financial accounting, but have often become very expensive to run and maintain, and not flexible enough to support the companies' initiatives to create a new digital core.

What most companies will need instead are more integrated and flexible data and system platforms that allow them to serve changing customer and business needs. Compared to traditional ERPs, the next generation of ERP systems are likely to have a much smaller 'core' (in line with our earlier observations) but may develop a relatively wide range of function- and industry-specific applications that can live on the cloud. As such, next-generation ERPs are able to balance both greater stability at the core and significantly enhanced agility and user experience at the 'edges':

- The evolution of these new systems takes time to mature, of course, and some companies may well decide to wait and maximize the investments in their current systems. But since the transition seems inevitable and rather time-consuming, it is a worthwhile initiative for companies to develop a longer-term transition strategy, including an understanding of which process changes could be enabled by or, vice versa, could facilitate the reimplementation of their ERP systems.

- The key business processes and operations that executives should evaluate most carefully include the core business processes (eg the transition to digital supply chains and networks, as well as smart manufacturing), core support processes (eg the digital transformation of core finance, procurement and employee management processes), as well as capabilities that a new ERP platform may help unlock to exploit changing consumer trends (eg the expected growth of e-commerce and omnichannel management) and the abilities to facilitate the participation in emerging digital business ecosystems (eg the need to collaborate more closely and more digitally with existing suppliers).

- In addition to that, ERP systems will of course continue to play an important role in enabling core transactional processes such as quote-to-cash (QTC), source-to-pay (STP) and record-to-report (RTR). While companies should evaluate carefully what does, and what does not, belong in their new digital core, there can be good reasons to use these processes as a stepping stone for a wider transformation.

DEVELOP CAPABILITIES FOR CONTINUOUS IMPROVEMENT

Many companies have established an 'intelligent automation factory', 'artificial intelligence factory' or 'digital foundry' to drive the digital transformation and optimization of their core business processes and operations – bringing together a wide range of skills including deep operational business insights, design thinking, coding, data science, user experience design, engineering and management skills. These factories tend to be situated close to the core business processes and operations, and connected to the enterprise business operations team, operations excellence team and/or global business services (GBS) team. In fact, several organizations have started to combine all of these capabilities through the creation of a global business operations (GBO) or integrated business services (IBS) organization, which is designed to run and develop the core operational processes, operations, capabilities and services in a more integrated and scalable way. Adding to this the management of a growing network of external partners and providers, these new organizations mark a significant evolution from traditional shared services organizations.

DO NOT UNDERESTIMATE THE BARRIERS TO CHANGE

Leaders should be reminded that many people in their organizations may not want to change existing ways of working, especially not in anticipation of a somehow uncertain future. Not only are changes to core business processes and operations hugely complex and inconvenient, they are also likely to result in short-term inefficiencies given that companies will have to introduce these changes *in anticipation* of a wider business and operating model change, rather than waiting until it has become a major business bottleneck or burning platform. Therefore, it is very important for leaders to have a well-articulated vision with clearly defined business benefits.

Some further considerations for sponsoring CFOs

The transformation of core processes and operations, as well as the creation of a new digital core, is a complex task that requires broad engagement and executive level support and governance. CFOs are often positioned as one of the main sponsors, and as such may find additional value in paying particular attention to the following three general aspects of digital business transformation.

ENCOURAGE THE MOVE FROM DIGITIZATION, TO DIGITALIZATION, TO DIGITAL TRANSFORMATION

In shaping the vision and strategy for a process transformation, it is often useful to distinguish between the terms *digitization*, *digitalization* and *digital transformation* to explain clearly what a company is aiming to achieve, and the types of decisions that may have to be made to realize this vision. In many companies these terms are used synonymously, thereby creating significant confusion, which diminishes the opportunity for structural change and true digital transformation. First, *digitization* refers to the fundamental task of translating and encoding analogue content into the digital language of zeros and ones so that it can be stored, processed and transmitted by machines. In contrast, *digitalization* refers to the use of technologies to automate, augment or optimize existing processes. Digitalization goes beyond the implementation of technology and aims to deliver a deeper, structural change to the entire business process and operating model. Although business leaders often use digitalization as an umbrella term for digital transformation, the terms should be differentiated further. *Digital (business) transformation*, as introduced before, may require a much more foundational and broader adoption of digital technologies (such as required for the creation of a digital core), even though the overarching ambition is less to do with the technology implementation and much more about the transformation of the core business and operating model to address the evolving needs of customers and employees.

For the majority of large, established companies, digital business transformation requires a much deeper structural and human-centric approach to reimagine business models, processes and operations to unlock and amplify new customer and employee potential. A company might undertake several initiatives to implement new technologies to improve the efficiency of existing processes. But executives who believe that there is nothing more to digital business transformation than the automation of existing process and activities may be making a profound strategic mistake. The key objective of digital transformation is to help an organization become better at dealing with ongoing change, essentially making agility a core competency as their business processes are transformed into customer-driven, data- and machine-enabled platforms. Such agility will facilitate ongoing *digitalization* initiatives but should not be confused with them. As such, digitization and digitalization are essentially about technology, but digital transformation is not. Digital transformation is about people – especially customers and employees.

ADVOCATE THE ART OF DESIGN THINKING TO ESTABLISH A RENEWED FOCUS ON LONG-TERM CUSTOMER AND EMPLOYEE VALUE CREATION

People tend to look at technology innovation through the lens of their own situation at work. They ask themselves how emerging technologies can help address the key challenges they are facing, or what opportunities they can find to optimize their current ways of working – for example, by automating or augmenting existing processes. This is a common phenomenon since most of us have been trained to think deductively; for instance, by using detailed upfront analysis and logic to derive solutions for well-defined problems. Indeed, many finance leaders would attribute their professional successes to their ability to structure problems clearly, and to derive solutions through rational thinking and reasoning.

Unfortunately, this approach, as valuable as it is in many aspects of finance, can hinder us in driving technology-enabled, transformational change. This is where design thinking can be very helpful. Rather than being trapped by the scope and challenges of our own existing work environment, design thinking can help leaders and their teams to focus on a long-term customer perspective, by asking questions such as: What do my customers (or employees) really desire? What can I possibly do to help them to use the new technologies offered to me? How sustainable is the solution in the long term?

The starting point is always at the human level – what the people you serve really need, and how you can make them feel better. Design thinking is not about implementing technologies, but the transformational change that technologies – in combination with other building blocks such as process or organizational changes – can do to enable new and enhanced ways of creating value to customers. Take the smartphone, for instance. The way it has been designed was not driven by technology alone, but by the way technology has been brought together with new software and other high-quality materials to enhance our user experience when it comes to taking a call, sending a message or accessing apps.

This is how design can help envision and deliver transformational change far beyond incremental efficiency savings. It is what Ford, knowingly or unknowingly, used to re-engineer his factories, and how CFOs should train themselves and their teams to reimagine and re-engineer core business processes and operations. As the CFO of a leading Fortune 100 company commented in a recent conversation on the role of finance in driving operational excellence: 'Every decision has to support a very customer-centric strategy. Everything we do on the back end is geared toward making us more effective and efficient as an organization in order to serve customers.'

BALANCE SHORT- AND LONG-TERM TRANSFORMATION OPPORTUNITIES AND RISKS

The creation of a new digital core is an important step in building the foundations for a wider digital transformation, which – there's no doubt about it – will be complex, resource- and time-intensive and risky.

CFOs have a very important role to play in helping to find the right balance and pace between necessary transformative changes and business continuity, and between the creation of new opportunities for growth and the need to protect value in the traditional model. Typically, this is not an 'either/or' decision, but important choices will need to be made about which processes can and need to be transformed, in which sequence, when and how. CFOs may be tempted to wait for new technologies to mature, or for best practices to emerge. In some cases, there might be many valid reasons for this approach. That said, in a fast-evolving connected world, the risk of doing nothing may rapidly grow faster than the risk of making mistakes along the way. CFOs and their teams will need to approach this journey with a mindset and an attitude that encourage continuous experimentation and learning, but also accept and embrace the set-backs. Design thinking is a key enabler to guide these efforts, and should be adopted and advocated widely.

Notes

1   Puiu, T (2020) Your smartphone is millions of times more powerful than the Apollo 11 guidance computers, *ZME Science*, 11 February, www.zmescience.com/science/news-science/smartphone-power-compared-to-apollo-432/ (archived at https://perma.cc/3MBR-W5SV)

2   Deloitte (2017) Bullish on the business value of cognitive: Leaders in cognitive and AI weigh in on what's working and what's next, 2017 Deloitte State of Cognitive Survey, www2.deloitte.com/content/dam/Deloitte/us/Documents/deloitte-analytics/us-da-2017-deloitte-state-of-cognitive-survey.pdf (archived at https://perma.cc/9NSL-B4AS)

3 Davenport, TH and Ronaki, R (2018) Artificial intelligence for the real world, *Harvard Business Review*, January–February, pp 108–16, hbr.org/2018/01/artificial-intelligence-for-the-real-world/ (archived at https://perma.cc/78Z7-URG4)

4 Davenport, TH and Ronaki, R (2018) Artificial intelligence for the real world, *Harvard Business Review*, January–February, pp 108–16, hbr.org/2018/01/artificial-intelligence-for-the-real-world/ (archived at https://perma.cc/78Z7-URG4)

5 Deloitte (2018) Robotic roll-outs reap results: 95% of organisations using RPA say the technology has improved productivity, Deloitte, 10 October, www2.deloitte.com/uk/en/pages/press-releases/articles/robotic-roll-outs-reap-results.html (archived at https://perma.cc/T8K9-4T6F)

6 HFS Research (2019) Integrated automation: Why you've been doing it all wrong, March, www.hfsresearch.com/research/state-of-intelligent-automation-2019 (archived at https://perma.cc/G2FU-PA7A)

7 Horton, R and Watson, J (2020) Automation with intelligence: Pursuing organisation-wide reimagination, Deloitte, www2.deloitte.com/uk/en/insights/focus/technology-and-the-future-of-work/intelligent-automation-2020-survey-results.html (archived at https://perma.cc/MN33-LXU4)

8 Garwin, DA (1998) The processes of organization and management, *MIT Sloan Management Review*, sloanreview.mit.edu/article/the-processes-of-organization-and-management/ (archived at https://perma.cc/GHQ3-S5VD)

9 Christensen, CM (2016) *The Innovator's Dilemma: When new technologies cause great companies to fail*, p 163, Harvard Business Review Press, Boston, MA

10 Iansiti, M and Lakhani, KR (2020) Competing in the age of AI, *Harvard Business Review,* January–February, p 30, hbr.org/2020/01/competing-in-the-age-of-ai (archived at https://perma.cc/HA3X-QGRV)

11 Building on: Iansiti, M and Lakhani, KR (2020) Competing in the Age of AI, *Harvard Business Review,* January–February, pp 9–11, hbr.org/2020/01/competing-in-the-age-of-ai (archived at https://perma.cc/HA3X-QGRV)

12 Iansiti, M and Lakhani, KR (2020) Competing in the Age of AI, *Harvard Business Review,* January–February, hbr.org/2020/01/competing-in-the-age-of-ai (archived at https://perma.cc/HA3X-QGRV)

13 Deloitte (nd) Welcome to the Center Office: The future of enterprise and shared services, *Deloitte Insights*, www2.deloitte.com/content/dam/insights/us/articles/6750_future-of-enterprise-services/DI_Future-of-enterprise-services.pdf (archived at https://perma.cc/K6ND-CHLA)

14 Deloitte (2019) 2019 Global Shared Services Survey Report, www2.deloitte.com/uk/en/pages/operations/articles/global-shared-services-survey.html (archived at https://perma.cc/3WKJ-9XDT)

03

Data, data, data

The quest for data

People say that data is the 'new oil'. Unlike the historical quest for the precious commodity, the data rush is only just beginning. Business has fallen in love with data. We can't get enough. The more we collect, the more we want. Companies are advised to hoard all the data accessible to them. Even when they are unsure whether it's useful or not, they are reticent to delete or not capture any data for fear of missing out. Tera-, peta-, zeta-, yeta- and soon also brontobyte (a 1 followed by 27 zeros) capacity is within reach. Now that storage and processing power is becoming so cheap, we are even more determined to use the 'new oil' to fuel the digital engine. After all, those that have the most data cannot lose, right?

Yet for all the impressive gains promised, only a few companies seem to have realized the expected benefits from their 'big data'. Many leading companies still struggle to get even the basics right, including core financial reporting and business performance management. The reason for this is usually not a lack of volume – it is an overflow of data that is lacking quality and context.

Nate Silver, a data scientist famous for beating the largest US research institutes in predicting the outcomes of the presidential elections in 2008 and 2012, highlighted:

> We're not that much smarter than we used to be, even though we have much more information – and that means the real skill now is learning how to pick out the useful information from all this noise.[1]

In other words, the key to Silver's highly accurate predictions was not the volume of data, but his systematic approach to focusing his data analyses on what mattered most within the context of the presidential elections:

asking the right questions, carefully defining key hypotheses and using a very thorough selection of a heterogeneous, high-quality data set to feed his prediction models. But high-quality data is pretty thin on the ground, as the statistics show.

The price of poor data

One study published by the *Harvard Business Review* in 2016 estimated that poor quality data was costing US businesses alone more than US $3 trillion annually.[2] The findings of another study published in *MIT Sloan Management Review* in 2017 estimated the cost of bad data at 15 to 25 per cent of revenue for most companies.[3] A key reason for these surprisingly high and still-rising figures has to do with the 'snowball effect' that poor data is creating at work: data that is of poor quality, or difficult to access, yet urgently required, becomes manipulated by people who are more likely to 'correct' errors themselves than establish the root cause of the problem. When this happens – and we all know that it is happening all the time – it is left to the recipients to deal with all the usual consequences: increasingly complex reconciliations, non-automatable processes, multiplication of costs for system changes and maintenance, inaccurate or misleading management information and insight, potential compliance issues, significant levels of complexity to execute business portfolio, business model or operating model changes, just to name a few.

As a result, and according to the previously mentioned studies, knowledge workers tend to spend up to 50 per cent, and data scientists up to 80 per cent of their time dealing with data quality issues. A cross-industry study published by the *Harvard Business Review* in 2018 indicated that, on average, less than half of an organization's structured data is actively used in making decisions, and that less than 1 per cent of its unstructured data is analysed or used at all.[4] More than 70 per cent of employees have access to data they should not, and 80 per cent of analysts' time is spent simply discovering and preparing data. Add to this that data quality issues can be very difficult to identify and to trace back, especially once manipulated or used for analytical calculations, and it is no surprise that many decision-makers have lost trust in data. In fact, according to the study, only 16 per cent of executives trust the data they use to make important decisions.

These challenges, limitations and costs caused by poor data are significant, and the scourge of established companies everywhere. Every industry suffers from it. Financial service companies are constantly launching new applications for consumers to connect, but struggle to calculate customer and channel profitability. The utility industry can measure energy consumption at the lowest level of granularity and by individual customer, but still has limited ability to track costs accurately. Leading healthcare companies are collecting significant amounts of patient data to drive preventive, value-based treatment strategies, but struggle to find quality data to feed their analytics solutions. As Vasant Narasimhan, CEO of Novartis, succinctly concluded in an interview with *Forbes*: 'I think people underestimate how little clean data there is out there, and how hard it is to clean and link the data.'[5]

While many companies have started to make investments in data and analytics, very few appear to be looking at the end-to-end operating model as a whole. As a consequence, a complex backlog of tedious data acquisition and preparation activities remain, driven by fragmented processes, disintegrated systems and functional data silos – most of which are deeply embedded in existing organizational silos following decades of driving efficiency at scale through functional specialization. This backlog may well be the most critical operational barrier and hazard in the connected world, hindering the digital transformation of core business processes, the use of AI at scale, cross-functional collaboration, the development of a 360-degree view of the consumer, the ability to participate in digital ecosystems, and so on. The majority of established companies will not be able to avoid significant investments in the transformation of their legacy systems into scalable data and technology platforms. Transforming a century-old data and technology landscape is not an easy task, and executives can easily underestimate the importance and urgency to get started. Getting it right may be an expensive and unglamorous task, but it is important. Those hoping for a silver bullet, or quick fix, to break up their deeply embedded data and technology silos will be disappointed.

The value of good data

So, does all this mean that data is not valuable? Far from it. However, data, like oil, unprocessed and raw, does not generate value. The process of turning (quality) data into insight, and to use these insights to improve business decision-making, or to feed machines and algorithms that run the company's core operations, generates the value. This, however, is only possible if quality data has been carefully collected and processed first; then selected, combined and used within the right context, be it by asking the right business questions, by developing and testing the right set of hypotheses or by developing and applying the right data analytics and algorithms. Take consumer analytics as an example. The vast amount of data that can be collected about consumer behaviours might, in isolation, not add much value, but combined with demographic and biographic data and set into the context of key business choices, it can help companies understand and anticipate customer preferences in context, and then be used to build better services and customer relationships.

Independent of the industry and business, the realities of the connected economy will offer significant advantages for companies with advanced data management and data analytics capabilities. A Deloitte study released in early 2019 found that digitally maturing companies are nearly three times more likely to derive significant business value from data.[6] Indeed, *data mastery* turned out to be the most important foundational capability that companies need to develop in driving their digital business transformation. Achieving data mastery requires the systematic development of several interconnected capabilities, starting with the creation of an enterprise data model, to the implementation of effective data governance and ownership structures, to the analytical use of data to provide insights for better decision-making – not just for senior corporate leaders, but for people throughout the enterprise. Let's explore these capabilities, and the role the CFOs can play in developing them, in more detail.

Taking collective ownership of data

If you leave it to the data scientists, they lack the domain knowledge. If you leave it to the businesses, they don't necessarily see the potential and power of data. So it's a challenge for finance here to be able to bridge the gap.

FTSE 100 CFO[7]

The opportunities and challenges that data generates are not new to CFOs, and have gained additional attention in light of companies' growing demand for analytical solutions to enhance business performance management and decision support, as well as the emerging role of CFOs in driving digital transformation initiatives.

A few CFOs who have been successful in addressing their data quality issues and in developing data capabilities to provide fact-based and analytical insights to business are regarded as the 'guardians of truth' for decision-makers.[8] This is flattering, but gaining this level of credibility and trust does not come for free. Most CFOs share the frustrations caused by poor data quality, which often impedes them from using analytics as effectively as they would like to. In fact, a large number of finance teams are still somehow caught up in complex data collection, validation and preparation activities, instead of spending their time on driving business performance.

In fact, data is both a blessing and curse for CFOs. There is no doubt that new digital technologies will help CFOs use data more effectively to drive performance, but to do so they must look beyond the 'shiny' capabilities needed to turn data into meaningful insights, and first address less 'glamorous' data quality issues. Tom Davenport, Professor of Information Technology and Management at Babson College, and Independent Adviser to Deloitte, neatly stated the core conundrum that many CFOs are facing: 'You can't be analytical without data and you can't be really good at analytics without really good data.'[9]

CFOs who are willing to step up to this 'data challenge', directly or indirectly, can create significant value for their organizations and should work together with other executives and functions. After all, it is critical that all parts of the company understand the immense importance and value of (quality) data. Unfortunately, in some organizations the discussion about data ownership has caused more friction than collaboration. Whatever differences CFOs, CIOs, CDOs, CMOs and other executives may have between them when it comes to data (many of which stem from not really taking the time to understand each other's roles), they should set them aside to avoid any adverse impacts these issues may have on the organization's ability to break down existing organizational barriers and silos.

Developing an enterprise-wide and business-led data strategy

Turning data into a common asset requires strong cross-organizational collaboration and a well-structured enterprise-wide strategy and approach that should consider the following key steps.

Positioning data as a strategic asset

There is little doubt that mastery of data is critical for participating in an economy that is increasingly shaped by digital business models and ecosystems. Unfortunately, improving data quality and capabilities is not an overnight job, especially for large, established companies. While the urgency of enhancing data capabilities and technologies across the enterprise is obvious, the creation of a financial investment case can be painful, especially if significant upfront investments are required. Companies may be able to achieve attractive short-term cost savings (eg improved productivity of data resources, reduced infrastructure costs or rationalizing data systems and vendors), but the investment in data capabilities should not be aimed at achieving a short-term payback; rather it should be targeted towards the creation of a strategic business asset – an important aspect that often requires particularly strong sponsorship and guidance from CFOs.

Developing a business-led data strategy

Developing a data strategy is an important step in positioning data as a common enterprise asset, and, if designed well, can be used to unlock critical business engagement and alignment at both senior executive and operational management levels. A data strategy should be clearly linked to the overall business's strategy and priorities and articulated in a way that is easily understandable for all employees across the company. Organizational alignment tends to be more challenging as you go down to operational business functions, units and applications – most of which, in the past, have created their own ways of sourcing and managing data. This fragmentation of data has created a proliferation of data silos and a lack of common ownership, which must be addressed upfront.

Creating a business-led information model and data taxonomy

As companies set out to develop and implement a new enterprise-wide data strategy, it is important to develop a business-led information model and data taxonomy, so that the organization can engage in meaningful dialogue about data in relation to its business priorities, impact and value. An information model and data taxonomy allows companies to reduce ambiguities driven by inconsistent definitions of metrics (eg a common definition of 'volume'), data hierarchies (eg a common customer and product hierarchy) and reporting concepts (eg a common way to calculate customer profitability). A well-defined information model and data taxonomy can make a big difference in providing context and meaning to a confusing and often abstract conversation about data, facilitating more effective collaboration between business and technical teams. While the taxonomy should be scoped to span across functions, it tends to be an asset that finance leaders, for example the Group Controller, are well placed to guard on behalf of the company.

Implementing a robust data governance and ownership model

Building on this, the development of a robust enterprise-wide data governance and ownership model is critical to position data as a strategic enterprise asset – from both a value-creation (eg data asset and capability development) and a value-protection (eg data protection and security) perspective. A data governance and ownership model should set out the long-term objectives, success criteria, responsibility framework, methodologies, capabilities and tools required to establish, safeguard and continuously improve data as an asset over time.

In developing the right governance and ownership structure, it is important to consider the company's business and operating model (eg a decentralized operating model will require a decentralized governance framework, and a centralized operating model will need a more centralized framework, and so on). In other words, the data governance and ownership structure should be – as far as possible – guided *by* the business and operating model. In fact, many companies have failed to create enterprise-wide data assets and capabilities because their data architecture, governance and ownership structures are not aligned to reflect how the business operates and uses data. Imagine, for example, a global consumer goods company that operates across multiple categories and markets. While a common, enterprise-wide strategy and approach to data management remains essential, the design and execution of that strategy should not ignore the complexities of a global business – for example, the need to balance data standardization on a global level (eg common metrics or master data for core financial management performance reporting)) and data specificity on a local level (eg local-, function- or process-specific, internal and external data for operational data analytics), as schematically illustrated in Figure 3.1.

Some finance leaders assume that data mastery is reserved for smaller companies or digital natives only and tend to regard it as too difficult to achieve for a large established and globally operating company. But this is not true. Many large, complex and global operating organizations have made advances in developing robust enterprise-wide data strategies, assets and capabilities, enabled by clear data governance and ownership – strategic

FIGURE 3.1 Alignment of global/local data and business model architecture (schematic)

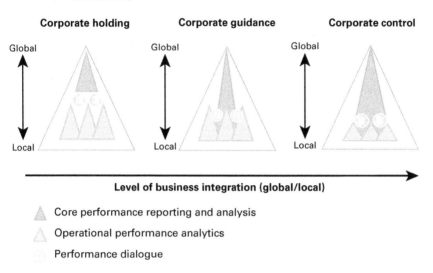

Level of business integration (global/local)

△ Core performance reporting and analysis

△ Operational performance analytics

○ Performance dialogue

investments that can generate significant long-term benefits in the connected world. Procter & Gamble (P&G), for example, has for a long time been recognized for its focused and disciplined, enterprise-wide approach to data management and analytics.[10] Driven by P&G's Shared Services organization, the company established and embedded common global data quality standards that allow the organization to aggregate, integrate and compare data across its many products, brands and geographies. The IT function has standardized the core process, data and systems landscape and largely automated the generation and visualization of performance reporting and analytics that can be consistently used across multiple business units. With consistent visuals, analysts and managers from one unit could step into a role, or even a meeting, with a different product or region and quickly understand the situation.

Reviewing the data architecture and infrastructure

Companies that want to fully participate and compete in an increasingly connected and data-driven economy need to be able to handle data that comes from an increasingly diverse range of internal and external sources, at exponentially growing volumes and across a widening variety of formats. Given the pace at which our technology-enabled economy is evolving, companies must be prepared to review and enhance their data architecture and infrastructure on an ongoing basis. From a finance perspective, they will have to consider both their centrally governed and controlled data flows and systems (especially the core data and system platforms that are necessary to support transactional processing, corporate planning and reporting, as well as master data management), and their explorative data analytics platforms and applications (Figure 3.2).

In reviewing the data architecture and infrastructure, companies should not only focus on their own internal requirements and needs, but increasingly also consider external developments – be it emerging reporting standards within their own industry sector or business ecosystem (for example, evolving data standards and commonly adopted solutions to meet sector-specific external reporting requirements and regulations), or innovative solutions that may have been used successfully in more digitally maturing companies and sectors (for example, sophisticated analytical solutions that could provide a new competitive edge). Equally, companies may want to prefer the adoption of standard platform solutions that can be enhanced continuously through vendor-driven software updates, rather than highly-customized solutions that are costly to implement and difficult to maintain as internal or external requirements change.

Leveraging cloud computing

The rapid evolution of digital technologies has, of course, a significant impact on the design and development of enterprise data assets and capabilities. One of the most important developments is the fast-growing use of cloud technologies. Many companies have started to adopt and leverage cloud technologies, yet the way in which cloud technology is used still varies significantly between companies – ranging from the development of standalone pilot applications to large-scale, cloud-enabled technology and business transformations.

During a poll of nearly 3,000 finance and business executives conducted during a Deloitte webcast in 2019, over 40 per cent indicated that they have cloud technologies in place or are in the process of implementing. Another 16 per cent said they are assessing cloud options, and nearly half of the executives said cloud technology would be critical to the performance of their organization in the near future.[11] But what exactly are the benefits that CFOs can expect from cloud-related investments?

FIGURE 3.2 Example data architecture (schematic)

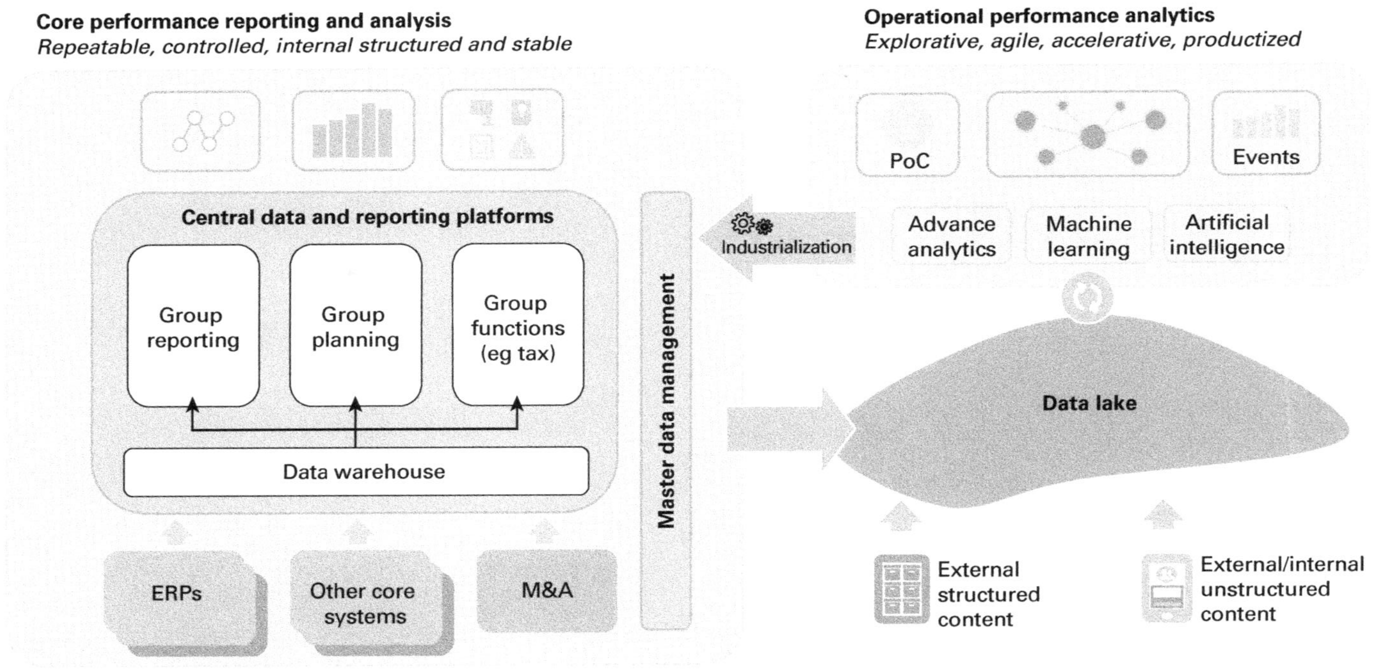

Core performance reporting and analysis
Repeatable, controlled, internal structured and stable

Operational performance analytics
Explorative, agile, accelerative, productized

Central data and reporting platforms

Group reporting

Group planning

Group functions (eg tax)

Data warehouse

Master data management

Industrialization

PoC

Advance analytics

Machine learning

Artificial intelligence

Events

Data lake

ERPs

Other core systems

M&A

External structured content

External/internal unstructured content

Operational cost reductions, for one. That said, while many organizations have been able to realize attractive IT-related operational cost savings (some companies, for instance, decided to shut down their proprietary data centres and consume computational power and attendant software as on-demand services; others use cloud computing software in their own data centres, as a means of increasing resources and working faster), the key benefits from cloud technology may come from transforming the technology, business and operating model.

TECHNOLOGY TRANSFORMATION

By transforming their existing technology landscape, most companies aim for enhanced agility (eg technology vendors are providing cloud-based service bundles to accelerate technology and product innovation and continuous improvement), speed (eg cloud platforms may enable companies to innovate and launch digitally-enabled products and services faster), scalability (eg the ability to flex core IT infrastructure components to increase or reduce its performance, resources and functionality according to the company's specific needs) and security (eg cloud allows companies to introduce new financial models, security and compliance considerations, and service monitoring requirements).[12]

Moreover, some companies are using cloud computing as an opportunity to accelerate the replacement of their fragmented and complex legacy data and technology systems landscape – a promising, albeit usually not a trivial strategy. Companies following this approach have learned that they need to do more than just 'lift and shift' their data and technology solutions into the cloud – a carefully planned and executed transformational approach that drives towards simplification of the data and systems landscape is still essential. An international airline group, for example, used cloud technologies to establish a new, harmonized, group-wide data and application layer that connects the group across several national airlines but it largely decoupled from local legacy systems. The cloud-based solution provides a standardized, simplified, scalable and agile environment that enables the group to plan, operate and manage business performance 'as one' – while providing direction and flexibility to the group's operating companies and airlines to plan and execute the modernization of their core operational processes and systems.

BUSINESS AND OPERATING MODEL TRANSFORMATION

Finally, established companies leverage cloud technologies to transform their core business processes and operations and to create new digital business models. Volkswagen, for example, has created the cloud platform Volkswagen Industrial Cloud to connect over 100 manufacturing plants, 500 warehouses and over 1,000 suppliers and partners, with a long-term goal to digitize and integrate its global supply chain across more than 30,000 locations. The cloud platform consolidates real-time data from machines, sensors and systems, while applying advanced analytics to track and optimize shop-floor processes. According to Martin Hofmann, CIO of Volkswagen, the company's core processes and operations differ across locations, which makes it very difficult to standardize and summarize data. Yet, as Hofmann explains:

> With the Volkswagen Industrial Cloud, we are able to do this: we consolidate the data from all locations. In the future, we will be able to evaluate and control all key figures from production and logistics, regardless of their type, globally. We will go live with Industry 4.0.[13]

In summary, the development of enterprise-wide data strategies, data assets and capabilities is an important and potentially business critical issue that business and finance leaders have to become familiar with. The use of digital technologies, and in particular cloud technologies, in its various forms and use cases, is not just about replacing legacy data and technology systems, but about enabling the digital transformation of the core operating model (as discussed in the previous chapter), as well as the creation of new digital business models (a topic that we will discuss in Part Three).

Companies that approach the transformation of data assets and capabilities with a narrow focus on short-term cost savings only may risk following in the footsteps of those short-lived companies that, about a century ago, used electricity to replace their steam engines to save energy costs, yet did not see the need to prepare their organizations for a new economic era to come (as mentioned in the introduction to Part One). Put simply, established companies that want to participate in the connected world have to accept that, regardless of their industry sector, data is going to be *the* key enabler to connect, interact and collaborate with clients, suppliers or other ecosystems partners (see Figure 3.3).

FIGURE 3.3   Data-enabled core business and operating model (schematic example)

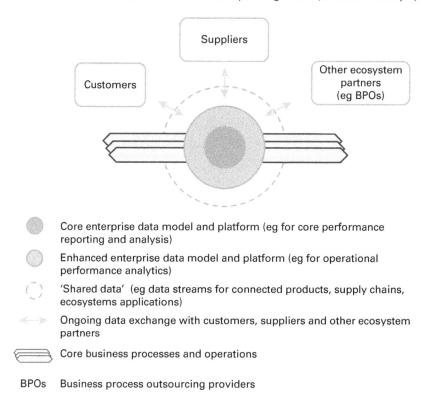

Core enterprise data model and platform (eg for core performance reporting and analysis)

Enhanced enterprise data model and platform (eg for operational performance analytics)

'Shared data' (eg data streams for connected products, supply chains, ecosystems applications)

Ongoing data exchange with customers, suppliers and other ecosystem partners

Core business processes and operations

BPOs   Business process outsourcing providers

Turning data into analytical insight

The role of finance in turning data into insight is often not well defined, which can create a lot of unnecessary confusion and tension – especially if other teams have been established to provide the business with performance insight that overlaps with intelligence that finance would have claimed as their own in the past. In many organizations these 'data and insight' teams have been created not to challenge the role of finance, but to develop analytical expertise that finance teams were not willing, or able, to provide. In order to play a role in analytics (beyond standard financial reporting and performance management), CFOs and their teams would have to move from 'managing the business' towards 'running the business', which requires day-to-day analytical support for operational decision-making; the latter traditionally residing outside the CFO's purview in markets and operations.

While finance can play a role in commercial decision-making, it would better serve the business as a whole by keeping a holistic and independent perspective and focusing on the implications of the regular performance cycle, rather than getting deeply involved in operational analytics and decision-making. However, business leaders are aware that a lot of value can fall between operational cracks, and that the creation of combined front-line teams that are bringing together deep commercial, financial and analytical skills to identify and unlock operational value opportunities can be a real game-changer (a topic we will explore further in Chapters 7 and 9).

Embedding data and analytics in the decision-making process

The impact of data and analytics on decision-making, and thereby on business performance, has been discussed extensively. A statistical correlation between data-driven decision-making and performance is generally difficult to quantify and prove. That said, a wide range of empirical studies suggest that the two are inextricably linked.

For example, a study conducted by Wharton School and IHS Markit in 2018 stated that 'data-literate' corporations tend to achieve a 3–5 per cent higher enterprise value than their less data-literate peers, and that many of the core capabilities and practices that data-literate companies have established, especially those that enable employees across the organization to make more data-informed and fact-based decisions, are positively related to key financial performance indicators, including productivity and gross margin.[14] A study conducted by Forrester in 2018 estimated that data-driven (and customer-centric) businesses were growing ahead of their peers at an average of more than 30 per cent annually.[15]

These findings confirm what many previous studies had indicated years earlier when the topic of data analytics become fashionable across many leading established companies. For example, already in 2011, MIT professor Erik Brynjolfsson and his colleagues surveyed the business practices and information technology investments of 179 large, publicly traded firms and found that companies that embrace data-driven decision-making have experienced productivity improvements that are 5–6 per cent higher than would be expected given their other investments and information technology usage.[16] The team also found some statistical evidence that suggests a positive association between data-driven decision-making and other business performance measures such as asset utilization, return on equity and market value. A survey of over 3,000 executives and business managers, by the *MIT Sloan Management Review* and the IBM Institute for Business Value, found that higher performing companies are far more likely to make use of data and analytics in decision-making than their lower performing peers.[17] Finally, an executive survey covering over 750 global companies, published in 2011 by Bain & Company, found that decision-making effectiveness and financial results correlated at a 95 per cent confidence level or higher for every country, industry and company size covered by the survey sample.[18] Indeed, the companies that were most effective at decision-making and execution generated average total shareholder returns nearly six percentage points higher than those of other firms.

These findings are impressive and indeed surprisingly consistent over time, and, of course, the question is: what can CFOs do to unlock these significant value opportunities? The answer is related and enabled by technology innovation but – as earlier findings indirectly suggest – driven by the (re-)design of the decision-making process.

When it comes to decision-making, people tend to think of the few, big and strategic decisions to be made by executives. But organizations make thousands of decisions every day. In fact, the way in which organizations operate could well be described and viewed as a series of decision-making processes. By breaking down a decision-making process, we can see that most business decisions, strategic and operational, tend to follow a similar pattern. First, data required to make a decision is collected to inform the decision. Then someone (or something) processes the data to formulate and evaluate alternative courses of action. Decisions that are acted upon will lead to an outcome that can be used to collect feedback, which generates new data points that can be used to inform the next decision-making process (Figure 3.4).

Breaking down the decision-making process in this way illustrates that data is an important input factor but also that there are other important factors to be considered, especially the *processor* of data and the *decision-maker*. In fact, we can see that, while data may hold the potential to better decision-making, it is the *processor* that generates insights to inform decisions, and that it is the

FIGURE 3.4   Data-driven decision-making process (schematic)

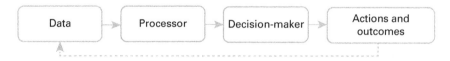

decision-maker that triggers action. In other words, it is the processor and the decision-maker that unlock the potential for value creation *from* data. We may assume that both the processor and the decision-maker are humans; however, in a digitally maturing organization, humans are increasingly supported or replaced by machines. Both humans and machines can be powerful processors and decision-makers, although with different, and in fact complementary, strengths and weaknesses that are important to consider.

Thus, in order to unlock the true value of data-driven decision-making, CFOs may need to make a more conscious effort to review and redesign their key decision-making processes. Following the principles of design thinking, they should pay specific attention both to the processor and to the decision-maker. In the broadest sense, CFOs can distinguish between three types of decisions:

1 **Strategic business decisions:** On one end of the spectrum, there are the few, big and strategic business decisions. Typically, strategic business decisions are made by humans (for example, executives), based on human interactions and judgement (for example, during an executive board meeting). The preparation of these decisions requires comprehensive use of data that will be analysed and aggregated (for example, through a board presentation) to inform the decision. In other words, data-driven decision-making is already the norm, therefore the opportunities for further machine-enabled enhancements are comparably limited. That said, the strategic decision-making process can be significantly enhanced by the use of data and machine-enabled scenario modelling and simulations – an opportunity that is schematically illustrated in Figure 3.5, and that we will be exploring further in Chapter 8.

FIGURE 3.5   Data-driven and machine-enabled strategic business decisions (schematic example)

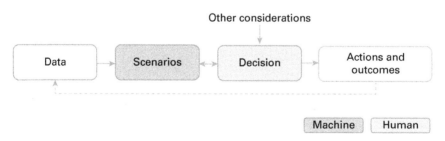

2   **Transactional decisions:** At the other end of the spectrum, CFOs can focus on the vast amount of transactional business decisions that drive the operational engine of the company (Figure 3.6). As discussed in the previous chapter, these decisions provide significant opportunities for enhanced data-driven decision-making and value creation. This is particularly interesting when large volumes of consumer- and process-generated data can be used to feed self-learning algorithms and machines to run, monitor and continuously improve core business processes and operations without direct human involvement – an opportunity that companies like Amazon have used very effectively to create a competitive advantage.

3   **Operational business decision-making:** Perhaps the most interesting value opportunity for established companies, and specifically for CFOs and their finance team, may be found in between these transactional decisions at the core, and the strategic business decisions at an executive level: the many operational business decisions that are made every day at the front line, spanning all parts of the business (Figure 3.7). These range from portfolio optimization decisions in R&D to pricing decisions in sales. Most of these decisions happen frequently, yet are also individually unique and complex, which requires a combination of machine-enabled, data-driven analytics and human judgement. Just imagine an AI-powered machine that processes data to make predictions and formulate a range of possible actions that humans can then use to decide on the best way forward.[19] The main advantage of this human–machine collaboration is that humans do not need to interface directly with data but rather with the possibilities and predictions produced by the machine's processing of the data. Humans can make use of additional information or other considerations, for example in the form of strategic priorities, human preferences and values, or dynamic systems complexities, to confirm or depart from the objective rationality of the machine.[20]

FIGURE 3.6   Data-driven and machine-enabled transactional decisions (schematic example)

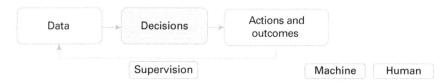

FIGURE 3.7   Data-driven and machine-enabled operational business decision-making process (schematic)

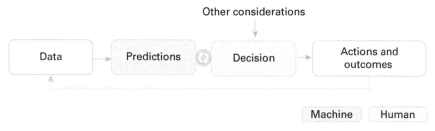

The opportunity to unlock and protect new value through the enhancement of these operational business decisions can be significant, yet has remained largely untapped. These opportunities can be particularly relevant for finance business partners and for front-line business teams in agile operating models – a topic that we will explore in more detail in Chapters 7 and 9.

DATA-DRIVEN TRADE PROMOTION MANAGEMENT AND OPTIMIZATION

For any consumer brand owner, trade promotions are the second-largest item on the P&L, behind cost of goods sold. In fact, trade spend has tripled during the 2000s and 2010s, and may reach up to 40 per cent of annual sales for many companies. Only very few companies have been successful in developing the analytical capabilities to optimize the effectiveness and efficiency of their promotional spend. Add to this the complexity of collecting a diverse set of data that is often trapped in a variety of disconnected functional systems, as well as external sources, and the widespread use of spreadsheets in most established companies. Most organizations find it very difficult to focus their promotional investments in a way that drives category growth.

Many companies are now looking at new ways to digitalize their workflows and use advanced analytics and artificial intelligence to optimize their spend on promotions, focusing on the two main aspects of the decision-making process with related but slightly separate solution options:

- First, the development and use of trade promotion management (TPM) solutions that apply machine learning to automate the labour-intensive processes of data collection and processing, and to automate the transactional workflows associated with planning, monitoring and optimizing promotional activities.

- And second, trade promotion optimization (TPO) solutions that use artificial intelligence to enable a more data-driven decision-making process to provide 'what if' scenarios (including advanced analytics for price elasticity calculations and cannibalization modelling) and related 'next best action' recommendations to decision-makers, which can use these inputs to optimize promotions to increase sales growth.

Companies have realized that by embedding these solutions into the traditional decision-making process, humans and machines can support each other in a way that can unlock a wide range of significant, measurable business benefits and value that was previously difficult to unlock, including increased sales and market share growth, optimized returns from promotional spend and significantly reduced time and effort in developing and tracking promotional plans.

Given the complexity of the business problem, AI-driven decision-making techniques can be applied but tend to be designed and implemented on a case-by-case basis across companies to meet the unique company needs.

Cultivating a data-driven decision-making culture

Despite all the conversation about data, the challenges and opportunities, it is surprising to see how little progress even leading global organizations are making in cultivating a data-driven decision-making culture. An annual survey conducted by NewVantage Partners found that the percentage of leading global companies that identified themselves as being 'data-driven' has declined significantly from 37 per cent in 2017 to 32.4 per cent in 2018 to 31 per cent in 2019.[21] Instead of seeing companies developing their data mastery and digital maturity, we seem to be witnessing a disappointing digital regression. Why is this?

In search of the key drivers for this significant decline, the survey found that by far the biggest challenge to becoming data-driven were *people* (62.5 per cent), followed by *processes* (30.0 per cent). These findings may come as a surprise to those companies that had hoped that investments in technology alone could help them catch up to their more data-savvy peers. Yet, while having the right technology is necessary, it is not sufficient. Despite the opportunities created by technology innovation, a 'shiny new data-driven culture' cannot be purchased or leased, it must be nurtured and developed.

The hardest challenge that companies may face in driving a data-driven culture is to shift the collective mindset of their leaders and people to embrace data. About 72 per cent of the survey participants, primarily C-level executives (97.5 per cent), stated that their organizations had not been able to achieve this mental and cultural change. Humans tend to be fond of their abilities to make rational judgements and are scared of the unknown. Taken together, it's hardly surprising that many executives and their teams still resist the idea that data-driven analysis, not mentioning advanced analytics and algorithms, might enhance their decision-making capabilities. In fact, many executives regard these solutions as 'black boxes' where magical things happen, more often bad than good.

Shifting people's perspective about data is not easy but it is an important leadership responsibility, especially also for CFOs who, by the very nature of their role, can make a real difference as sponsors, role models and ambassadors for data-driven decision-making. If CFOs don't believe in using data in the decision-making process, it is going to be very difficult to expect others to adopt a data-driven mindset. Leading by example is one of the most powerful levers that CFOs can pull. Others include the demonstration of tangible results (for example, for selected high-value opportunities in operational decision-making), as well as the development of data skills and capabilities across the wider organization (rather than just pockets) – ranging from basic data management skills to data analysis and storytelling.

CFOs will need to be both diligent and patient. The creation and cultivation of a data-driven culture takes time and cannot be rushed, but it must absolutely be addressed, with much more attention paid to it now than in the past. The investments are likely to pay off over time: an executive survey conducted by Deloitte in 2019 found that organizations with a strong *cultural* orientation towards data-driven decision-making are twice as likely to 'significantly exceed' in their business performance goals.[22]

A final thought on data

In the connected world, data is not scarce, but abundantly available. Its entropic nature has the potential for infinite expansion, which means the supply of data is practically unlimited. In fact, the costs of sourcing data, and as such also the price and value of (raw) data, is declining at an accelerating pace. Generating value *from* data is not about sourcing and storing it but about converting the flow of data into meaningful and actionable insights. Data should not be compared to the 'new oil' after all. Rather, CFOs should envisage data as an unlimited flow of energy that they can tap into and convert into the 'new electricity' of the connected world – when used in combination with self-learning algorithms and machines, human imagination and courage, data enables us to reimagine how our businesses and economy can operate.

Notes

1 NPR (2012) 'Signal' and 'Noise': Prediction as art and science, NPR, 10 October, n.pr/UPXRS4 (archived at https://perma.cc/C59G-SXFQ)

2 Redman, TC (2016) Bad data costs the US $3 trillion per year, *Harvard Business Review,* 22 September, hbr.org/2016/09/bad-data-costs-the-u-s-3-trillion-per-year (archived at https://perma.cc/QKL4-MZWH)

3 Redman, TC (2017) Seizing opportunity in data quality, *MIT Sloan Management Review,* sloanreview.mit.edu/article/seizing-opportunity-in-data-quality/ (archived at https://perma.cc/CAK3-V4KQ)

4 DalleMule, L and Davenport, TH (2017) What's your data strategy?, *Harvard Business Review,* hbr.org/2017/05/whats-your-data-strategy (archived at https://perma.cc/F9TL-ZUHC)

5 Shaywitz, D (2019) Novartis CEO who wanted to bring tech into pharma now explains why it's so hard, *Forbes*, 16 January, www.forbes.com/sites/davidshaywitz/2019/01/16/novartis-ceo-who-wanted-to-bring-tech-into-pharma-now-explains-why-its-so-hard/amp/ (archived at https://perma.cc/99BJ-WJTZ)

6 Gurumurthy, R and Schatsky, D (2019) Pivoting to digital maturity: Seven capabilities central to digital transformation, *Deloitte Insights*, 13 March, www2.deloitte.com/us/en/insights/focus/digital-maturity/digital-maturity-pivot-model.html (archived at https://perma.cc/E8CU-T6QB)

7 Ehrenhalt, S (2016) Crunch time: Finance in a digital world, Deloitte, www2.deloitte.com/content/dam/Deloitte/uk/Documents/strategy/deloitte-uk-so-crunch-time.pdf (archived at https://perma.cc/6D7J-5JZ4)

8 Friedman, F (2014) Why CFOs should 'own' analytics, *CFO*, 29 October, ww2.cfo.com/analytics/2014/10/cfos-analytics/ (archived at https://perma.cc/Z5H8-LUAY)

9 Davenport, TH (2010) *Analytics at work: Smarter decisions, better results*, p 23, Harvard Business Review Press, Boston, MA

10 Smith, T, Stiller, B, Guszcza, J and Davenport, T (2019) Analytics and AI-driven enterprises thrive in the Age of With, *Deloitte Insights*, www2.deloitte.com/content/dam/Deloitte/ec/Documents/technology-media-telecommunications/DI_Becoming-an-Insight-Driven-organization%20(2).pdf (archived at https://perma.cc/PF85-YU88)

11 Deloitte (2019) Crunch time 8: The CFO guide to cloud, www2.deloitte.com/content/dam/Deloitte/global/Documents/Finance/gx-the-cfo-guide-to-cloud.pdf (archived at https://perma.cc/Z6JZ-E6MP)

12 Deloitte (2018) Transform with cloud. Drive your future. The cloud journey ahead is dynamic, fast moving, and full of competitive advantages. Capitalize on it, www2.deloitte.com/content/dam/Deloitte/global/Documents/About-Deloitte/us-about-deloitte-transform-with-cloud-drive-your-future.pdf (archived at https://perma.cc/6B5U-R6M9)

13 Volkswagen (nd) Interview with Martin Hofmann, CIO of the Volkswagen Group, and Gerd Walker, Head of Volkswagen Group Production, www.volkswagen-newsroom.com/de/storys/industrie-40-wir-schalten-live-4779 (archived at https://perma.cc/C4HG-X4M8)

14 Hitt, L and Morrow, J (2018) How to unlock the business value from data, *Management Today,* www.managementtoday.co.uk/unlock-business-value-data/innovation/article/1520754 (archived at https://perma.cc/S9X6-XYSM)

15 Hopkins, B, McCormick, J, Schadler, T with Sridharan, S (2018) Insights-driven businesses set the pace for global growth, Forrester, www.forrester.com/report/InsightsDriven+Businesses+Set+The+Pace+For+Global+Growth/-/E-RES130848 (archived at https://perma.cc/H66W-RZJH)

16 Brynjolfsson, E, Hitt, LM and Heekyung Hellen, K (2011) Strength in numbers: How does data-driven decision-making affect firm performance? 22 April, ssrn.com/abstract=1819486 (archived at https://perma.cc/M7KG-KKZP) or dx.doi.org/10.2139/ssrn.1819486 (archived at https://perma.cc/Z6GS-QTK2)

17 Kiron, D, Shockley, R, Kruschwitz, N, Finch, G and Haydock, M (2011) Analytics: The widening divide, *MIT Sloan Management Review*, sloanreview.mit.edu/projects/analytics-the-widening-divide/ (archived at https://perma.cc/DT2C-YEBE)

18 Blenko, MW, Mankins, MC and Rogers, P (2013) Decision Insights, *Compendium* (Issues 1–5), Bain & Company, media.bain.com/Images/DECISION%20INSIGHTS_Compendium_Issues1-5.pdf (archived at https://perma.cc/M3DY-ZT6M)

19 Agarwal, A, Gans, J and Goldfarb, A (2018) *Prediction Machines: The simple economics of artificial intelligence,* p 76, Harvard Business Press, Boston, MA

20 Colson, E (2019) What AI-driven decision making looks like, *Harvard Business Review,* hbr.org/2019/07/what-ai-driven-decision-making-looks-like (archived at https://perma.cc/8KY6-VBX3)

21 Bean, R and Davenport, TH (2019) Companies are failing in their efforts to become data-driven, *Harvard Business Review*, 5 February, hbr.org/2019/02/companies-are-failing-in-their-efforts-to-become-data-driven (archived at https://perma.cc/3EQF-J8K8)

22 Smith, T, Stiller, B, Guszcza, J and Davenport, T (2019) Analytics and AI-driven enterprises thrive in the Age of With, *Deloitte Insights*, www2.deloitte.com/content/dam/Deloitte/ec/Documents/technology-media-telecommunications/DI_Becoming-an-Insight-Driven-organization%20(2).pdf (archived at https://perma.cc/PF85-YU88)

04

It's all about people

The changing conception of human work

In March 1964, President Lyndon Johnson received a memorandum signed by a committee of leading Nobel Prize-winning economists, publishers and scientists that warned the president that computers and 'automated self-regulating machines' would gradually replace humans in all areas of labour. According to the memo, this so-called 'cybernation' was already taking place by 'reorganizing the economic and social system to meet its own needs'. In fact, the committee was convinced that cybernation would ultimately lead to long-term human mass unemployment.[1]

In many ways, the committee's prediction was correct: computers have dramatically changed or taken over many jobs that were traditionally performed by humans. Yet the memo also conveyed a major misconception: far from creating mass unemployment, 'cybernation' has become the infrastructure of the global economy, thereby triggering a significant net increase in information-driven work, the creation of new jobs and a major recomposition of the workforce, resulting in a globally operating workplace. The evolution of our connected world will not only accelerate these trends, but is set to reach new levels – impacting knowledge and information-driven work across all parts of business, including finance.

It is not the first time that our conception of work has been changed so dramatically by the evolution of technology. The definition of work developed throughout the 20th century was based on the idea that products and services could be manufactured much faster, cheaper and better if core business processes could be decomposed into predictable and repeatable tasks in which workers could specialize. This definition of work still holds true in many large organizations, especially in operational and functional areas, including finance. Work in these areas can, and should, of course, be automated as technology evolves. If there is a choice between humans and machines to perform routine activities, for instance a standard process procedure or control, machines should win every time.

However, technological innovation both eliminates and *creates* new human work. The World Economic Forum predicts that by 2025 more than 130 million new jobs can be created, while only 75 million may disappear.[2] The majority of jobs will continue to exist, even though the work itself may change significantly. As machines take over repeatable tasks and the work people do becomes less routine, the work of the future will either focus on creating and running the newly created machine-powered operations, or will become much more concentrated on activities that machines cannot perform, such as complex problem-solving, interaction and communications.

For successful change to happen, leaders will need to take time to adjust the way they conceive work. What exactly should be, or indeed could be, considered work in future? If machines can take over routine activities, how can we unlock and leverage human potential to create value in new areas and ways, and what (new) human capabilities will be required? In an age of machine-run companies, these are important and potentially powerful questions to ask, yet few leaders seem to pay enough attention to such people-related change.

According to Deloitte's Global Human Capital Trends Survey, considerably less than 20 per cent of all participating executives feel that their people and organizations are prepared for the transformational changes ahead.[3] While they admit that much more attention needs to be paid to the people-related aspects of change, very few have taken the time to step back and reflect on the following key points: first, the way in which *work* (the what) itself will be impacted and changed – not only how existing work will be impacted by redesign and automation but, very importantly, how new work will be created by the digital transformation of the business. Second, how *workers* (the who) need to develop the capabilities required to operate effectively in future, and how these future capabilities can be met by a combined human and machine workforce. Third, the way in which *workplaces* (the how) need to be redesigned – especially how work and workers need to be organized to meet the needs of our fast-changing, connected world.

Refining work for the future

Instead of focusing on the automation of existing work only, leaders should explore the rapidly evolving and expanding spectrum of newly created work and value-creation opportunities – the refinement of work itself, and the implications for their people. As John Hagel highlights: 'It seems while executives and thought leaders are engaged in a rich conversation about the future of work, few are asking the most basic, fundamental question about what work should be.'[4]

While digital transformation can be a key catalyst for freeing up more capacity of workers, it is not just about replacing or augmenting workers with machines, or the recomposition of the workforce, or simply redeploying workers elsewhere. Rather than the 'future of work', it is about defining 'the work of the future' by identifying and addressing previously *unseen* problems and value-creation opportunities in (new) work, for everyone, at all levels, at all times.

The traditional roles in operational finance, for example, are set to disappear entirely during the 2020s, as the digital transformation of core processes and operations advances. At the same time, however, new work will need to be created, for example, the ongoing design, configuration and maintenance of algorithm-enabled processes – requiring a mix of core finance capabilities, augmented with data science, UX design and technology architecture. And the situation is no different for business-facing finance leaders: they face fast and continuously changing business, operating and profit models, as well as ongoing regulatory changes and associated business opportunities and risks, which will increase the demand for advanced finance capabilities to help unlock and protect value.

Finance teams are used to change, but many are not prepared to cope with such an accelerated pace. In many organizations, this lack of preparedness and the resulting lack of finance capabilities create real problems, especially for business leaders looking for finance's help in navigating major business turbulence, opportunities and risks. In 2014, a bi-annual study conducted by Deloitte in the UK indicated that, on average, less than 10 per cent of leading global companies regard the analysis provided by finance as a primary source of decision-making[5] – an alarming trend that is only going to continue without focused interventions refining the work, role and capabilities of finance business partners.

Ironically, the opportunity for CFOs to refine the work of finance in supporting a changing business and in demonstrating the value that finance can bring has never been greater. But only a few finance leaders have stepped up to the opportunity and challenge – too many remain influenced by ever more challenging cost benchmarks that seem to continuously indicate that the cheapest finance function is, by definition, also 'world-class'.

Where does this mismatch between business needs and finance-driven business support come from? According to the Deloitte study, the answer is clear: less than 20 per cent of finance leaders feel that the opportunities for finance to add value in our fast-changing businesses are sufficiently defined.[6] Consequently, finance teams remain focused on existing work activities – many of which have lost relevance and rightfully become automatable over time – rather than proactively preparing and pursuing new opportunities for value creation.

Moreover, the accelerated rate of technology innovation that has been available to finance has rarely resulted in a comparable rise of analytical capabilities to generate better business insights. In fact, the business and finance leaders surveyed indicated that while their teams may possess some analytical skills and experience, they increasingly lacked capabilities to create the insights needed to partner a fast-changing business. Many respondents reported that their teams still spent significant time on spread-sheets to prepare mostly backward-looking, cyclical reporting and forecasting, rather than the information that business leaders need to unlock the next wave of value opportunities across the business. No wonder many business leaders decided to develop their own capabilities rather than rely on finance.

There are also some finance teams that stand out – not always in terms of efficiency but in terms of business impact. Their relentless focus to reinvent themselves so that they add value to a business sets them apart. They tend to reallocate resources more often than others to meet changing priorities, invest more in people development and make more effective use of technology – automating existing routine activities as soon as they can, digitalizing processes and using data analytics to enhance their decision-making processes in order to address newly emerging value opportunities and risks. These teams are convinced that digital transformation is not reducing but increasing the role of finance in a connected world – a belief that will endure assuming they continue to be open to learning and refining their work continuously as driven by business needs, a concept I call 'following the value'.

FOLLOWING THE VALUE

Several leading global companies have adopted the 'follow the value' mindset and concept with significant positive impact on business transformation, performance and growth. Some have developed simple and practical mechanisms and tools to operationalize the concept in practice.

The finance leadership team of a leading global pharmaceuticals and consumer healthcare company, for example, initiated this change journey by bringing together key finance and business leaders across all parts of the organization to jointly identify, specify and prioritize emerging, unseen *value-creation opportunities* for the short and long term, and to discuss the resources and capabilities needed from finance to help the business address these opportunities to make a step-change in business value creation and protection.

The development of so-called *finance value maps* (Figure 4.1) captured the outcomes of these working sessions, illustrating the main value opportunities across each business area, for example: opportunities to allocate capital more dynamically at corporate or divisional level, enhanced portfolio investment in R&D, enhanced trade promotion management and optimization in sales and marketing, and so on. The finance and business leadership teams were able to use these finance value maps to select a small number of high-priority value opportunities that could unlock significant unseen or untapped business value, and that could be addressed and validated in a first wave and pilot.

For each of these prioritized value opportunities, a new front-line team with representatives from the company's wider business, finance and technology communities were formed. The team's initial task was to analyse how value opportunities can be addressed and unlocked in practice, considering the decision-making process, the use of advanced analytics, as well as other forms of targeted interventions. Providing clear evidence of the value-creation opportunity through practical use cases was a key element of the piloting stage, and required an iterative approach to refine, test, validate and optimize the true 'moments that matter' during the decision-making process, so-called *value events*.

The teams were not only asked to describe the tangible inputs, activities, decision points and outputs for each of the value opportunities, but also the intangible aspects that they felt were important for teams to display, specifically the mindset, capabilities, experiences and behaviours that they felt were critical to succeed. Being anchored in real-life business situations and

FIGURE 4.1 Example finance value maps

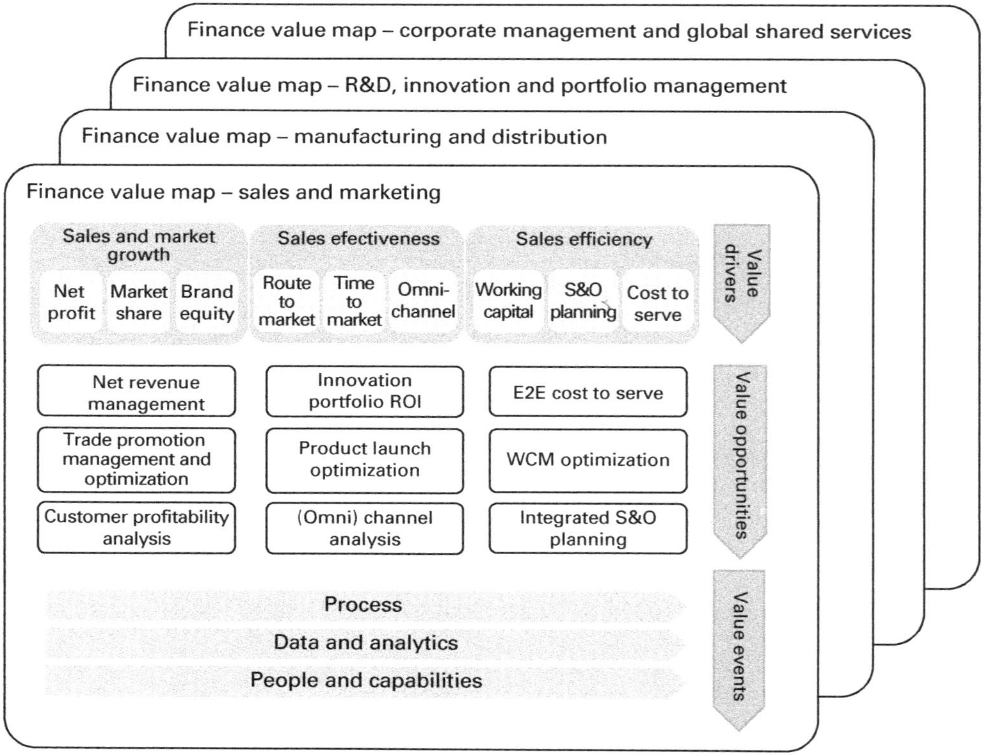

Finance value map – corporate management and global shared services

Finance value map – R&D, innovation and portfolio management

Finance value map – manufacturing and distribution

Finance value map – sales and marketing

Value drivers

Sales and market growth		Sales effectiveness		Sales efficiency		
Net profit	Market share	Brand equity	Route to market	Time to market	Omni-channel	Working capital	S&O planning	Cost to serve

Value opportunities

- Net revenue management
- Trade promotion management and optimization
- Customer profitability analysis

- Innovation portfolio ROI
- Product launch optimization
- (Omni) channel analysis

- E2E cost to serve
- WCM optimization
- Integrated S&O planning

Value events

Process

Data and analytics

People and capabilities

practical examples, as well as linked to the company's core competency framework, the team's resulting findings and recommendations were highly specific, relevant and implementable.

Following this relatively simple approach, this company was able to identify around 140 value-creation opportunities that could be implemented over the short and medium term, representing an untapped value-creation and -protection potential of around 3–5 per cent of the company's total net revenue.

The idea of 'following the value' creates an opportunity for the continuous, value-oriented refinement of work, which allows CFOs to shift the focus of work from automatable, routine activities towards further evolving and newly emerging business value opportunities and risks. While the automation of routine activities remains an important transformational step to free up capacity, the people- and capability-related aspects of digital transformation must go far beyond automating people's jobs away, or augmenting the human workforce with machines to improve productivity. 'Following the value' means that everyone, at all levels, and at all times, is proactively trying to find new ways to unlock new business value opportunities, or to mitigate new business risks. Adopting the 'follow the value' concept, or employing similar approaches to refine work for the future, can help CFOs and their leadership teams unlock and protect significant business value – usually at a multiple of what automation of existing work can deliver. It confirms the critical role and contribution that finance teams can make, while highlighting the need to cultivate and develop core human behaviours and capabilities – but it needs a significantly greater and ongoing focus on the refinement of work, the development of new cognitive capabilities, and the creation of a workplace that enables much greater organizational agility and inspiration to grow and learn continuously, at scale.

Preparing knowledge workers for a new future

The need to develop more varied people skills to adapt to a changing business, and to keep pace with technology innovation, is a major challenge for companies. The list of skills required to address new business opportunities and risks often grows faster than the rate at which workers can be trained. In these cases, focusing on trainable skills alone is not enough to build an adaptable workforce for the future.

Businesses keen to 'follow the value' should focus more on the cultivation of core capabilities such as curiosity, empathy and creativity – skills that underlie the ability to identify, acquire and apply new skills continuously and proactively. A greater focus on capability development may unlock human drive and imagination to identify and explore new ways of value creation – for instance, by connecting with and understanding the changing needs of customers, employees and other people; recognizing and adapting to highly specific and fast-changing business contexts; communicating and collaborating with other humans and developing new ways of working. These activities, unlike skills, are applicable across multiple domains, and take place over time.[7] Unfortunately, few companies focus enough on the development of core human capability – there might be some exceptions within more creative functions and roles, but usually not in finance.

Cultivating core cognitive capabilities

Core cognitive capabilities are those that we are born with and tend to differentiate us as humans – eg curiosity, empathy, creativity and imagination. They are not fixed, and can be cultivated and developed through deliberate practice and the right working environment. If neglected, however, they may become underdeveloped and dormant.

In his book *A Whole New Mind* business author Daniel Pink describes how the predictable and methodical nature of work in the 20th century influenced people to use and develop so-called 'left-brain' capabilities, such as analytical and methodical thinking, at the expense of 'right-brain' capabilities such as curiosity, empathy and creativity.[8] This is a common challenge for finance teams entering the connected world. While not scientifically proven from an anatomical perspective,[9] the 'left-brain/right-brain' *model* can still be a very useful framework and reminder for CFOs to pay attention to the development of both sides of the spectrum. The ability and drive to identify new opportunities for value creation, to create new ideas, to reimagine new ways of working, to connect and communicate across domains, and so on, increasingly requires highly developed core cognitive capabilities.

CFOs can support their people by helping them develop enhanced cognitive capabilities, specifically those needed to navigate ever-increasing levels of organizational connectedness and information complexity. Enhanced cognitive capabilities are established and refined over time – allowing people to adapt their ways of thinking, communicating and collaborating within a constantly changing context.

Thinking differently

Our ability to adapt to new ways of thinking plays an important role in navigating the connected world, and requires the development of two important, cognitive abilities – contextual thinking and metacognition:

- **Contextual thinking** refers to our ability to look at changing needs and information from different perspectives and angles, ie different contexts, and to expand our horizons to understand the forces, opportunities and risks that shape the environments within which we operate in a connected world. Moreover, contextual thinking is essential to seeing the world from the perspective of others, for example to understand other people's desires and needs. Doing so helps us to create trusted relationships within the context of increasingly cross-functional, cross-organizational, cross-sector or cross-border interactions and collaborations.

- **Metacognition** is related to contextual thinking. It describes the ability to step back and reflect on how existing and emerging problem-solving strategies are performing, as well as the mental flexibility to quickly switch to alternative strategies. In many ways it is the most foundational, cognitive capability to learn, as it refers to the ability to 'think about thinking', specifically the ability to question previous ways of thinking, and, if needed, to adopt new ways of thinking. Metacognition helps avoid dead ends and allows us to identify new opportunities and risks by encouraging important behaviours, such as the ability to ask good questions, rather than jumping to 'proven solutions'; the capability to take proactive steps to search for alternative solutions; and the skill of challenging and changing deeply ingrained mental models and ways of working.

Both contextual thinking and metacognition represent capabilities that machines cannot perform, and are therefore important capabilities for people to develop.

Communicating differently

The intellectual, empathic and cognitive capability required to interact effectively with a wide range of diverse stakeholders in different and constantly evolving contextual settings is often underestimated, but nevertheless remains a core aspect of the cross-organizational role of finance. The constantly growing organizational connectedness and the explosion of information and communication channels further increases the need for people with effective and finely tuned communication abilities.

With machines taking over more and more routine, methodological and analytical tasks, finance leaders and their teams should be prepared to spend considerably more time on developing their communication capabilities than they may have in the past. Several studies show that the demand for people with enhanced communication skills (such as the ability to connect and coach with empathy, to draw conclusions despite ambiguity, to provide clear explanations of complex analytical analyses or express recommendations through storytelling) is increasing and will continue to increase.

Low-complexity communication may be taken over or at least supported by emerging cognitive technologies, such as natural language recognition and processing, but empathic and contextual communication will remain a human domain for many years to come. In fact, the introduction of communication platforms will, if anything, require new capabilities such as the ability to share purposeful, clear and concise messages by using and combining a wide range of verbal and non-verbal, visual and digital means.

Collaborating differently

Effective collaboration has never been more important in the workplace, but getting it right is not easy. When an organization lacks collaboration and teamwork, it either ends up functioning as a collection of silos, or – at the other extreme – allocating too much time to unproductive meetings.

Collaboration skills are all about the ability to work effectively with others on a common task, to take action with respect to intentions, needs and contributions of others, and to align different perspectives to find the most beneficial solutions for the team and company. Yet collaboration is becoming more complex – driven by a more diverse workforce, cross-functional collaboration and agile and remote working, as well as the 'collaboration' with machines, as discussed in previous chapters. Complex collaboration may require some adaptation, but offers an exciting opportunity for finance to remain the 'glue' of our increasingly modular organizations.

Creating an inspiring working environment

The refinement of work as well as the cultivation of corresponding workers' capabilities is not a one-off exercise, but a continuous process that should become a key aspect of future work itself. CFOs should create a working environment that encourages and supports continuous evolution, capability development and learning at scale.

Creating a growth mindset

Inspiring continuous learning is an essential aspect of creating the workforce of the future. CFOs can support their people by helping them develop a growth mindset – as individuals, and as a team. People with a growth mindset believe that their capabilities will develop through continuous effort and practice. According to Stanford University psychologist Carol Dweck, people with a growth mindset are generally more self-driven and eager to take on new challenges to enhance their capabilities.[10] Unlike people with a fixed mindset, people with a strong growth mindset thrive on constructive feedback and perceive failures and mistakes as opportunities to learn faster.

A growth mindset is a critical enabler and driver for a continuous learning culture. Many leading companies have started to make significant investments in supporting their people and teams on this journey. For instance, when one company moved to an 'AI-first' growth mindset, the firm introduced a new capability development programme for more than 18,000 employees across all its global functions. To encourage a continuous, experimental learning culture, the company created an organic support model that allows future talent to develop and flourish, from formal coursework to informal knowledge sharing between employees.

Some companies have started to set aside time for employees to put their new capabilities into practice by driving AI-based innovation and piloting projects that they feel passionate about. In return, the company not only benefits from meaningful and practical digital innovation, but also a workforce that feels motivated, valued and nurtured. Being able to strengthen employees' growth mindset and passion, as well as encourage greater organizational collaboration and learning at scale, creates an environment that attracts future talent and encourages continuous capability development.

Creating organizational agility

In response to continuous change, many large, established companies have started to break down rigid organizational structures. The creation of modular team structures, especially at the front line, operating around digitalized core business processes and operations, is a key aspect of digital transformation in large companies – and an important topic that we will explore further in Part Two. Moving the business as a whole in this direction, energized by the intention to create more flexibility within finance front- and back-office teams in order to 'follow the value', will likely give rise to the pioneering of new organizational models and ways of working.

From a shared-services perspective, for example, companies like Procter & Gamble (P&G) have introduced the so-called 'flow-to-the-work' concept. P&G first introduced this concept in their Global Business Services (GBS) organization. The 'flow-to-the-work' concept addresses the fluctuating, project-related nature of service requests by creating more flexibility for GBS teams to focus on changing business priorities. While some jobs remain pre-assigned to permanent service roles, a large proportion of resources are allocated continuously to serve the business needs and initiatives with the highest urgency, strategic relevance or pay-off. Workers are not constrained to stay in one business unit in one region, but instead are assigned to working in flexible, temporary teams organized to tackle pressing events and assignments in succession. The acquisition and integration of Gillette in 2005 was one such assignment – adding 30,000 employees at a cost of US $57 billion, involving one of the most challenging aspects of the integration of all back-office functions and information technology systems. The 'flow-to-the-work' concept allowed P&G to assign a significant number of their flexible workforce to priority integration tasks, allowing them to accomplish large parts of the back-office integration within a mere 15 months, less than half the time normally required for an acquisition of this size. With synergy savings from integration estimated at US $4 million a day, this translated into savings close to US $2 billion.[11]

The concept of 'agile business partnering' is similar to P&G's 'flow-to-the-work' concept. The agile approach provides finance business partners with more flexibility to 'follow the value' by operating in agile front-line teams that focus on key business events and value opportunities rather than being strictly assigned to a business line or functional leader. Unilever's finance function has pioneered and implemented this concept successfully as an enabling step for their 'Future Finance' transformation. This initiative focuses on a 'deliver more for less' approach by matching the right finance capabilities with the right business requirement at the right time, along with the agility to support the business in driving differentiated growth across more than 150 markets and three global divisions.

By using resources more effectively, the 'agile business partnering' concept allows companies to reduce costs, improve productivity and enhance speed and agility. Most importantly, it creates an environment that allows finance teams to focus their attention on new, continuously emerging and evolving business needs and, at times unexpected, high-priority business events, or so-called 'moments that matter' – where finance teams identify new, significant opportunities to unlock or protect significant, measurable business value. To help people transition away from 'partnering the organization' in fixed roles, to 'following the value' in flexible roles and assignments, Unilever paid particular attention to the definition and cultivation of core behaviours and capabilities.

In a CFO panel discussion moderated by myself, and further commented on in an article published in the CFO Journal page of *The Wall Street Journal* in 2017,[12] Mark Shadrack, former VP Future Finance at Unilever, stated:

> Transformation is fundamentally about change management, about people. We needed to bring clarity and confidence to our finance team, to ensure that everyone was confident moving away from a model where business leaders each had a finance person as their dedicated resource, towards a new balance between excellence teams and more agile business partners.

To do that, Shadrack explained:

> We articulated and demonstrated the behaviours we wanted finance to display, which included courage and ownership, among others. We also got rid of silos and made it a point to over-communicate the case for change: what's in it for individuals, teams, the finance organization and the business as a whole.

The implementation of a new, agile organization structure was an important step in Unilever's journey towards a widely recognized, future-oriented finance function – and was further enhanced by investments in creating a collaborative and learning-oriented workplace, for example the implementation of digital collaboration and learning platforms that allowed agile teams to stay connected, and share learnings quickly and at scale.

Notes

1 Levy, F (2005) *The New Division of Labor: How computers are creating the next job market*, p 1, Princeton University Press, Princeton, NJ
2 World Economic Forum (2020) Annual Meeting, 21–24 January 2020, www.weforum.org/events/world-economic-forum-annual-meeting-2020 (archived at https://perma.cc/G88Z-DR2U)
3 Deloitte (2020) 2020 Global Human Capital Trends report: The social enterprise at work, Deloitte, www2.deloitte.com/cn/en/pages/human-capital/articles/global-human-capital-trends-2020.html (archived at https://perma.cc/8PDT-4ZLF)
4 Hagel, J III and Wooll, M (2019) What is work?, *Deloitte Insights*, 28 January, www2.deloitte.com/us/en/insights/focus/technology-and-the-future-of-work/what-is-work.html (archived at https://perma.cc/5AJ3-QJJG)

5   Horton, R (2014–16) Finance business partnering: Less than the sum of its parts, Deloitte, www2.deloitte.com/content/dam/Deloitte/uk/Documents/finance/deloitte-uk-finance-less-than-the-sum-of-the-parts.pdf (archived at https://perma.cc/96GP-ZLA4)

6   Horton, R (2014–16) Finance business partnering: Less than the sum of its parts, Deloitte, www2.deloitte.com/content/dam/Deloitte/uk/Documents/finance/deloitte-uk-finance-less-than-the-sum-of-the-parts.pdf (archived at https://perma.cc/8DR5-H8CD)

7   Hagel, J III, Wooll, M and Brown, JS (2019) Skills change, but capabilities endure: Why fostering human capabilities first might be more important than reskilling in the future of work, *Deloitte Insights*, 30 August, www2.deloitte.com/us/en/insights/focus/technology-and-the-future-of-work/future-of-work-human-capabilities.html (archived at https://perma.cc/38RH-MY9F)

8   Pink, DH (2005) *A Whole New Mind: Why right-brainers will rule the future*, Riverhead Books, New York, NY

9   There is truth to the idea that some brain functions reside more on one side of the brain than the other, which for example has been observed from what is lost when a stroke affects a particular part of the brain. So, location does matter. But for more individual personality traits, such as creativity thinking, or a tendency toward the rational rather than the intuitive, there is little or no scientific evidence supporting a residence in one area of the brain. See Robert H Shmerling (2017) Right brain/left brain, right? Harvard Health Publishing, Harvard Health Blog, www.health.harvard.edu/blog/right-brainleft-brain-right-2017082512222 (archived at https://perma.cc/62HK-TPTN)

10 Dweck, CS (2006) *Mindset: The new psychology of success*, Random House, New York, NY

11 Martin, RL (2013) Rethinking the decision factory, *Harvard Business Review*, October, hbr.org/2013/10/rethinking-the-decision-factory (archived at https://perma.cc/SSU8-2NFT)

12 CFO Journal (2017) For CFOs, disruption gives rise to new leadership challenges, *The Wall Street Journal,* 25 October, deloitte.wsj.com/cfo/2017/10/25/for-cfos-disruption-gives-rise-to-new-leadership-challenges/ (archived at https://perma.cc/RC4U-AVPL)

05

The engineer perspective

Summary

Key insight

As we approach the end of Part One, it might be worth pausing for a moment to reflect on the key insights that we uncovered in these last three chapters, specifically the application of the art of design thinking in developing digital maturity.

There is no doubt that digital transformation continues to be a top priority for companies across all sectors. For many established companies, this journey requires the reimagination and re-engineering of their operating model, in particular the core business processes and operations, the core data infrastructure and the core organizational structures.

In doing this, the impact on people must not be underestimated. The transformational change that we are talking about here is not just about the adoption of new capabilities or organizational models, but essentially about the reconception and continuous refinement of work itself. As such, it is not just about change management but placing the human at the very centre of the transformation itself.

Design thinking is more than a powerful 'tool' that allows us to focus our transformational focus and efforts on addressing human needs and desires. More specifically, the art of design thinking, facilitated and amplified through the use of digital technology innovation, allows us to tap into and unlock the immense forces of human desire and potential – be it the needs of customers, or the imagination and drive of employees.

If there was only one thing that CFOs may want to take away from Part One, it is that digital transformation, at its most fundamental level, is not just about the automation of work, but the use of technology to refine work in a way that can unlock and amplify human potential.

Leaders who are truly adopting this new perspective will be able to shift from a mindset of scarcity to abundance – they will be able to see that digital transformation can create and attract more opportunities for growth and value creation than any organization can possibly pursue.

Within this context, however, they will also recognize that the structural transformation of an organization, as discussed so far, can only ever be the first step towards digital transformation. The next important step is about making sure that this liberated and amplified human potential is going to be channelled and leveraged effectively to generate sustainable organizational growth and performance improvement in the connected world. This is the focus of Part Two.

Key findings

- **Pressure to adapt:** The combination of the fast-expanding connected economy, fast-changing customer needs and expectations, and the ever-accelerating evolution of digital technologies is creating growing pressure on an established company to transform its core business and operating models to become a digitally maturing company – a company that is able to adapt its strategy, structure, capabilities and culture to a connected world that is increasingly defined by technology innovation.

- **Adopting the art of design thinking:** History reminds us that business and operating models of leading companies were designed to excel by achieving scalable efficiencies in a comparatively predictable business environment, and that they now need to be transformed – at pace and at a fundamental level, and using new digital technologies – in order to meet the new requirement of a fast-changing, and largely uncertain, connected world. The adoption of a more human, and customer-centric approach, which leverages the art of design thinking, may unlock significant benefits.

- **Starting the transformation with finance:** Finance operations can be a good starting point for driving the transformational change of core processes and operations. However, too many finance leaders still seem to hold on to old paradigms, and have limited their focus on digital to automating selected process activities. For organizations with an already well-developed technology infrastructure, this approach may deliver attractive returns (in the short term), but for companies with fragmented processes, data and systems the incremental approach will limit the ability to deliver transformational change at the scale and pace needed.

- **The next frontier of technology is transformational:** The next frontier of technology innovation has arrived, and it involves the use of cloud-based platforms, analytics and artificial intelligence solutions at scale. However, it may require a fundamental reimagination and redesign of how today's cross-functional operations work. The art of design thinking can help transformational leaders to break through traditional silos and build the foundations for new ways of working.

- **Use of data is still sub-optimal:** Data may be regarded as the 'new oil', but for all the impressive gains promised, in practice only very few companies have actually realized the true benefits from 'data' – owing to a lack of data quality, a lack of business context and a lack of capabilities to turn large amounts of data into meaningful and actionable business insights.

- **Turning data into insights:** In turning data into meaningful insights, CFOs need to overcome four leadership challenges and adopt the following disciplines:

  o position data as a strategic asset;

  o set data into context;

  o create an ownership and governance model for data; and

  o embed data and algorithm-based decision-making into the company's culture.

- **Need for change is both important and urgent:** Data is at the heart of emerging digital business and operating models that dominate each industry sector. Companies must not underestimate the urgency and importance of transitioning towards this new data- and algorithm-enabled operating model, nor the time and efforts needed to get there.

- **Get ready for the augmented workforce:** The acceleration of digitization means that most roles in finance and related back-office operations will undergo a process of fundamental reinvention in the next few years, leading to the creation of an 'augmented workforce'. CFOs planning to undertake a digital business transformation at scale must pay attention to the changing conception and required redefinition of knowledge work, the cultivation of corresponding cognitive capabilities of workers, the redesign of the overall working environment and the need to change their own leadership approach.

- **Following the value:** To redefine work for the future, both now and going forward, CFOs can help their teams by adopting the 'follow the value' concept – a primarily behavioural change that motivates people to proactively and continuously identify and pursue important opportunities for value creation and protection, while encouraging them to develop new perspectives and skills continuously.

- **Agility and continuous learning:** Agility and continuous learning have been identified as the most important criteria for future success – both at an individual and an organizational level. CFOs can help their teams to become more agile and more focused on learning by creating the right workspace and working environment.

Guiding questions for practical application and further exploration

- Core business processes and operations:
  - o To what degree is your company's business and operating model designed to drive efficiencies at scale, versus agility to keep up with change?
  - o In which areas of the business is your current model creating competitive advantages or disadvantages, both now and going forward?
  - o Which core business processes and operations are essential for creating value in your business, but are not (yet) designed to meet changing consumer needs and expectations?
- Data and technology infrastructure:
  - o What is the state of your data and technology infrastructure?
  - o Will you be able to generate, store and leverage the exponentially growing amount of data to fuel advanced analytics, machine learning and AI-enabled decision-making?
  - o How does your company's current infrastructure allow you to use, and potentially connect, data from various internal and external sources, while protecting the integrity of data overall?
  - o What is the data culture in your company? To what level is data owned and regarded as a strategic asset?
- People and the work of the future:
  - o To what extent is the conception of work changing across your company?
  - o Do you have a clear perspective on the work of the future, the expected value this work will be able to unlock and the capabilities needed to help people fulfil these roles?

o Do you have a work environment and culture that encourages individual and organizational agility and continuous learning?

o Which leadership style and skills will be required to help unlock and amplify human potential in this environment?

HOW TO GET STARTED

Mobilize a cross-functional team with the task to:

1 Develop a vision and a *target operating model* (TOM) for a digital core that aligns to your business strategy (at a 10-year+ horizon) (Figure 5.1).

2 Define *key design requirements and principles* across multiple layers (eg processes, data, people and technology).

3 Identify and prioritize *key user needs* (eg clients or employees). Apply design thinking to create *draft user journeys* that span and integrate across layer.

4 Use an iterative approach to explore, test and develop solutions for each of the draft user stories – potentially using a *digital foundry* or factory concept (as mentioned earlier).

5 Update the KDRs and the TOM accordingly after each iteration.

FIGURE 5.1   Multi-layered target operating model (TOM) (schematic)

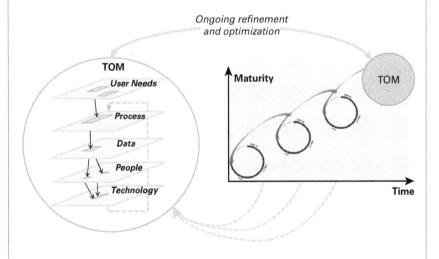

Recommended sources for further exploration

- Deloitte Technology Trends (2018) The new core: Unleashing the digital potential in the 'heart of the business' operations.[1]
- *Deloitte Insights* (2018) Can we realize untapped opportunity by redefining work?[2]
- Deloitte Global Human Capital Trends (2019) Leading the social enterprise: Reinvent with a human focus.[3]
- *Deloitte Insights* (2019) Analytics and AI-driven enterprises thrive in the Age of With.[4]
- *Deloitte Insights* (2019) AI-fuelled organizations: Reaching AI's full potential in the enterprise.[5]

Notes

1 Deloitte (2017) The new core: Unleashing the digital potential in 'heart of the business' operations, *Deloitte Insights*, www2.deloitte.com/us/en/insights/focus/tech-trends/2018/new-technology-enabled-core.html (archived at https://perma.cc/6LUQ-S8XZ)

2 Hagel, J III, Brown, JS and Wooll, M (2018) Can we realize untapped opportunity by redefining work? *Deloitte Insights*, www2.deloitte.com/us/en/insights/focus/technology-and-the-future-of-work/redefining-work-organizational-transformation.html (archived at https://perma.cc/UKN6-REG8)

3 Deloitte (2019) Leading the social enterprise: Reinvent with a human focus, Deloitte Global Human Capital Trends, *Deloitte Insights*, www2.deloitte.com/content/dam/Deloitte/cn/Documents/human-capital/deloitte-cn-hc-trend-2019-en-190411.pdf (archived at https://perma.cc/3GE4-UN74)

4 Smith, T, Stiller, B, Guszcza, J and Davenport, T (2019) Analytics and AI-driven enterprises thrive in the Age of With: The culture catalyst, *Deloitte Insights,* www2.deloitte.com/content/dam/insights/us/articles/6308_Becoming-an-insight-driven-organization/DI_Becoming-an-Insight-Driven-organization.pdf (archived at https://perma.cc/U27D-Z388)

5 Mittal, N and Kuder, D (2019) AI-fueled organizations, *Deloitte Insights,* www2.deloitte.com/us/en/insights/focus/tech-trends/2019/driving-ai-potential-organizations.html (archived at https://perma.cc/G7BG-TGTE)

PART TWO

The entrepreneur perspective (and the art of systems thinking)

06

Introduction

Beyond engineering

In Part One, we explored the evolving role of CFOs in driving the digital transformation of core processes, data platforms and people capabilities. But this isn't where the story ends. While one would expect productivity to rise as companies make use of technology innovation, research led by Deloitte's Center for the Edge across US public companies shows that returns on assets (ROA) have dropped significantly, by over 70 per cent, in the late 20th and early 21st centuries – a trend illustrating a steady decline in corporate performance that not many have even noticed, much less investigated.[1] Indeed, according to Deloitte's research leads, there continues to be a profound cognitive dissonance around this point: on one hand, we would all acknowledge experiencing increasing stress as performance pressures mount; on the other hand, we seem reluctant to accept that many of our transformational efforts continue to produce deteriorating results.[2]

The situation across many other advanced economies, in particular Western Europe, is not much different. According to a report published by the McKinsey Global Institute in 2018, labour-productivity growth has been declining across Western Europe since a boom in the 1960s, and has decelerated further after the financial crisis to historic lows.[3] Does this mean that for all the efforts of (digital) business transformation, companies are only able to capture a very small fraction of the value offered by technology innovation? And, if so, why is this?

Customers, for one thing. Fast-changing needs, growing expectations and consumer power have led to a demand for tailored products and services. Add to this the increased level of economic uncertainty and the constant pressure from new competitors and new business models around the world, it is little wonder that established companies are struggling to create and capture the value they need to thrive in the connected world.

Moreover, while the digital revolution contains the promise of significant productivity improvements, many companies are only just at the beginning of their journey and benefits have not been materialized at scale – in fact, based on the previously mentioned report, the McKinsey Global Institute estimated in 2018 that the United States operates at 18 per cent, and Europe overall at only 12 per cent of their 'digital potential'.[4] The productivity challenge might get amplified by the fact that many large, established companies have continued to use technology innovation primarily to drive efficiency. Yet, while scalable efficiencies might have helped them to grow and dominate their sectors in the past decades, it also leaves them with complex and rigid structures that are hostile to change – a significant limitation to compete in a fast-changing business environment.

The main driver of corporate productivity and performance, however, is not the customer, the competition, technology innovation, or any other external factor. It is corporate management – or, more precisely, the capacity of corporate management to use available resources most effectively in response to changing customer needs, competition, technology innovation, and so on. Making sure that resources are used carefully and productively is *the* major responsibility of any corporate leader, in particular the CFO. It is not just a responsibility towards shareholders, but a responsibility towards *all* stakeholders, including a company's employees, suppliers, communities – as well as the environment and society (an important topic that we will explore further in Part Three). Put simply, productivity is the key driver for business and economic value creation – and it is to a very large extent driven by the practices of corporate management, especially those owned by the CFO.

The evolution of corporate performance management

The key mechanism and lever for CFOs to manage corporate-wide resource planning and allocation, productivity and performance is the company's Performance Management System. (Note: the term 'system' is not limited to a technical solution, but the interconnected processes, methods, tools and ways of working used to drive business performance.)

In most established companies, the performance management system has developed gradually, reflecting the evolution of the business and operating model, changing leadership styles and performance culture. These companies are still applying many practices that were designed to help CFOs deliver efficiency at scale within a relatively stable business environment. They were built on the assumption that the future is predictable, and that financial performance can be planned and controlled. Within this system, financial plans and targets are revisited during the year, but apart from a few course corrections, no dramatic changes are expected.

Monthly performance forecasts and reports are used to identify and assess plan deviations, and to agree actions to 'get performance back on track' for the next quarterly performance review. The dominating style of the performance management dialogue often reflects a command-and-control culture where performance review meetings are used to recognize overachievements, but also to put underachievers on the spot. As a result, the prevailing performance culture is competitive, with neither insights nor failures shared amongst peers and resolved as a team, thereby significantly limiting the opportunity for collaboration and learning.

The long-term impact of these management practices has been well documented – a plethora of targets, budgets and policies that have left large companies behind with bureaucracy, uninspired operational leaders and uncommitted teams. Whatever benefits these practices have delivered in the past, they are presenting one of the biggest barriers for established companies aiming to succeed and survive in the connected world.

A new paradigm for performance management

Every economic success and failure depends on the choices being made about how capital and resources are invested to meet evolving customer needs. Customer needs are changing faster than ever before, so companies must adapt accordingly – even if this involves changing their business models, products and operations continuously. Preoccupied with short-term financial results, some CFOs tend to forget that a company is not in business for making a quarterly profit, but first and foremost for developing and delighting its customers. This does not mean that driving efficiencies is not important. But, rather than focusing on efficiencies alone, CFOs must pay much more attention to enabling their organization to become more agile, get faster and better at anticipating and responding to changing customer needs, and faster at capturing new sources of value – from an operating model *and* a performance management perspective.

From an operating model perspective, companies must, as discussed before, strive for the right balance between stability at the core, and enhanced agility at the front line. When either of these is missing, performance suffers. From a performance management perspective, the same principles apply. A performance management system must provide structure but also promote agility and entrepreneurship. Getting this balance right requires all aspects of a performance management system (both formal and informal) to be well aligned – specifically, the core performance management cycle (for example, planning and forecasting, resource allocation, performance tracking, and so on), as well as the company's performance culture.

Promoting stability and agility simultaneously, from an operating model and performance management perspective, enables organizations to provide a balance between the continuous search for new value-creation opportunities (exploration) and the maximization of pay-offs from already existing value sources (exploitation) – the core principle of long-term performance management and accelerated performance improvement.

Applying systems thinking in performance management

The transformation of performance management may well be the most important responsibility for CFOs in driving digital transformation and value creation in the connected world. Liberating the organization from the shackles of old ways of thinking and working, most of which are no longer relevant and valid, is important and urgent – but also difficult. Abandoning the traditional practices may be easy; the challenge is filling the gap with something new. Removing the old processes and structures in favour of self-management and -governance may work in start-ups, but tends to fail in large, established organizations.

So if traditional structures do not work, and a self-governing approach is too much of an ask for a large organization, how are CFOs able to help? First, they can create a new generation of performance management systems that empowers people to think and act with entrepreneurial spirit and agility. Second, the system itself must be adaptive to meet the needs of a constantly changing business. And third, the system must encourage and promote individual and organizational learning at scale, allowing the company to systematically learn and improve how it creates value for customers.

In designing a more adaptable and generative performance management system, CFOs may have to draw on another important discipline: the *Art of*

Systems Thinking. Systems thinking is a discipline developed to observe, understand and navigate complex and adaptive systems – such as human beings, organizations or ecosystems. Systems thinking is not new; it was first conceived and developed in the 1950s and has since been used successfully across a number of domains, including physics, biology, social sciences, engineering – and, increasingly, economics and business.

Arguably, the most popular academic understanding of systems thinking was developed by Professor Jay Forrester at the Massachusetts Institute of Technology (MIT). Forrester founded systems dynamics in the 1950s, and decades later, in 1990, Peter Senge, a student of Forrester's, raised awareness of systems thinking for business leaders in his book *The Fifth Discipline.*[5] As an introduction to Part Two, it is worth introducing a few core principles of systems thinking, and how these may be applied to business performance management.

Connectedness

Systems thinking is a discipline that allows us to observe and interact more consciously in an increasingly dynamic, complex and connected world. In many areas, including performance management, this can mark a significant shift in how business teams, organizations and ecosystems operate. Most of us have been taught to deal with complexity by breaking the whole into its atomic components, to look at things in small and manageable chunks, to reduce dependencies into a set of linear cause–effect relationships that can then be analysed in simplified models. Unfortunately, this is not how the connected world works. Everything we encounter, including ourselves, is an interconnected, complex adaptive system – a human, an organization, a business ecosystem, a society.

To understand complex systems, or have any influence over them, it is not enough to analyse the parts – we also need to look at the whole. A complex adaptive system is much more than just the sum of its parts. The essence of complex adaptive systems is defined by the things that keep the parts connected, most of which we cannot see: its intrinsic purpose, goals and connecting flow of information that drives adaptive, dynamic, goal-seeking, self-organizing and preserving, and creative behaviours.[6]

Companies are complex adaptive systems. By breaking down traditional structures and silos to enable more modularity and agility, as discussed in Part One, a company's performance becomes increasingly influenced by setting the right performance goals, effective and efficient collaboration and interaction, as well as the seamless flow of information to accelerate learning – rather than formal processes and structures only (except for the small, selected group of fully automated and machine-driven operational processes).

Emergence

Another key reason why our 'understanding and managing the bits' approach does not work when applied to systems is that systems can display new and unexpected qualities that emerge from the connecting structure of the system as a whole, and are not properties of any of the parts. In the most abstract sense, 'emergence' describes the universal principle of how living organizations emerge from individual elements in diverse and unique ways. Emergence is the result of the connectedness and the synergies of the parts – it is what creates non-linearity and self-organization. A simple example of emergence is a snowflake – when the temperature is right, freezing water particles form in beautiful fractal patterns around a single molecule of matter.[7] While the temperature and humidity under which a snowflake appears is predictable, the emerging structure is nevertheless entirely unpredictable.

The same principle can be applied to multiple business situations – for example, the generation of new insights through dynamic teaming, which is an essential aspect of agile organizations, and a characteristic of high-performing organizations. Teams themselves are adaptive systems, and the performance of teams is only partly determined by individual capabilities; the rest depends on the level of motivation, workplace environment and culture that enable effective teaming, as well as the 'chemistry' between individuals that amplifies their skills and learnings as a team.

Dynamic complexity

Dealing with complexity is a major challenge for companies in the connected world, and is a recurring key theme in annual reports, analyst conferences and conversations with business leaders. Failing to manage the fast-growing complexity of a large organization affects the ability to make quick decisions, drive innovation and accelerate growth, identify and develop promising talents, and gives rise to significant operational, transactional and organizational inefficiencies.

A key challenge for CFOs is that commonly established performance management practices and solutions struggle to deal with dynamic complexities – situations where cause and effect are subtle and where the effects of interventions over time are not obvious. For example, even the most sophisticated analytical solutions are not equipped to deal with dynamic complexity. They may provide accurate insights for short-term performance improvement, but they are not able to recognize the long-term dynamics of a complex business: balancing investments in research and development, people development, innovation and capacity expansion, improving quality while reducing costs and satisfying customers in a sustainable manner are all examples of system dynamics.

Many of the problems we face, such as climate change, are driven by the inability to deal with dynamic complexities and arise as unanticipated side effects of our own past actions. And the policies we implement to solve these important problems often fail, make the problem worse or create new problems. Understanding dynamic complexities is difficult but important as it creates leverage in driving long-term, sustainable growth and performance improvement.

In essence, the art of systems thinking lies in the ability to see through the details of a whole complex and adaptable system; to observe, and potentially even influence them. Systems thinking challenges us to acknowledge the limitations of the linear perspectives and solutions we use to drive performance–such as our inability to predict, plan and control long-term performance. It helps us become aware of the drawbacks of systems, such as the limits to growth due to exploitation of human or natural resources, and as such provides us with a more holistic approach to creating long-term value.

Designing a new performance management system

Applying the principles of systems thinking to both strategic and operational aspects of performance management raises some important questions for CFOs to focus on:

- From a strategic perspective:
  - What are the new strategic performance goals and drivers in this uncertain, complex and fast-changing connected world?
  - How do we balance our long-term performance and growth ambition while responding to ongoing change and uncertainty?
  - How do we balance accountability and autonomy?
  - How do we create organizational agility and speed in decision-making, while managing risk proactively?

- From an operational perspective:

  o How do we translate and embed our strategic goals into the fast-evolving realities at the front line?

  o How do we become faster and more adaptable in (re-)allocating our resources across a continuously changing portfolio of value opportunities and risks?

  o How can we accelerate decision-making, while encouraging a more data-driven and fact-based decision-making process?

  o How can we capture key operational insights and turn them into a virtuous cycle of organizational learning, innovation, growth and performance improvement?

Systems thinking teaches us that in order to approach these questions effectively, we need to design a new performance management system that enables so-called 'generative learning'. Traditional performance management systems are at best 'adaptive', which means that they can help us identify deviations between where we are and where we want to be, so we can take actions to close the gap. A 'generative' performance management system goes significantly further. It not only allows us to identify and fill gaps in performance, it also drives the continuous adaptation and improvement of the performance

FIGURE 6.1   Concept of a new, generative performance management system (schematic)

management systems itself – an important, if not critical, feature in times of ongoing change. From a systems thinking perspective, a generative performance management system requires an ongoing, two-level feedback loop and dialogue, as schematically illustrated in Figure 6.1.[8]

The first feedback loop and dialogue, the so-called 'Strategic Performance Dialogue', addresses the main aspects of strategic enterprise performance management – specifically the definition of a performance goal, the growth model, the accountability model, the management information system (MIS) and proactive risk management. The second feedback loop and dialogue, the so-called 'Operational Performance Dialogue', covers key aspects such as generative planning and budgeting, dynamic resource allocation, performance tracking and team learning; all of which need to be embedded within a strong learning and growth-oriented generative 'Performance Culture'. All aspects are highly interconnected.

Mastering both performance dialogues can create significant organizational benefits, especially: greater organizational agility and resilience, accelerated speed of decision-making, organizational learning at scale and continuous business performance improvement.

Part Two (Figure 6.2) of this book is dedicated to exploring each element of the proposed strategic and operational performance dialogue (Chapters 7 and 8) in more detail, as well as the importance of creating a growth- and learning-oriented performance culture (Chapter 9).

FIGURE 6.2   Introduction to Part Two

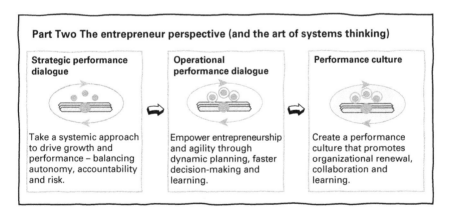

Part Two The entrepreneur perspective (and the art of systems thinking)

Strategic performance dialogue	Operational performance dialogue	Performance culture
Take a systemic approach to drive growth and performance – balancing autonomy, accountability and risk.	Empower entrepreneurship and agility through dynamic planning, faster decision-making and learning.	Create a performance culture that promotes organizational renewal, collaboration and learning.

Notes

1 Hagel, J III, Brown, JS, de Maar, A and Wooll, M (2018) Moving from best to better to better, *Deloitte Insights*, 31 January, www2.deloitte.com/insights/us/en/topics/talent/business-performance-improvement/process-redesign.html (archived at https://perma.cc/DYF8-BFEB)

2 Deloitte (2019) Beyond process: How to get better, faster as 'exceptions' become the rule, *Deloitte Insights*, www2.deloitte.com/content/dam/insights/us/articles/4158_Business-process-redesign/beyond-process.pdf (archived at https://perma.cc/3HG7-8T52)

3 Remes, J, Manyika, J, Bughin, J, Woetzel, J, Mischke, J and Krishnan, M (2018) Solving the productivity puzzle, McKinsey Global Institute, www.mckinsey.com/featured-insights/regions-in-focus/solving-the-productivity-puzzle (archived at https://perma.cc/377K-KFA7)

4 Remes, J, Manyika, J, Bughin, J, Woetzel, J, Mischke, J and Krishnan, M (2018) Solving the productivity puzzle, McKinsey Global Institute, www.mckinsey.com/featured-insights/regions-in-focus/solving-the-productivity-puzzle (archived at https://perma.cc/DYQ5-F8P3)

5 Senge, PM (1990) *The Fifth Discipline: The art and practice of the learning organization,* Doubleday/Currency, New York, NY

6 Meadows, DH (2009) *Thinking in Systems: A primer,* Earthscan Ltd, Abingdon

7 Meadows, DH (2009) *Thinking in Systems: A primer,* p 79, Earthscan Ltd, Abingdon

8 Argyris, C (1977) Double loop learning in organizations, *Harvard Business Review,* hbr.org/1977/09/double-loop-learning-in-organizations (archived at https://perma.cc/FJH4-NJ7A)

07

The strategic performance dialogue

The certainty of uncertainty

Peter Drucker was one of the first business advisers to call out the 'certainty of uncertainty', particularly in relation to the implications for planning and performance management. As far back as 1992, Drucker stated that uncertainty in the economy and society had become so great as to make the kind of planning and performance management approaches that most companies were still practising pointless, if not counterproductive.[1] To survive, companies need to embrace uncertainty, and thereby accept that traditional approaches to planning and performance management are useless and indeed dangerous. What may have been an early warning 30 years ago has become an urgent issue for many established companies.

The performance management systems found in most companies are based on the assumption that business performance is predictable and hence can be planned and controlled. In fact, and in some ways ironically, the advancements of digital technology – such as new information and analytics solutions – have encouraged some CFOs to revert to a more centralized performance management approach. According to this line of thinking, technology allows us to 'drill down' to predict and track everything that's going on, instantly and at the most granular level. This approach assumes that, as long as granular information about past and current business performance is accessible, accurate and instantaneous enough to inform rational planning and decision-making, business can be managed with clockwork precision. Potential uncertainties are assumed to be statistically 'well behaved' and can be handled by algorithmic prediction models. While this might be (partly) true for selected, highly-standardized and automated operational processes (as discussed in earlier chapters), unfortunately these assumptions do generally not align to the realities of large organizations and markets, which have become too connected, complex, dynamic and sensitive to be predictable, other than in the very shortest of terms.[2]

But, if true, where does this leave us? The reality – whether we like it or not – is that most companies are just muddling through. CFOs, business leaders and investors still very much rely on the reductionist theories and models developed decades earlier, and designed for a very different economy to inform 'rational' decision-making. They plan, target, forecast and track company performance as best they can, and then deductively define the supposed 'best way forward'. Accepting a new reality is essential for business and finance leaders. It may strip away any illusion of being able to predict and control the long-term performance of companies in times of uncertain change, but it also offers a way forward.

Although we might not be able to predict and control business performance, we can change our perspectives of how organizations really work, and how we may positively influence their performance. Some CFOs may find this comforting, in that a potential solution is at hand; others might be daunted, particularly as it requires a different way of thinking about performance management – one that is much less focused on 'controlling organizational performance', but rather on driving performance systemically through 'self-management and -control'.

This chapter explores this new way of thinking, paying particular attention to the key leverage points of an organizational system – places within a complex adaptive system where targeted interventions and small changes in selected areas can trigger big changes for the whole. To quote Donella Meadows, a leading systems thinker, who has explored and introduced the concept of leverage points: 'We can't control systems, or figure them out. But we can dance with them.'[3]

We start by looking at the strategic performance dialogue, which has two main objectives: to encourage the leadership team to engage in an ongoing, focused dialogue on the strategic direction and performance ambition of the company; and to maintain the continuous discipline of reflection and adoption of the performance management system itself. As illustrated in Figure 7.1, there are five key leverage points for CFOs to consider: the performance goal, the growth model, the accountability model, the management information system (MIS) and proactive risk management.

The performance goal: how to set a company-wide performance ambition

The **performance goal** is the first key component and leverage point of the **strategic performance dialogue**. It reflects the company's philosophy and aspiration for driving longer-term performance improvement. A performance goal that is clear, inspiring, easily understandable and sharable by employees can permeate every level of the organization, and thereby drive organizational focus, alignment and commitment without commanding, controlling or micro-managing individuals. If accepted and shared widely across the organization, it can also have a very positive influence on the relationship between employees and the company, as well as between people themselves – both of which are essential for making an agile and entrepreneurial organization work effectively.

From an individual employee perspective, a performance goal must not feel like an imposed target but an invitation to contribute to the organization's overall desire and effort to learn, grow and improve. Organizations often neglect the significant positive impact that goals can have on employee engagement and motivation. For example, goals that have traditionally been defined between CEOs, CFOs, shareholders and the board, and that are articulated in financial terms only, may be important for investor relations, but tend to carry little meaning for employees – many of whom will have problems understanding, visualizing and emotively connecting to a common goal. These goals may create a greater sense of company compliance, but do not necessarily encourage self-drive and entrepreneurial commitment.

From an organizational perspective, performance goals must help mitigate misalignment and focus, both of which can have a significant impact on decision-making and performance management. Leaders have a responsibility to avoid ambiguity by defining clear and tangible performance goals, especially during times of change or crises, or when supporting major business transformation. In turn, failing to deliver against this important leadership responsibility can amplify organizational confusion, misalignment, fragmentation and inhibited decision-making. Many companies struggle with this. Although some companies have a proliferation of well-meant leadership statements and manifestos displayed on colourful posters, decorating office walls and coffee corners, these tend to have little impact on employee behaviour.

A performance goal is not to be confused with the purpose. Even though the purpose can have a positive impact on performance, it is more about the rationale, the 'why'. As such, the purpose often describes a potentially unachievable vision and aspiration that drives an organization forward. It goes far beyond improving performance, making money or winning in the marketplace. Disney's 'Disneyland will never be completed, as long as there is imagination left in the world',[4] or Microsoft's 'To empower every person and every organization on the planet to achieve more'[5] are good examples of company purpose. It is what drives people forward, inspires their imagination, gives meaning and unlocks their energy – but it is not directed towards a measurable outcome.[6] A performance goal, in contrast, is performance-oriented, specific, ambitious and achievable – in other words, it channels the human energy of a purpose-driven organization towards a clearly defined and commonly agreed business outcome.

Take, for example, Jack Welch's famous dictum 'To become #1 or #2 in every market we serve, and to revolutionize the company to have the speed and agility of a small enterprise' that he set out when becoming the CEO of General Electric in 1981, which had been a low-performing, hugely complex and bureaucratic business conglomerate.[7] The performance goal that Welch set was so clear, precise, challenging and emotive that its employees had no difficulty in understanding or embracing it. It even provided a clear articulation of how the performance goal was to be achieved.

Ideally, the performance goal should be designed to encourage organizational collaboration by aiming for extraordinary outcomes that simply cannot be achieved in silos or isolation – and, once achieved, should provide a reason to celebrate together. Performance goals can be amended over time so as to keep a company in constant motion, thereby encouraging continuous innovation, learning and improvement.

The growth model: how to shift the focus towards long-term growth

The **growth model** – sometimes also called the **growth algorithm** – is the second core component and leverage point of the strategic performance dialogue. It augments and amplifies the performance goal by describing how performance improvement can be achieved and accelerated systematically over time. Most importantly, the growth model helps leaders define and articulate the company's systematic approach to generated, and indeed accelerated, growth and performance improvement.

Many established companies remain too focused on achieving scalable efficiencies as the primary drivers for performance improvement. A quick look at the annual report is usually enough to provide evidence of the prevailing philosophy; for example, showing that, over several years, more capital has been devoted to cost-oriented restructuring initiatives and share repurchases than on driving research and development, product innovation or capability development.

CFOs talk about their intentions to drive growth, but all too often a coherent and systemic strategy and approach to growth is missing. In fact, only a few companies seem to have made the effort to develop a growth model, and even fewer have embedded a growth model at the heart of their performance management system. For those who do, however, the growth model plays an important and powerful role. While the performance goal can propel an organization forward, it is by nature static; the growth model, however, is by nature dynamic, and can help shift the paradigm from achieving performance by pursuing scalable efficiency to pursuing generative growth. Specifically, it provides an intuitive model and framework for leaders to observe and reflect on, and enables the discussion of complex dynamics of growth by leveraging key principles of systems thinking.

In systems thinking, then, growth is usually represented by a *self-reinforcing feedback loop* – meaning that a change in one direction results in a self-reinforced, and therefore accelerated, change in that same direction.[8] A reinforcing feedback loop will result in a virtuous (+) or vicious (-) cycle of growth which, left unchecked, will send a system's growth rate to either infinity or zero, respectively. Viral marketing is a typical example of a virtuous cycle; global warming of a vicious cycle.

Every business, from the largest global multinational to the smallest corner shop, tries to make the basic virtuous cycle work. Once it's established, the ambition of reaching accelerated growth and performance improvement seems achievable – all the company needs to do is to create an environment that allows the self-reinforcing feedback loop to spin faster and faster, accelerating learning and growth with every turn.

Despite the best growth strategies, leaders should not expect their businesses, not even the digital giants, to accelerate growth forever without any sort of limitation. In systems thinking, growth is typically limited because of the counterbalancing, internal and external forces that impact all companies. Typically, these forces are related to market or capacity constraints, such as the saturation of markets, or limitations to internal and external resources. The way to illustrate these counterbalancing forces and dynamics is by augmenting the self-reinforcing feedback loop with a balancing feedback loop, as illustrated in Figure 7.1.

Growth in constrained environments, caused by internal or external limiting factors, is very common, in fact so common that in systems thinking it is defined as the 'Limits to Growth' archetype model. Applying this basic model to performance management can significantly enhance the strategic performance dialogue by enabling leaders to think more holistically and

FIGURE 7.1   'Limits to Growth' archetype[9]

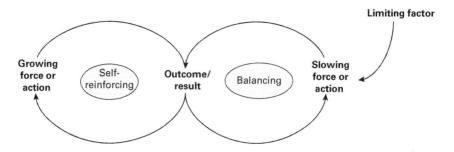

consciously about growth and performance improvement. Specifically, it provides leaders with a simplified model that helps them to understand and illustrate some of the complex, non-linear dynamics of growth in an inter-connected world – many of which may feel non-intuitive and perhaps unexpected, for example:

- **Dealing more consciously with the uncertainty of systems:** Traditional performance management systems have been created based on two fundamental, often implicit assumptions: first, that one can make confi-dent plans and predictions of the future; and second, that one can use these plans and predictions to create competitive advantage and improve performance. According to systems theory, neither assumption holds true. The dynamic complexities of large organizations operating within an ever more complex, connected world are, by nature, unpredictable. The tools and techniques that have been developed to help management teams to predict the future can help in the short term by making assump-tions about statistical distributions and well-behaved randomness, but they are hardly applicable for long-term planning and performance management. For some, this may be difficult to accept, but the truth is that systems, no matter how advanced our approaches to planning and prediction may be, will continue to surprise us. This must not prevent us from taking a long-term perspective, but we do need to think more consciously about our limitations in dealing with uncertainty. For exam-ple, rather than relying on complex planning models and rigidly controlled execution, companies may have a better chance to succeed in the long term by creating an environment that encourages experimentation and learning – a topic that we will explore in the next chapter.

- **Paying attention to barriers to growth:** The concept of balancing feedback loops and associated limiting factors seems simple, but it is mostly neglected or misunderstood. Even those few companies that have created a growth model tend to pay little attention to limiting factors, ranging from limitations in market growth and organizational capacity to, ultimately, and most often neglected, limited natural resources of our world. Shifting focus from abundant factors, such as a new product innovation in high demand, to limiting factors, such as employee or capacity constraints to cope with the demand, is the real key to growth. But leaders are often unaware of systems dynamics, and they tend to respond wrongly – typically, by pushing harder. For instance, if you can't make the team work more, push harder and pay a bonus; if demand goes down and impacts profit, lower prices to increase sales; and so on. These are all typical human reactions – when we taste success, we tend to want more, but when the growth starts to slow down, we often react by increasing pressure on the system to compensate for it. Unfortunately, the harder we push, the more we restrict the limiting factors, and the harder the system pushes back on us. The only way we can deal with this situation is to accept that in every system the true leverage for growth will transition towards the balancing loop, not the reinforcing loop. This is also the reason that leaders should not try to enforce growth and performance by command and control, but rather focus their efforts on removing organizational bottlenecks that may create limitations to customer- and employee-driven growth and development. A well-designed growth model will not only facilitate the timely identification of the most limiting factors but also help leaders understand that growth itself depletes or enhances limitations, and that growth itself will define what the next limiting factors will be.[10] As such, identifying and addressing potentially limiting factors before they start to create a bottleneck is to gain true control over growth.

- **Taking leadership responsibility for long-term growth:** Many significant challenges arise because leaders address short-term symptoms rather than look for the long-term solution to cure the underlying disease. Automating activities rather than re-engineering processes is one example; mapping data instead of fixing data quality issues at source is another. The main challenge with short-term interventions is that many of them deliver impressive short-term results at first and leaders may regard the problem as being resolved. In many instances, however, if the root-cause problem remains unresolved, the dynamic complexities of systems will push back – usually with a delayed, but accumulated force.

The phenomenon of short-term improvements leading to long-term problems is so common across all domains, including business and finance, that it represents one of the main archetypes in systems thinking, called 'shifting the burden' (which indicates that in most cases, the next generation of leaders and employees will have to carry the burdens triggered by their predecessors).[11] Embedding a growth model in the strategic performance dialogue can prevent these typical but often devastating mistakes. Used actively and consciously, it encourages leaders to consider the long-term implications of their actions, to focus more on interventions that strengthen the organizational system as a whole, and thereby the system's ability to shoulder its own burdens over time. We return to this important topic in Part Three, where we discuss the importance of managing business ecosystems' health, and the implications of growth on wider societal and natural ecosystems.

- **Growing faster and better by design:** Focusing on growth does not mean that growing faster is always better. In fact, systems theory reminds us that every system has an intrinsically optimal rate of growth. In most systems, the optimal rate of growth is far slower than the fastest possible growth, and pushing growth beyond that optimal rate will put the system's health seriously at risk. But this does not mean that the optimal rate of growth cannot be improved: rather than pushing the existing system to grow faster, the system itself must be enhanced. This principle emphasizes the important role and relationship between the company's operating model (Part One), the performance management system (Part Two) and its business model (Part Three) in driving growth – or, perhaps more accurately, in designing an integrated organizational system that is able to unlock, channel and amplify human potential (such as the desires of customers, or the imagination of employees) in a way that allows growth to accelerate and improve.

The 'Limits to Growth' archetype usually provides a good starting point for leaders to model and illustrate the core logic, drivers and dynamic complexities of their core business and growth models. Figure 7.2, for example, illustrates the application of the model archetype for a service business.

Developing and using a growth model is a simple but powerful way to enhance a strategic performance dialogue and performance management system. It is a tool that is increasingly adopted by leading global companies and one that we will come back to in subsequent chapters.

FIGURE 7.2   'Limits to Growth' archetype model application (simplified and schematic example)

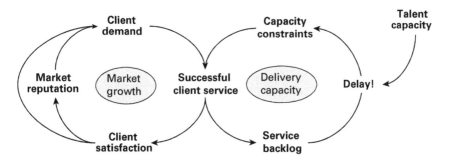

The accountability model: how to balance autonomy and accountability

The **accountability model** is the third core component and leverage point of the strategic performance dialogue. Building on the desired balance between agility and stability (and exploration and exploitation, respectively), it plays an important and powerful role in creating an organizational environment that balances autonomy and accountability.

Driving performance by defining and assigning accountabilities involves specifying a desired outcome and contribution, putting someone in charge, and letting the responsible person decide how to accomplish the objective. There is no need for leaders to define detailed reporting lines, tasks and activities; rather – as discussed in Part One – their role is to help and encourage people to create and collaborate in agile teams focused on delivering clearly defined and aligned outcomes, to provide them with easy access to data and information, to create a workplace that facilitates the teams' access to data and information, their ability to collaborate and communicate, and to regularly review progress, allowing teams to pivot as they identify what is and isn't working.

A leading European media streaming company, for example, supports its customer offerings through the efforts of small autonomous teams, known as squads. These squads define their own missions and develop their own goals, as well as hypotheses outlining how they will meet their goals. The progress made by the squads is shared and discussed regularly, in internal reviews and through customer feedback. Time is set aside to hold a meaningful dialogue and reflect on successes and failures to ensure learning. Some

THE ENTREPRENEUR PERSPECTIVE

squad rooms even have 'fail walls' where failures are pasted on walls to give everyone the opportunity to learn from the mistakes of others. Every few weeks, squads conduct a retrospective to evaluate what is going well, what needs to improve and what individuals can do to improve – a process designed to encourage people to take ownership for outcomes, make contributions and drive personal improvement and growth.

This model may not be applicable and appropriate for every company – and that's not the point that I am trying to make here – but every company should create a model to drive accountability that balances organizational autonomy and accountability for driving performance. In doing so, the following three steps should be considered.

1. Designing the company's accountability architecture

For a large company to work effectively and efficiently, the different parts of its organization must work well together towards a common performance goal. Unfortunately, this is often not the case. In many large companies, complex organizational structures and a lack of clarity around accountabilities have resulted in significant misalignment and friction. Even though everyone is working hard, the impact on overall performance is barely noticeable, resulting in wasted energy and disappointment. CFOs facing these challenges may have to refine the overall accountability architecture – basically, the macro level of an accountability model.

Figure 7.3 illustrates what a (significantly simplified) accountability model might look like, based on an example of a leading global technology company group. Historically, this company was focused on manufacturing hi-tech products (and as such, on creating value by maximizing product profitability). A key objective of the company's digital transformation journey was to shift the business and operating model away from a product-focused structure towards servicing the end-to-end customer journey – and as such, on driving performance with a much greater focus on maximizing customer lifetime value.

Supporting this fundamental change required a transformation of the steering mechanism and dialogue, one that considered all aspects of performance management systems, including a new accountability model. This involved shifting greater P&L ownership towards customer operations, introducing a new set of customer- and channel-oriented key performance indicators (KPIs) and revising the previous charging logic and underlying performance metrics that reflected the accountabilities of other contributing

FIGURE 7.3   Example of a customer-oriented accountability architecture (schematic)

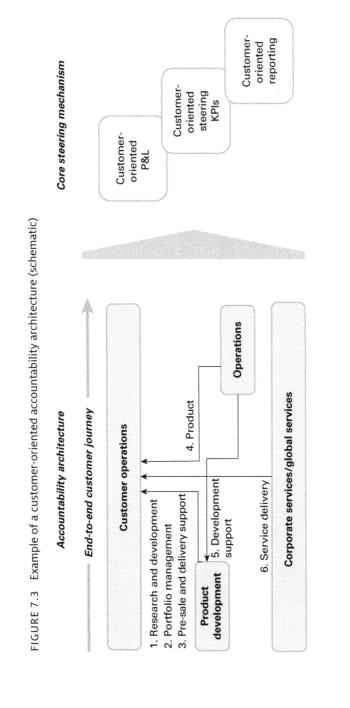

Accountability architecture

End-to-end customer journey

Customer operations

1. Research and development
2. Portfolio management
3. Pre-sale and delivery support

4. Product

Operations

5. Development support

Product development

6. Service delivery

Corporate services/global services

Core steering mechanism

Customer-oriented P&L

Customer-oriented steering KPIs

Customer-oriented reporting

business units. All of these steps, but in particular the refinement and clarification of the accountability model, played a significant role in enabling a shift away from a rather rigid design- and product-oriented, to a more agile and customer service-oriented business model and mode of operations.

The accountability architecture creates the blueprint for designing the company's performance management systems, in particular the core financial steering mechanisms. These featured a customer-oriented P&L structure, a focused set of steering KPIs and core performance reporting to reflect and align individual accountabilities and contributions towards achieving company-wide performance and growth ambitions. There was a greater focus on driving end-to-end customer service value that permeated across all organizational levels. The key insight here is that in order to minimize organizational ambiguity and friction across a business, both the new operating model and performance management system must channel the organizational focus and energy towards the same steering object (in this example, the customer).

2. Defining the decision-making structure

Another way for CFOs to achieve greater operational agility is by simplifying and accelerating the company's vertical decision-making progress. The decision-making processes in large organizations often span multiple management layers, thereby creating a significant distance between the point of decision-making and the point of action. As the management adviser Peter Drucker once observed, these management layers were:

> … like tree rings; they grow by themselves with age. […] Every additional level makes the attainment of common direction and mutual understanding more difficult. Every additional level distorts objectives and misdirects attention. Every link in the chain sets up additional stresses, and creates one more source of inertia, friction and slack.[12]

The problems created by a proliferation of management layers are amplified in a matrix structure, which requires people to interact across an even wider range of stakeholders during the decision-making process – specifically key trade-off decisions requiring multiple parts and functions to align. This is where the creation of cross-functional front-line teams can make a real difference. Front-line teams are a key characteristic of an agile organizational model and can be created to address permanent or temporary business priorities across all areas of the business. As illustrated earlier, front-line teams are expected, and able, to see change earlier, make decisions faster, experiment more, pivot and learn. But front-line teams are not just an organizational feature to drive agility, they are essential to enable a more streamlined decision-making process. Having said this, to help these front-line teams operate successfully and effectively, it is important for business and finance leaders to define, align and specify team-specific expected outcomes and contributions, as well as the associated performance goals and metrics, the key decision rights and organizational interdependencies (see following box).

DESIGNING AN ACCOUNTABILITY MODEL FOR FRONT-LINE BUSINESS TEAMS (EXAMPLE CASE STUDY)

A global manufacturing company operated in a complex and often uncertain business environment, driven by multiple factors such as constantly changing growing conditions, fluctuating customer demands and commodity prices and climate change, to name just a few.

In developing a more agile and customer-centric management approach, the company decided to establish multiple market-facing front-line teams. Specifically, these teams operated at the intersection of key product groups and markets, with an expectation to accelerate and improve the end-to-end decision-making process across R&D, procurement and commercial decision-making in order to improve long-term customer satisfaction, product and service quality and profitability. Each team brought together cross-functional local leaders to address specified and agreed *key trade-off decisions* that spanned the value chain (for example, to align commercial campaign decisions with product range and production decisions), recognizing that past decision-making was often slow, complex and sub-optimal due to functional silos across the company's matrix structure.

The primary mandate for these newly established front-line teams was to deliver a better customer experience with continued and accelerated improvement of profitability, quality and reliability (see Figure 7.4). Specifically, the teams were expected to accelerate and optimize the decision-making process for key trade-off decisions required in the market to align between category-driven strategic growth ambitions and short-term cost and profitability targets. In addressing these trade-off decisions, the front-line teams had to deal with a high degree of dynamic complexity driven by highly interconnected long- and short-term performance cycles, especially a complex combination of multi-year research and development investment cycles, two- to three-year production cycles and a weather-dependent in-season sales cycle, with daily decision points.

FIGURE 7.4 The role of front-line teams in optimizing the end-to-end value-creation path (example)

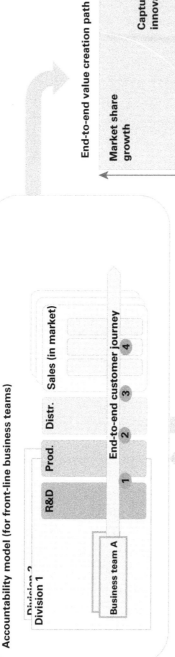

Accountability model (for front-line business teams)

Division 1

Business team A

| R&D | Prod. | Distr. | Sales (in market) |

End-to-end customer journey

1 2 3 4

End-to-end value creation path

Market share growth

Capture/ innovate

Profitability growth

Key trade-off decisions (for front-line business teams)

1 Portfolio management trade-offs (eg breadth vs focus)

2 Product development trades-offs (eg customization vs complexity)

3 Operations planning trade-offs (eg risk of shortage vs surplus)

4 Commercial strategy trade-offs (eg localization vs hubs)

THE STRATEGIC PERFORMANCE DIALOGUE   107

The first step in approaching these complexities was the definition and prioritization of the most important trade-off decisions, based on commonly agreed criteria, such as the multi-functional impact of a decision, the financial impact on business performance, and so on. Sponsored by the CEO and CFO, the front-line teams then came together to discuss the overarching performance ambitions and execution strategy, and ensure alignment. Leadership expectations were clearly defined and articulated in respect of growth, gross margin and profitability-based performance targets, and underpinned by a systematic growth and accountability model that illustrated how these targets could be achieved. The aims were a strengthened focus on the customer, improvements to product and service reliability and better end-to-end alignment of R&D, production and commercial decision-making. These cross-functional leadership sessions, led by finance, were subsequently translated and embedded into the company's performance management system.

The definition and formalization of performance expectations and goals, trade-off decisions, key accountabilities and decision rights, and ways of working constituted a step change in leadership focus and alignment. The reforms helped the front-line team to see the whole picture, and helped them understand the dynamic complexities, systemic interdependencies and consequences of choice on other global, local and functional units, which was absolutely critical.

3. Setting clear expectations on outcomes and contributions

Leaders have to ensure that the organization is always pulling in the same direction – even if that direction changes regularly. In order to do this, they need to define which outcomes and contributions are expected from individual employees or teams, and how these are going to be measured and evaluated within the context of the overall performance goal. People like to understand how their work contributes to the success of the enterprise – it makes them feel appreciated, and that their efforts are not being wasted or misdirected. Performance objectives should not only describe individual contributions, but also how these contributions will help others to perform better and, in turn, will highlight the support required from others to meet the objectives. While this may sound complex, it's important that right from the start the conversation about objectives is focused on measurable outcomes and contributions, not just on tasks and activities.

Each performance objective should be clearly linked to the company-wide top priorities or performance drivers (such as the key growth drivers, or barriers, defined in the growth model). Although not every employee will be able to influence every priority or driver, it's important to create a level of understanding of what the company is trying to achieve as a whole – and to consider different ways in which individuals can contribute. Employees should be allowed to develop and set their objectives, both for themselves and within their teams – with limited direction from their managers. In fact, employees should be actively involved in developing the objectives of their managers and business unit – something that helps employees develop a sense of genuine responsibility for the success of the company, not just their own.

Finally, and perhaps the most impactful principle of all, employees should be allowed to track their performance themselves, with full access to the information they need to reflect, learn and improve. Then, and only then, can leaders unlock one of the most powerful aspects of systems: the quality of self-organization and -control.

The principles outlined here are to a large extent based on the concept of 'Management by Objectives', and have since been applied and practised successfully across many large organizations.[13] Another well-known example of applying the proposed principles is the concept of OKRs (objectives and key results). An important feature of OKRs is the emphasis on transparency and frequency in developing and reviewing objectives. OKRs are primarily team-focused and are meant to be shared openly to facilitate the alignment with team objectives. Confidentiality is not always an option since team members may need to be aware of what others are trying to achieve. Equally, OKRs operate under the premise that goals and objectives need to be reviewed more frequently, allowing teams to pivot based on current information rather than waiting until the end of a performance cycle.

Larry Page, the CEO of Alphabet and co-founder of Google, openly praised the impact of OKRs by stating that:

> OKRs have helped lead us to 10x growth, many times over. They've helped make our crazily bold mission of 'organizing the world's information' perhaps even achievable. They've kept me and the rest of the company on time and on track when it mattered the most.[14]

Since becoming popular at Google, OKRs have found favour with many other leading organizations seeking to balance agility, autonomy and accountability to boost business performance.

The management information system: how to enable self-management and -control

The **management information system** (MIS) represents the fourth core component and leverage point of the strategic performance dialogue.

One of the great advantages of a well-designed accountability model is that it makes it possible for people and teams to manage their own performance. Self-management fuels ambition, accountability, agility, entrepreneurship, collaboration, creativity and motivation – the desire to learn, develop and grow – in teams – rather than just delivering what one has been told to do. Yet, to make self-management a reality, people need to get access to high-quality information, so they can track and analyse progress to enhance performance continuously.[15] More than this. All individuals and teams across the company should be able to access the same information from 'one common source of truth', a common MIS, which enables them to have a meaningful performance dialogue.

That said, this source of information should be used for self-management and -organization, not to impose top-down performance pressure and control from above. Executives who misuse modern technology to create information systems for the purposes of command and control may achieve the opposite – the impediment of self-management by conformity, compliance, competition, bureaucracy, distrust and demotivation. This does not mean that performance expectations and standards are lowered – on the contrary. Self-management and -organization aims to achieve a higher form of learning and performance improvement, and every individual and team will continue to be held accountable for the results being achieved. Yet, the way in which results can be achieved should be largely self-controlled, with the boundaries of the company's risk, compliance and ethical standards (as discussed in the next section).

Building on our exploration in Chapter 3, the development of an MIS that provides access to cross-functionally harmonized, enterprise-wide performance information, potentially enhanced though self-service reporting and analysis capabilities, is an essential asset for any agile organization. CFOs – in close collaboration with other executive members, as well as senior business and technology leaders – are well placed to drive and own the development of an MIS, and to set and protect the principles of an effective performance dialogue within an 'information democracy': ie an environment where critical performance information is made available anytime, anywhere, for everybody.

The CFO at a leading consumer-products company, for instance, has sponsored the deployment of an Enterprise MIS with self-service capabilities. Rather than making people wait for standard reports, management and staff are able to access pre-defined dashboards and analytics capabilities 'within three clicks' on their mobile devices in order to track and analyse cross-functional KPIs and other sets of performance information. Drill-down functionality allows them to specify their information needs by breaking down performance indicators by core business perspectives and dimensions (eg organizational profit and cost centres, geographies and markets, customer and channel, products and brands, projects and internal orders, and other parameters, as required), as well as by key corporate events (eg weekly sales analysis, monthly performance review meetings, S&OP planning cycle, etc). The MIS has not only enabled a more effective and agile performance dialogue, but also delivered significant efficiencies – the move to self-serve reporting and analysis has cut the cost of performance reporting by 30 per cent.

Proactive risk management: how to liberate through boundaries and controls

Proactive risk management represents the fifth core component and leverage point of the strategic performance dialogue. Risk management, perhaps contrary to common perception, plays an important role in enhancing agility, autonomy and entrepreneurship. Put simply, leaders who want more routine activities to be performed by algorithms, who want to delegate decision-making rights to the front line, and who want to encourage their people to become faster and more entrepreneurial in their decision-making, must not only be prepared to deal with an increased likelihood of mistakes, but also to control failures and ethical errors.

The spate of management mistakes, control failures and ethical errors that made headlines in the first two decades of the 21st century should be a reminder of the consequences of poor proactive risk management; in severe cases, resulting in an instant loss of significant business value due to damaged reputation, lost business opportunities, diversion of strategic resources to deal with the consequences and material fines – with some cases resulting in further legal action. It is not surprising that, according to a survey conducted by MIT and Deloitte in 2019, digitally maturing companies are much more likely to have enhanced risk and controls mechanisms in place than their less mature peers.[16] Even more so, a wide range of CFO and executive interviews and studies has consistently confirmed a significantly increasing awareness of, and focus on, proactive risk and controls management across all sectors.

However, while more and more company leaders are rediscovering the need for enhanced risk management and controls, the models and the approach required for the connected world are different than previously. Rather than pursuing the traditional approach to risk and controls management – characterized by highly technical, formal, rigid and compliance-focused activities executed by a specialist finance team operating in isolation from the rest of the business, companies will have to create a model that leaves sufficient room for autonomy, speed and agility.

Many leading companies have stopped perceiving risk and controls as a barrier to improving performance, and instead view them as a value-creating activity and mechanism for accelerated learning. CFOs following this approach will look upon the performance risk and controls management model as an art which involves a systemic combination of a variety of risk and controls mechanisms to meet the company-specific business context, need and performance ambition. The design of a risk management and controls system requires a wide range of company-specific considerations, which is not possible to cover within this section. The two key learnings here are that, first, proactive risk management should be regarded an integrated element and leverage point of the performance dialogue; and second, that integrated performance and risk management should involve a systemic approach, aligned with the key principles of systems thinking. Within this context, CFOs may consider a combination of the following elements:[17]

- **Diagnostic systems:** Diagnostic systems use formalized processes, procedures and metrics to track potential business risks and compliance issues – for example by detecting deviations from core process flows or pre-defined performance thresholds. Diagnostic systems are broadly applicable, specifically for monitoring and protecting the company's core processes and operations. Most finance functions have already made good progress in automating and enhancing their diagnostic controls systems to minimize costs, for example using RPA and other process-specific technologies. In selected areas, leading finance functions have started to leverage predictive analytics, machine learning and artificial intelligence technologies to enable risk sensing and early risk prevention, for instance the detection of early warning signs, exceptions or other forms of abnormal functioning within the company's core business operations.

- **Belief systems:** Belief systems help embed core values within the organization. The articulation of the company's purpose and performance goal – and to some extent even the growth and accountability model – represent key aspects of the belief system. Many leading companies – especially those already operating in highly decentralized organizations with increasingly autonomous teams – are investing significant time and resources into educating and embedding a clear and consistent understanding of core company values and beliefs, thereby helping their people to identify risks or potential compliance issues. These organizations are also drawing a line between acceptable and non-acceptable behaviour, especially in relation to unexpected or high-pressure situations. Perhaps the most visible and impactful way for leaders to shape the company's belief systems is to lead by example by being genuine in their efforts to recognize and encourage value-conforming behaviours in their communications and individual performance conversations.

- **Boundary systems:** Boundary systems are based on the philosophy that in order to help employees become more creative and entrepreneurial, it is much better to provide clear guidelines on what not to do, rather than commanding them what to do. In other words, telling people what to do discourages creativity and entrepreneurship; but telling them what not to do leaves space for innovation and experimentation, set within clearly defined limits. As such, boundary systems usually express limits or minimum standards, such as a code of conduct. Every company needs them, not least the most entrepreneurial, agile and performance-oriented ones. People generally want to do the right thing and act ethically but because of uncertainties, or pressure in the workplace, individuals are sometimes tempted to bend the rules.

- **Interactive systems:** Interactive systems enable CFOs to manage risk proactively, with a true focus on value creation and protection, which requires ongoing, interactive dialogue about balancing business opportunities and risks at all levels of the organization. This process can be initiated by establishing proactive risk management as a core component of the performance management system, beginning with the strategic performance dialogue. Without an ongoing and interactive leadership dialogue on risk, together with a performance management process that links the strategic directions with operational actions and decisions at the front line, all other measures will have limited effect. In a *Harvard Business Review* survey in 2011, 41 per cent of the respondents stated that the lack of strong and active senior management involvement was the primary barrier to embedding risk management in the company.[18] Building on these findings, risk-related aspects should also be fully embedded in the company's operational performance management dialogue, for example by including a balanced set of financial and non-financial risk indicators and drivers in all planning, resource allocation, decision-making and learning processes. Some companies, for example, have created an enhanced version of the Balanced Scorecard (or similar performance management frameworks) to highlight the importance of proactive and integrated risk and performance management.[19]

Ultimately, proactive risk management must become part of the performance culture – as a joint responsibility to protect the company in times of greater uncertainty, as well as an opportunity to identify and create new sources of value in the connected world. The goal of proactive risk management is not to avoid risk-taking, but to help people find the right trade-off between value-creation opportunities and risks – and to take conscious and proactive steps towards handling these trade-offs in day-to-day decision-making.

Notes

1 Drucker, P (1992) Planning for uncertainty, *The Wall Street Journal*, July

2 Beinhocker, E (2007) *The Origin of Wealth: Evolution, complexity and the radical remaking of economics,* p 323, Random House Business, London

3 Meadows, DH (2009) *Thinking in Systems: A primer*, p 170, Earthscan Ltd, Abingdon

4 Disney (2015) 'Disneyland will never be completed, as long as there is imagination left in the world' – Walt Elias Disney, Twitter, t.co/k2ub1rmRfl (archived at https://perma.cc/U8WR-ZFTZ)

5 Microsoft (nd) Microsoft, www.microsoft.com/en-gb/about/ (archived at https://perma.cc/SA6Q-LA9U)

6 A survey conducted in 2018, and considering approximately 500,000 survey responses, identified that purpose-driven firms come in two forms: firms characterized by high camaraderie between workers and firms characterized by high clarity from management. The first type, high Purpose–Camaraderie organizations, includes companies that score high on purpose and also on dimensions of workplace camaraderie (eg 'This is a fun place to work'; 'We are all in this together'). The second type includes high Purpose–Clarity organizations that score high on purpose but also on dimensions of management clarity (eg 'Management makes its expectations clear'; 'Management has a clear view of where the organization is going and how to get there'). When analysing and comparing these two types of purpose organizations, the research revealed that only the high Purpose–Clarity organizations exhibit superior accounting and stock market performance. See Gartenberg, CM, Prat, A and Serafeim, G (2018) Corporate Purpose and Financial Performance, 9 October, *Organization Science*, 30 (1), pp 1–18, ssrn. com/abstract=2840005 (archived at https://perma.cc/AT9V-ZGFX) or dx.doi. org/10.2139/ssrn.2840005 (archived at https://perma.cc/KA5Z-LURW)

7 Collins, J and Porras, J (2005) *Built to Last: Successful habits of visionary companies,* p 95, Random House Business, London

8 Meadows, DH (2009) *Thinking in Systems: A primer*, p 172, Earthscan, Abingdon

9 Clancy, T (2018) Systems thinking: Three system archetypes every manager should know, *IEEE Engineering Management Review*, 46 (2), pp 32–41, June, doi:10.1109/EMR.2018.2844377 (archived at https://perma.cc/U3XU-ZWQV)

10 Meadows, DH (2009) *Thinking in Systems: A primer*, p 102, Earthscan Ltd, Abingdon

11 Meadows, DH (2009) *Thinking in Systems: A primer*, p 148, Earthscan Ltd, Abingdon

12 Drucker, P (2001) *The Management Challenge for the 21st Century,* HarperBusiness, London

13 Drucker, P (2006) *The Practice of Management*, Reissue edn, pp 105–18, HarperBusiness, London

14 Meejia, J (2018) This simple method is used by Bill Gates, Larry Page and even Bono to tackle their biggest goals, CNBC, 14 August, www.cnbc. com/2018/08/14/this-goal-setting-method-is-used-by-bill-gates-larry-page-and-bono.html (archived at https://perma.cc/U8GR-RLPJ)

15 Also compare: Drucker, P (2007) *The Practice of Management*, pp 113–15, in *The Classic Drucker Collection* (2007), Elsevier, Amsterdam

16 Kane, GC, Palmer, D, Phillips, AN, Kiron, D and Buckley, N (2019) Innovation inside and out: Agile teams, ecosystems, and ethics, *MIT Sloan Management Review*, 4 June, sloanreview.mit.edu/projects/accelerating-digital-innovation-inside-and-out/ (archived at https://perma.cc/YEC4-VKSR)

17 The risk and controls mechanisms outlined in this section follow the categorization proposed by Paul Simons in Simons, R (1995) Control in the age of empowerment, *Harvard Business Review*, 73, 1/2, pp 80–88

18 Harvard Business Review Analytic Services (2011) Risk management at a time of global uncertainty, *Harvard Business Review*, hbr.org/resources/pdfs/tools/17036_HBR_Zurich_Report_final_Dec2011.pdf (archived at https://perma.cc/VLF4-9USC)

19 Homburg, C, Stephan, J and Haupt, M (2005) Risikomanagement unter Nutzung der 'Balanced Scorecard', *Der Betrieb*, 58 (20), pp 1069–075

08

The operational performance dialogue

In Chapter 7, we explored five core elements and leverage points of the **strategic performance dialogue**. For the strategic performance dialogue to become effective operationally, it must be embedded into the day-to-day operational performance management practices and interactions, the **operational performance dialogue**. The link between both performance cycles and dialogues should be mutually supportive: the strategic context and direction set by the strategic performance dialogue needs to be operationalized to become effective; at the same time, operational insights and learnings generated through the operational performance dialogue should be fed back regularly into the strategic performance dialogue. When both dialogues are inter-linked and aligned, the wheels of organizational learning, business growth and performance improvement can start to accelerate.

Validity- and reliability-oriented (performance) management

Leading agile organizations demonstrate how the agile model can be applied in practice, and how much it differs from the traditional approaches still followed by many established companies. Long-term business strategies are – despite all the uncertainties within the current business environment – defined by looking 10–20 years into the future, and to a large extent are operationalized by creating a portfolio of innovation and performance improvement projects to help the company take important next steps towards the envisioned future. While the portfolio of initiatives might be governed centrally, most projects have been delegated to the front line and are led by interdisciplinary teams. Most of these teams have been encouraged to follow an experimentation-driven approach to specify and test the *validity* of their project as early as possible. Progress is reviewed regularly based on a wide range of predominantly non-financial indicators, most of which are focused on assessing the project's impact on long-term value creation for customers, employees, society or other key stakeholder groups. Depending on the project's progress and impact, resources are throttled up or down to accelerate and scale the most promising business opportunities. To accelerate this process, the company has established a high degree of cost consciousness that drives an ongoing, collective focus on identifying and eliminating operational waste, and on freeing up precious resources from lower-performing business investments of the past to fuel the growth of tomorrow.

Comparing this to a more traditional approach to performance management, the contrast is sharp: in a more conventional approach, the allocation of resources shuffles around strictly governed, annual financial budgeting and planning cycles. Even though some companies have replaced their spreadsheet-based budget and planning models with a more enhanced planning solution, the creation of financial plans and budgets is still largely based on fixed templates that are used to adjust last year's revenue and cost baseline. The cadence of quarterly and monthly performance forecasts and reviews is not meant to challenge the assumptions of the annual plan, but to identify and call out deviations early enough to get the business back on track. Unexpected changes tend to be handled rather cautiously and with an intention to protect the organization and deliver the plan. Managers who meet their agreed 'last year +' financial targets, or at least manage to stay within their agreed cost budgets, are rewarded for their *reliability*. Innovative opportunities and ideas are welcome as long as they are aligned with existing annual leadership priorities and meet pre-defined, short-term financial payback criteria; however, most of these investment opportunities need to be qualified and scheduled for the following year's round of investment planning due to the current year's budget constraints.

The business rationale and implications of *validity-* and *reliability-*oriented management, as described by Roger Martin in his book *The Design of Business*, are important to understand and consider in shaping the appropriate approaches to operational performance management.[1] As Martin explains, the primary goal of validity-oriented (performance) management is to renew and expand the company's knowledge advantage by generating new and innovative ideas and hypotheses for value creation, but which then need to be *validated* following an iterative and experimental approach. In contrast, reliability-oriented (performance) management mainly builds on

FIGURE 8.1   Reliability-biased performance management focus and trap[2]

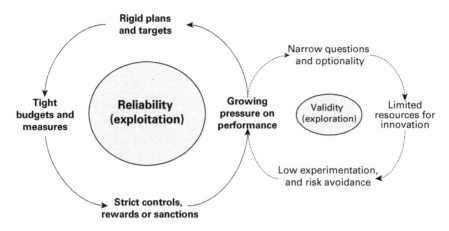

existing knowledge advantages by focusing all resources and efforts on producing the same, consistent outcomes with greater predictability and efficiency in a highly *reliable* manner (Figure 8.1).

The reality is that large companies require both, reliability- *and* validity-oriented practices. A common challenge, however, is that the planning and performance management approach of many established companies has become too focused on reliability, resulting in ever-growing performance pressures.

Rigid plans and targeted, ever tightening budgets and measures, stricter controls and rewards focused on incremental cost efficiency have systematically eroded the exploration of new opportunities to drive innovation and experimentation, thereby hindering the organization's ability to learn, develop and adapt to an increasingly dynamic business environment.

The key task for CFOs is to combine validity- and reliability-oriented approaches to planning and performance management in a way that balances the organizational focus on exploration and exploitation, according to the company-specific situation and ambition. This becomes even more important – but also more challenging – in times of uncertainty. First, CFOs cannot assume that the future (or even the near future) will be an extension or extrapolation of the past. They must proactively plan and prepare for dealing with unexpected change. Second, CFOs have to keep their organizations lean, liberated from any unnecessary weights of low-performing businesses or investments, yet at the same time strong enough to deal with sudden crises and new opportunities. Third, CFOs need to allocate resources more carefully and more dynamically, able to throttle resources up or down based on progress and performance.

The practices of planning, budgeting, forecasting and resource allocation remain the most powerful levers that CFOs can use to accomplish this task. In combination with enhanced practices of performance tracking, as well as accelerated decision-making and learning, they represent the key leverage points of the operational performance dialogue. We will pay particular attention to the introduction of validity-oriented practices to performance management. This does not mean that reliability-oriented practices are not relevant, but in most companies CFOs face a much greater challenge in shifting the balance towards validity-based management to enhance organizational entrepreneurship and agility.

Generative planning and budgeting: how to fuel organizational learning and growth

The first leverage point in establishing a more balanced operational performance dialogue involves the introduction of alternative practices to planning and budgeting that are less rigid and deterministic than traditional approaches, and that support a more agile, entrepreneurial and learning-oriented approach to performance management.

At the beginning of the 20th century, leaders from large industrial organizations set in motion the development of the foundations of financial planning, budgeting and resource allocation. At the time, this was a significant step forward in terms of keeping control of their financials, which gave a sense of reliability to outside investors, and ultimately became one of the most important drivers of profitable growth in the industrial age.

It was not until the later decades of the 20th century that a new generation of executives started to question the increasingly complex and rigid practices of creating annually fixed financial plans and cost budgets. Jack Welch, for example, famously proclaimed in 1995 that the practices of rigid financial planning, budgeting and deterministic resource allocation were 'the bane of corporate America', stating that for most companies, it:

> has to be the most ineffective practice in management. It sucks the energy, time, fun and big dreams out of an organization. [...] And yet [...] companies sink countless hours into writing budgets. What a waste![3]

Decades later, many business leaders can still relate to Welch's criticism, especially those who recognize the enormous amount of time and resources consumed by financial planning and budgeting, and the challenges this creates in responding to a fast-changing business environment. Responses to a survey conducted by Deloitte in 2014, involving over 600 senior executives of leading global organizations, found that financial budgeting and planning processes not only demand significant time and effort, but are also facing remarkably similar challenges across organizations and sectors.[4] The main challenge highlighted by the survey is the rigidity of practices and the consistently high, self-inflicted level of detail in preparing financial plans, budgets and forecasts, with well over 50 per cent of the respondents admitting that their organizations have a 'culture of financial detail' which involves spending excessive time and effort to produce rather limited additional insights and value. More than 40 per cent of respondents said that they needed three months to complete the annual plan and budget, while over 30 per cent took up to six months. A third of the respondents felt frustrated that once developed, plans and budgets were often changed at the top, with no clear action or reasonable feedback to the front-line business. For most respondents, this was an unacceptable waste of time, effort and resource.

Some companies have resolved the number-crunching problem by implementing sophisticated planning solutions; in many cases, however, these tools have not been used to simplify planning models and processes, or to create insightful planning scenarios, but to unveil even more details in order to predict and control performance across each area of the business. The main motivations for doing this are obvious: leaders are looking for reliability. The more uncertainty they face, the more granularity they seem to be seeking to 'recreate certainty'.

Perhaps most interestingly – at the time of writing in March 2021 – the incoming results of Deloitte's 2021 Global Planning, Budgeting and Forecasting survey indicate that on average, companies around the world and across all sectors are still facing many of the same key challenges that they had highlighted in the 2014 survey. This means that – despite all the significant technology advancements over the last seven years – leading companies have *not* been able to make a step-change in planning, budgeting and forecasting. But, why?

Planning as a learning opportunity

For most established companies, planning is a fundamentally reliability-driven management process. Enabled by modern planning solutions or not, the underlying planning processes and models are largely fed on assumptions and data derived from the past to predict the future. Even some of the most sophisticated planning models – in fact, often especially these – are based on the assumption that a large organization works like a big machine, with interacting parts that can produce consistent results based on predictable, largely linear relationships between internal and external input factors and corresponding outputs.

However, apart from a few highly automated operational processes at the core (as discussed in Part 1), this Newtonian perspective of a company rarely matches the realities of our complex, connected world. Large and interconnected organizations are much more determined by the non-linear dynamics of complex, adaptive systems than by clockwork mechanisms. For CFOs and business leaders, this means that instead of following the traditional, reliability-focused approach to planning and performance management, where deterministic plans and agreed financial budgets are followed by focused and controlled execution, a more validity-focused approach is required, and where experimental action comes *before* financial commitment. By shifting the focus from reliability to validity, the planning process itself can become an opportunity to accelerate organizational learning, rather than being a corporate instrument of prediction and control.

Looking at planning as a learning opportunity can have a number of positive effects on the performance dialogue. Not only does it remind us of our limitations in predicting the future, but it also prompts us to act differently – in particular, to focus more on asking the right questions rather than finding the right answers. A simple question like 'What else can we do to create value for our customers?' can help us to step back and challenge long-held assumptions and beliefs, and to explore what is really going to be relevant and possible in the future. Asking the right questions also helps us to remain humble and realistic, while remaining open to identifying new ideas and opportunities to break out of traditional incrementalism.[5] Questions can make us think beyond current ways of working – not just to make people work harder, but to change the rules of the game.

There are different practices which the CFO can adopt, to introduce and facilitate a more learning-oriented approach to planning, two of which we are going to look at here: zoom-out/zoom-in and scenario planning.

ZOOM-OUT/ZOOM-IN
One alternative planning practice known as 'zoom-out/zoom-in' appears to be particularly applicable in times of heightened change and uncertainty.[6]

According to Deloitte's Centre of the Edge, the approach first emerged among Silicon Valley technology companies, which adopted this approach to develop and refine their plans in response to a fast-changing business environment. The management teams of these companies knew that things would change, perhaps faster than expected, but they were unsure of exactly how. Since then, some large, established companies in more traditional sectors have adopted this approach to navigate change and to avoid the risk of falling into incremental and reactive planning habits.

The key motivation of zoom-out/zoom-in is the desire to generate new perspectives and ideas, expand knowledge and enable accelerated learning. Planning teams are asked to iterate between two time horizons: a long-term horizon looking far ahead into the future by 10 to 20 years (zoom-out), and a short-term horizon, looking at the immediate next steps to be accomplished within the coming six months (zoom-in).

In developing the zoom-out perspective, the planning teams should focus on economic trends and changing customer needs, asking questions like: What will our market look like 10 to 20 years from now? What kind of company will we need to become to be successful in that market? The goal is not to create a blueprint, but to build alignment on a desired future and to gain clarity on trends and opportunities that could help frame near-term actions.

Once the long-term perspective has become clearer, the planning teams will focus on the zoom-in perspective to discuss and agree on a (limited) number of near-term initiatives that can lead the company toward the agreed future. Here, the teams focus on questions like: What are the (few) initiatives that we could pursue in the next 6 to 12 months that get us closer to our longer-term destination? Do we have the right resources to deliver with impact? How are we going to measure whether we achieved the impact we intended?

By going back and forth, the planning teams are encouraged to revisit the different time horizons continuously, specifically to reflect on what the company could be doing differently in the short term to build new capabilities and unlock new sources of customer value for the future. The zoom-out/zoom-in method assumes that if long- and short-term plans are aligned, the mid-range will fall into place. This approach prevents the teams from becoming too focused on annual budgets and quarterly results – and also from spreading resources too thinly across initiatives. Most importantly, it facilitates an agile and entrepreneurial, validity-based approach that reduces the risk of being blindsided by developments that may appear trivial today, but are important in the long term.

SCENARIO PLANNING

The practice of 'thinking in alternative futures', or scenarios, can be traced back to the 16th century.[7] The idea to combine the practices of scenario thinking and planning in a systemic way emerged in the late 1940s, when a young defence analyst Herman Kahn put forth a new technique to describe how nuclear technology might be used by hostile nations.[8] In the 1960s, members of the corporate planning team at Royal Dutch/Shell sought to leverage Kahn's techniques to develop business planning scenarios that helped them navigate the 1970s OPEC oil embargo better and faster than their peers, thereby setting the foundations for significant long-term business growth. Since then, many leading global corporations have adopted scenario planning during times of turbulence and uncertainty.

Despite the continuous surge in popularity, many misconceptions remain about what scenario planning is, when it should be used, and what benefits can be derived. At one extreme, it is used just to enhance forecasting, involving the assignment of explicit probabilities to potential outcomes. At the other extreme, it appears to have evolved into a complicated and often abstract exercise that takes up significant time but has little or no practical application for operational decision-making. Neither extreme is effective, but how can CFOs find the right middle path?

Scholarly research and literature defines scenario planning as:

> a process of posting several informed, plausible and imagined alternative
> future environments in which decisions about the future may be played out,
> for the purpose of changing current thinking, improving decision-making,
> enhancing human and organization learning and improving performance.[9]

In other words, scenario planning does not aim to predict the future, but to provide leaders with a broader understanding of the organizational and economic complexities in order to prepare and assist the present (strategic and operational) decision-making process. While traditional planning practices seek to 'create certainty' by asking leaders to place a high level of value and focus on a single plan (ie a process that seeks answers to initiate a controlling process), scenario planning practices seek to create optionality by embracing uncertainty (ie a process that looks for questions to initiate a learning process).

Essentially, developing a planning scenario is like creating a story that illustrates and explains how the business environment might evolve over time, and which consequences this might have on an organization. In times of uncertainty it is important to create stories that encompass a wider range of plausible future developments, including less obvious risks and opportunities that may occur and that could endure well into the future (for example, a shift in consumer behaviours and preferences that may affect the company's products and service portfolio). In developing these stories, plausibility is more important than probability. Ultimately, scenarios are intended to set a stage that invites leaders to see themselves as actors in a possible future situation, and that thereby encourages them to reflect on their expectations, assumptions and intended course of actions. At this stage, the outcome of a scenario is not as important as the storyline's clarity of logic and how it helps open the mind to new dynamics.

From a systems thinking perspective, the introduction of alternative, learning-oriented planning approaches – be it zoom-in/zoom-out, scenario planning, a combination of those or with other practices – is necessary to understand and navigate the complex dynamics of the connected world. Embedding these new practices into the strategic and operational performance dialogues can not only enhance the planning but also the decision-making and learning process, specifically:

- **Expanding horizons**: From a systems thinking perspective, distinctions between time horizons do not make much sense. In a complex and dynamic environment, any action taken now will have some immediate effects and some that radiate out for decades to come. Equally, any experience now is the consequences of actions that were taken a few days and decades ago. Systems are always coupling and uncoupling actions and effects across multiple time horizons. Imagine, for example, we are driving on a tricky, unknown and curvy road. It would be foolish to keep our heads down and look just a few metres ahead. That said, it would be equally foolish to peer far ahead into the distance and pay no attention to what is immediately in front of us.[10] Once we accept that predictions are not possible, the best thing we can do is to apply practices that allow us to watch and evaluate both the short and the long term, the whole system.

- **Embracing new realities**: Organizations, like humans, tend to make plans based on agreed-upon assumptions, existing mental models and conventional wisdoms. The problem is that these assumptions, mental models and wisdoms derive from extrapolations of the past – most of which are poor indicators for the future, and are biased towards incrementalism.[11] Learning-oriented planning approaches try to break this habit by placing more emphasis on asking questions, or by introducing uncertainties, thereby broadening the perspectives of leaders for planning and decision-making.

- **Enhancing responsiveness and agility:** Alternative planning practices encourage leaders to think through a broader range of plausible future outcomes, and the sequence of events that could lead up to them. By exploring how, and why, things could quite quickly become much better or worse, it aims to increase readiness for action and thereby enhances business agility, responsiveness and resilience. In times of discontinuous, unpredictable change, performance improvement becomes less dependent on the ability to predict the future than on being prepared to identify and respond earlier and faster to emerging opportunities and risks.

- **Encouraging future-oriented decision-making and actions:** Finally, alternative approaches not only assist leaders in envisioning a desirable future, but also in shaping an actionable path for bringing it about – thereby embedding planning into the operational decision-making and learning process. From this perspective, the main benefit is not the plan itself but the ongoing, interactive process and dialogue of creating and adjusting the plan. By treating planning as a learning opportunity, organizations come to gain a much deeper understanding of their environment, and – most importantly – the decisions and actions that they need to take to realize their desired future. While traditional planning is primarily concerned about the predictability of the future (which can be used to derive controllable targets and plans for execution), alternative planning approaches are more concerned about the quality of decision-making at present (which can be used to invent and drive the right set of actions to achieve, and indeed *shape* the desired future).

From a practical perspective, some CFOs will be concerned about the difficulties and efforts required to introduce and embed a new planning approach. These concerns are of course valid, but should be assessed relative to the recurring investments of time and resources in traditional planning and budgeting – which, in many companies, create very little or no business value (if not damage). The reality is that, for many decades, established companies have used planning to create a greater sense of certainty and control. In doing so, they followed pretty much the same approach they always have. This may still work for a few organizations that are operating in a relatively stable and predictable business environment, but it creates significant challenges and barriers for those exposed to volatility and uncertainty. Alternative, learning-oriented planning approaches, such as those introduced in this section, can help CFOs replace or enhance their traditional practices to drive greater agility and entrepreneurship.

Some companies have developed innovative approaches to combine key aspects of traditional and new planning practices in an effective and efficient way. A leading manufacturing company, for instance, instituted a 'Corporate Planning Lab' that requires the wider leadership and planning teams to travel to one location for a five–seven working day period to focus solely on the creation and alignment of plans, leveraging different techniques including scenario modelling. This Lab follows a well-prepared and facilitated hour-by-hour timetable, with offline consolidation and analysis completed overnight as required. The success of the Lab relies on and reinforces the importance of cross-functional trust, collaboration, learning and ownership – a significant cultural shift from the past where a lack of organizational trust and dialogue resulted in an overwhelmingly complex, detailed and political planning process.

Finding the right balance between traditional and learning-based planning practices, as well as the most appropriate way to facilitate the planning process, is a company-specific choice and design question. The good news is that when it comes to planning, CFOs can make their own rules. It also means, however, that if planning practices are not delivering the expected value, CFOs will have to take ownership to drive the changes needed on behalf of the company.

Budgeting as a growth opportunity

Building on this, one does not have to search long to find a finance or business leader who does not like the practice of budgeting. Given all the stress and efforts associated with budgeting, it is no wonder that most financial leaders would be tempted to erase the exercise from their calendars. However, despite all the pain, the criticisms and the pressure of balancing reliability and validity, companies continue to count on CFOs to make sure that the expenditures and investments are under control, and that resources are used to maximize business performance and growth. To do this job effectively, financial budgeting, investment planning, cost management and resource allocation remain important and powerful tools. Companies may not be able to cut their way to growth, but they must have the discipline to cut out today's waste in order to fuel tomorrow's growth.

New methods of cost control and budgeting have emerged, or come back into vogue – including zero-based budgeting (ZBB), an approach adopted by many global organizations in the consumer-products and manufacturing industry, as well as increasingly in other sectors. ZBB is not a one-off exercise to 'rebudget from zero', rather a systematic, ongoing process to developing greater cost consciousness. While the budgeting process does start from a 'zero base', this approach facilitates a more agile, interactive and meaningful dialogue about cost improvement opportunities. That said, in practice, there are significant differences in the way budgeting methods, such as ZBB, have been applied. Many companies have used ZBB with a focus on radical cost-cutting. Although their cuts are impressive, evidence of accelerated growth is hard to come by. Indeed, some companies have experienced falling revenues over time, which in turn impacts organizational capability development, innovation capacity, morale and entrepreneurship.

Although promoted by private equity investors, many long-term oriented business leaders have called into question a heavy-handed approach to ZBB. Both sides could be right or wrong – the key difference here is driven by the way budgeting is being positioned and executed in practice. Even more aggressive budgeting methods, like ZBB, can be applied to focus on long-term growth and value creation. Simple principles and steps, such as a more conscious and clearer distinction between budgets assigned to generating growth and building capabilities, versus the hidden costs of low-value activities, organizational empire building, or historically grown operational complexities, can make all the difference.

The CFO of a leading global consumer healthcare company, for example, was able to make a significant contribution to the company's digital transformation journey by embedding ZBB as a continuous process, which allowed finance to reduce and reinvest a material budget to prioritize restructuring activities. Key features of the approach included a clearly defined and continuously updated and aligned analysis of savings potentials and targets in all areas that – according to business leaders – were not going to be essential for long-term customer value creation; and an ongoing reassessment and reallocation of realized savings across a portfolio of prioritized initiatives.

Other companies have pursued similar objectives very successfully, yet may have adopted different approaches. A leading media company, for instance, decided to conduct a 'light touch' budgeting process that sets a challenging 'baseline budget'. To avoid complex and time-consuming budget negotiations, business leaders have been given confidence by the CFO and wider executive team that additional expenditure will be made available over the course of the year, and that they will not be held to account against this number in a 'black and white' fashion. During the year, finance facilitates a highly interactive and collaborative dialogue where additional expenditure from a central pot is reviewed and approved in light of business performance, opportunities and market dynamics. Leaders from all divisions are involved in regular meetings to assess the rationale for new approval – therefore all functions feel part of defining the solution and driving business performance, while the organization overall benefits from a challenging budget being adopted. According to senior finance leaders, the approach has resulted in a cultural shift away from purely individual interests to collective accountability, as well as a much leaner and far more responsive approach to allocating operational budgets.

Dynamic resource allocation: how to build the business of tomorrow

Every company has to balance two types of resource requirements: those needed to keep the business of today running (operational expenditure), and those needed to build the business of tomorrow (capital expenditure). While resources needed to run the business of today should be *satisfied* through budgeting, the resources available and needed to build the business of tomorrow should be *optimized* through resource allocation.[12] In established companies, the resources needed to run the business will be much greater than the resources available to fuel new opportunities – yet CFOs should give at least the same amount of attention to the latter.

That said, traditional approaches to resource allocation are based on the assumption that the company's investment choices can be planned and prioritized well in advance. The goal is to increase reliability by narrowing down the range of investment choices and corresponding budget implications, which is a sensible approach to adopt in a stable and predictable business environment. In times of change and uncertainty, however, companies can be better served by following a more dynamic and validity-based method, for instance by creating a portfolio of investment opportunities that can be validated and funded following an iterative, experimentation-based approach. This approach does not only promote agility and entrepreneurship, but can also reduce risks by focusing larger investments on well-progressing and gradually validated opportunities. Put differently: in times of change and uncertainty, *optionality* becomes more valuable and less risky than *reliability*. Therefore, establishing a more dynamic approach to resource allocation is the second key element and leverage point for CFOs to consider.

Adopting a 'validity'-oriented, dynamic approach to resource allocation can be perceived as a challenge, risking the ability to control company resources. But that is not the case at all. In practice, most companies that transition from a traditional, reliability-oriented to an alternative, validity-based approach to resource allocation will experience a much higher demand for fact-based analysis, clearly guided decision-making and robust governance. Dynamic resource allocation may also require more, and indeed more ongoing, management attention than a traditional approach – to build a portfolio of innovation projects and to monitor and assess the progress and validity of each project, and to reassess and change the allocation of resources, for instance through a cadence of quarterly reviews.

Interviewed in 2011, Patrick Pichette, the former CFO of Google and a passionate advocate of the company's entrepreneurial culture, described the funding approach taken to grow several 'billion-user' services such as Google Search, Google Android or Chrome.[13] 'To feed the winners and hold back the ones not performing the way they should', said Pichette, 'you need to shift a lot'. Every project is assessed from three key perspectives:

- First, the project progress: what did it do in the last 90 days and what will it do in the next 90 days?
- Second, the trajectory: are we gaining or losing momentum? If momentum is lacking, are more resources needed?
- Third, the strategic positioning assessed in the context of a fast-changing landscape: are the internal or external conditions changing, and what is the impact of these changes on the project?

The allocation of company resources has been and will continue to be a major responsibility of the CFO. It is neither the business environment, nor the economic situation, that makes resources more or less productive – but the decisions made by CFOs on how to use available resources most effectively. The trend of declining business productivity, as stated at the beginning of Part Two, indicates that resource allocation has become a challenge, not just for individual organizations but for the economy as whole. In fact, several studies indicate that many large established companies operate on relatively low levels of resource productivity, and that one of the main reasons for that is that these companies have been too focused on driving productivity through efficiency only.[14] Yet, while efficiency and productivity are related, they are not the same – one aims to deliver the same for less, the other aims for delivering more for the same. In order to drive, and indeed accelerate, productivity improvement, many companies must pay more attention to the balance between cost reduction and growth generation.

According to a McKinsey study, 83 per cent of the executive respondents would identify resource allocation as the top management lever for spurring growth, yet a third of companies surveyed only reallocated 1 per cent of their capital from year to year: the average is 8 per cent.[15] Failing to engage in dynamic reallocation can be a huge, missed opportunity, especially when evidence suggests that actively reallocating resources increases both company and economic value. According to the McKinsey research, a company that actively reallocates delivers, on average, a 10 per cent return to shareholders, in contrast to 6 per cent for companies that remain static. This means that within two decades, dynamic resource allocation could help a company become worth twice as much as its less agile counterpart – a divide likely to increase further with growing levels of change and uncertainty.

A study published by the *Harvard Business Review* looked at the performance of 4,700 public companies in times of turbulent change, using the periods during and after the past recessions.[16] The study found that 17 per cent of the companies did not survive the turbulence, and that 80 per cent of the surviving companies were struggling years later to match their pre-recession growth. Only 9 per cent of the surviving companies posted results that exceeded both their pre-recession performance, outperforming their industry peers by at least 10 per cent in terms of sales and profit growth. Most interestingly, however, is the fact that these companies did not outperform others by being overly aggressive in cutting costs, or by investing in growth. According to the research, these companies outperformed all others because they mastered the delicate balance between cutting costs to survive today and investing to grow tomorrow by adopting a more dynamic yet systemic approach to improve both operational efficiency along with market and asset development.

At the heart of adopting a more validity-based approach to planning, budgeting and resource allocation, as introduced in the previous paragraphs, lies finance's ability to assess where the finite amount of business focus, management attention and company resources will deliver the most value and impact. Adopting validity-based approaches, however, can have its challenges, not just from a change management perspective but also because CFOs are not able to access the information needed to support these practices effectively. High-level aggregated financial reporting and performance metrics are not enough to enable a more dynamic and interactive performance dialogue at an operational level, but need to be augmented by strong operational performance-tracking and analytics capabilities, as well as more effective, data-driven decision-making processes.

Performance tracking: how to accelerate decision-making and learning

Companies like Google, and other well-known digital leaders, are not only known for their adoption of a validity-based approach to planning, budgeting and resource allocation, but also for their strong data- and analytics-driven decision-making culture. Many business executives regard their data-driven and fact-based decision-making culture as an important aspect of the company's DNA. Important decisions are made using data-driven analysis and scientific experimentation, which usually begins by asking the right questions and clearly defining the type of information needed to make a key management decision. As Google's former executive chairman Eric Schmidt says:

> We run the company by questions, not by answers [...] You ask it as a question, rather than a pithy answer, and that stimulates conversation. Out of the conversation comes innovation [...] I think you get a better innovative culture if you ask it as a question.[17]

Once a question is clearly defined and prioritized, the relevant facts can be collected and analysed to enhance the decision-making process.

Building on the discussions about data-driven decision-making in Chapter 4, there are two additional practices that CFOs may want to consider to embed and enhance the operational performance dialogue: performance analytics and analytical forecasting.

Performance analytics

A common problem with performance is that it is simply not measured properly. Traditional performance reporting is often dominated by backward-looking financial metrics, which scarcely answer the most important question of all: Are we continuously getting better at achieving our performance goal? Not only that, but in times of more rapid change – when consumer preferences, technologies, competition and market contexts change so rapidly that incremental improvement can't keep pace, the important questions to consider become: Are we getting better at achieving our goals quickly enough? Are we deciding, learning and improving fast enough?

Being able to answer these questions positively is the key to accelerated performance improvement, yet they are rarely asked, or their responses adequately measured.

In times of rapid change, it is essential for finance to move away from retrospectively measuring the attainment of a financial goal, or the deviation of the same, and to focus more on measuring the progress being made in accelerating the learning and performance improvement cycle. Yet the reality is that despite technological advancement, many companies still rely on predominantly static performance targets, plans and reports dominated by lagging financial metrics. While financial metrics have a place in providing an overall view of financial performance on a corporate level, and in communicating financial performance expectations externally, they are often meaningless at an operational level where, especially in an agile organization, decisions need to be made rapidly and in anticipation of future developments. Here, at the front line, decision-makers are looking for consumer-, market- and process-related operational metrics that help accelerate decision-making and learning.

DEVELOPING A PERFORMANCE-TRACKING SOLUTION FOR DRIVING DIFFERENTIATED MARKET GROWTH

Following years of global business and operating model integration and centralization, the executive team of this leading global consumer goods company decided to tackle growing local competition by refocusing management attention and resources into selected top-tier markets – specifically the creation of dedicated cross-functional front-line teams to unlock opportunities for differentiated, innovation-driven, market- and segment-specific growth. While the growth fundamentals for most product categories appeared to be stagnating on an aggregated level over the medium to long term, a more detailed analysis of the local consumer and market segments, and operations, highlighted clear opportunities for differentiated growth at a local, country, consumer and product-specific level.

To validate these growth hypotheses, the company developed a performance-tracking tool and approaches that would enable fast decision-making and learning (Figure 8.2). The primary goal was to enable the new front-line teams to facilitate continuous growth and performance improvement by making better, earlier, more informed and fact-based investment choices about where, when and how to compete, using highly granular, predominately locally specific internal and external data analysis.

FIGURE 8.2   Growth performance tracking (example)

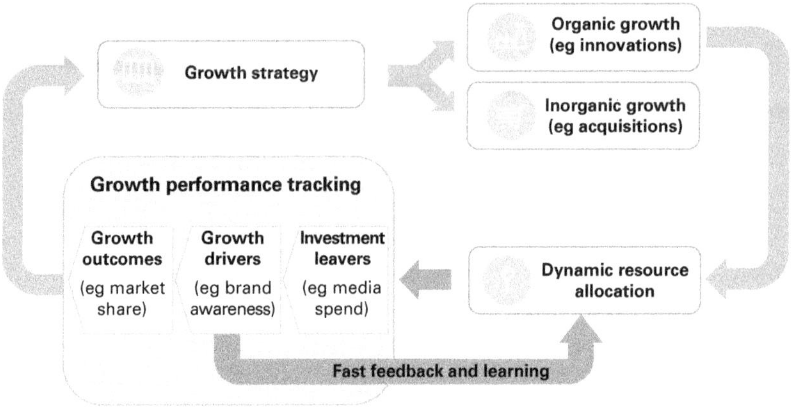

To enhance the decision-making process on this operational level, the performance-tracking tool had to be designed to process and analyse carefully selected, mostly non-financial metrics that would allow the local teams to observe and understand the causal effects between three core parameters: first, the key investment choices (ie the key trade-off decisions that teams had to make on where to spend time, money and management attention in order to drive growth – for example, local advertisement and media spend); second, the performance drivers (ie measures to influence performance and growth improvement, such as brand awareness); and third, the performance outcomes (ie the key indicators reflecting superior local growth and performance improvement, such as net sales or market share).

Iterative experimentation, tracking and analysis of the relationship between these three parameters at a granular level provided the teams with timely feedback and insight on 'what is working, what is not working, and – most importantly – *why*?' In other words, the performance-tracking solution enabled not only a much faster and more data-driven decision-making process, but also the opportunity for fast and continuous learning.

Algorithmic forecasting

When CFOs are asked what a 'good' forecast should look like, the answers are usually very clear and coherent: accurate enough to help anticipate near-term business outcomes; timely enough to highlight potential performance risks or opportunities; and just about detailed enough to provide additional data points for upcoming business decisions. But asking finance leaders what purposes the forecast should be used for yields a different, far less homogeneous picture – typically ranging between operational optimization activities (to minimize inventory levels), the identification of corrective interventions required to get 'back on track' against plan (to inform performance reviews between the group, business units and markets), the basis for mid- and long-term planning (by using a rolling forecast), the prediction of upcoming quarterly financial results (to help prepare for investor meetings), the anticipation of tax liabilities (to optimize the company's cash position), and so on.

The list of applications for a 'good' forecast is usually rather long – and that's where the dilemma begins. Creating a 'good' forecast is context-specific and may need to be tailored to be able to answer sector-, company- or event-specific questions. In an attempt to solve too many problems at once, many companies have ended up with hugely complex and time-consuming forecasting models and processes, often resulting in sub-optimal timeliness and accuracy, which impedes fact-based decision-making. CFOs, therefore, should keep the following two principles in mind:

- **First, be specific about the problem that needs to be solved:** Developing a highly granular forecast to help run operational activities more efficiently requires a very different approach to the preparation of upcoming investor guidance. From a performance management perspective, forecasting should not be mixed up with the planning, budgeting or resource allocation processes (which should be addressed by the corresponding practices discussed earlier), but should remain focused on providing fact-based, analytical insight to support a rational decision-making process. Forecasts are by nature future-oriented, but they are not predictions or any other form of a subjective perspective about what is expected to happen; rather they are fact-based, analytical, objective hypotheses about what could happen and what that means for the business or for finance. As such, they provide new data points that managers can consider in the decision-making process, particularly when it comes to identifying and addressing risk and opportunities under a range of outcomes.

- **Second, let machines do the work:** In many organizations, forecasting is still a highly manual and very time-consuming, recurring process that requires armies of people and significant management time to compile and manipulate data and insights. Despite all efforts, human biases, guesswork and errors are likely to creep in, impacting the timeliness and accuracy of results. Algorithmic forecasting, which involves people working alongside data-rich predictive technology solutions, can significantly improve the timeliness and accuracy of forecasting, while relieving finance and business teams of tedious and repetitive work.[18] Within finance and performance management, algorithmic forecasting can be applied to support either top-down forecasting (for example, profit or cash forecasting), bottom-up forecasting (for example, product or market-level forecasting) or external reporting and guidance. Access to more granular and richer data sources, as well as the use of machine learning, can help further improve accuracy over time. The real lift from algorithmic forecasting, however, comes when it is combined with human intelligence. Algorithmic forecasting models help keep people rational and honest as they can use the machine's conclusions to evaluate and inform their own fact-based decision-making.

Enhanced operational decision-making processes

The ability to enhance operational performance tracking through advanced analytical methods and solutions, such as performance analytics and algorithmic forecasting, is an important capability to develop. Building on our discussions in Chapter 3, however, CFOs should pay at least as much attention to improving the decision-making process itself. As Tom Davenport observed, in most organizations, decision-making is viewed 'as the prerogative of individuals – usually senior executives', but not as a process, and hence is rarely the focus of systematic analysis.[19] Yet there are just as many opportunities for creating differentiating competitive advantages in decision-making as in any other processes. One of the most powerful, but also most neglected, aspects of the decision-making process is the opportunity for individuals and teams to step back and reflect on newly gained insights and learnings – the next key leverage point of the operational performance dialogue.

Team learning: how to accelerate organizational learning and improvement

The performance of teams has long been recognized as one of the most important drivers for company performance. For a savvy investor, for example, the management team is the single most important non-financial indicator for expected company performance. That said, good teamworking is important not only at an executive level but also operationally, especially as agile organizational models, new technologies and remote working arrangements are refining how work gets done. Creating an environment that encourages and supports the formation, collaboration and interaction of teams is a top priority for many leading companies (as discussed in Chapter 7). Several aspects play an important role for establishing an effective operational performance dialogue, in particular team composition and alignment, but also team dialogue and learning, These are our key focus areas for this section.

Team composition and alignment

The starting point for great teamwork and performance is the composition and alignment of the teams. In general terms, a team should not become too big (ie some suggest not bigger than the number of people needed to eat two pizzas) to avoid the creation of sub-teams. At the same time, a team should also be big enough to bring together a diverse set of individual skills and experiences (leaders may consider how complementary skills could be brought together to form cross-functionally operating front-line teams).

It is one thing to get the right team composition, but only when people start working together does the character of the team begin to be revealed. What is it that makes the difference between a team of all stars and an all-star team? A wide range of research across domains ranging from high-performance sports to management teams has tried to answer this question – not always revealing consistent results but with some common findings. One of the most often mentioned drivers for team performance is the need for a team to have a compelling, clearly defined and aligned direction: an articulated statement of 'this is what we'll achieve and this is how we'll achieve it'. Teams need to have a shared vision and belief in achieving an overarching goal and ambition, as well as clarity about the team's role, responsibility and accountability in getting there – a finding that underpins and confirms many aspects that we have discussed in earlier chapters.

Team dialogue and learning

Another common driver of team performance is the way in which members communicate and interact with each other, in particular the team's ability to identify and address new, unseen business opportunities and challenges through collaboration and dialogue. Although 'dialogue' is a commonly used term, its importance and potential for performance management will be underestimated if it is seen as a matter of exchange or negotiation of individual perspectives only. People commonly assume that the *di-* in 'dialogue' refers to a conversation between *two or more* parties – for example, in contrast to one person delivering a monologue.[20] The corollary of this conventional view is that the potential of team interaction and dialogue is reduced to the exchange of perspectives and opinions. In fact, the *di-* of 'dialogue' indicates *through*, implying that dialogue, as the physicist David Bohm stated, creates 'a new kind of mind' that is carried by the participants as a team.[21] This newly emerging, collective 'super-mind' is not located in any or even in all of the individual participants, but rather in a whole that is incommensurable with the sum of the parts – a powerful phenomenon that is increasingly understood and used to enhance the decision-making process, for example, through the use of crowdsourcing and collaboration platforms (see next box).

When teams learn how to navigate change and complexity, and especially when they are confronted with new and unseen opportunities and challenges, dialogue becomes essential. While new and unseen situations can create chaos through confusion, their resolution through team dialogue will create order through insights and meaning. To look for insights and meaning as a team is to filter multiple data points, facts and perspectives in order to connect to the core of a particular opportunity and challenge. When teams learn to do this, by paying attention, understanding and analysing what is changing within, across and outside their organization, and by bringing the information that each individual has attained back to the group through dialogue, they enable the elucidation of system-level insights. In other words, the practice of team dialogue enables teams to find new insights, meaning and learnings from within chaos and confusion. As such, the concluding perspectives of well-composed, diverse teams can provide a systemic approach and pathway to navigate change and complexity, and as such accelerate insight generation and learning.

Research carried out by MIT and Deloitte showed that less than 30 per cent of people in organizations at the beginning of a digital business transformation agreed that the process was collaborative;[22] this is in stark contrast to the 90 per cent of people working in digitally mature organizations, who reported that collaboration was key to the transformation process. Yet the research also showed that not all collaboration is beneficial, particularly when it either involves people who are dominating the conversation to enforce a singular perspective, or when it involves a group of people who share similar viewpoints. To curtail the negative impacts on decision-making, companies have started to explore the use of collaboration and crowdsourcing technology.

THE USE OF CROWDSOURCING AND COLLABORATION PLATFORMS TO ENHANCE ORGANIZATIONAL DECISION-MAKING AND LEARNING

To enhance business decision-making, many organizations are exclusively focusing on the use of data analytics, machine learning and artificial intelligence. In doing so, they may neglect the adoption of less widely known but powerful digital solutions, especially collaboration and crowdsourcing platforms.

Collaboration and crowdsourcing platforms are not only helping groups of people to connect and collaborate more efficiently, but can also enhance the creative process of generating new ideas and solutions to solve complex problems. By creating a vastly larger set of possibilities for connecting and organizing groups of people, these technologies enable people with diverse knowledge and problem-solving approaches to communicate, collaborate and learn together at a scale that has not been possible before.[23] These platforms are comparatively easy to implement and use but can offer a wide range of relevant opportunities to leverage the power of collective intelligence, both within and outside an organization.

The GPS navigation platform Waze, for example, uses the collective intelligence of its users to track and predict changing traffic conditions. Henkel, a multinational chemical and consumer goods company headquartered in Germany, devised a plan to improve forecasting accuracy by using an internal prediction market that is designed to gather the collective wisdom from its own employees with impressive results: the company found that using its own internal prediction market resulted in a 16 per cent increase in forecasting accuracy.[24] Plenty more examples exist and should encourage corporate leaders to consider the use of collaboration and crowdsourcing platforms as a pragmatic and powerful alternative to further enhance and accelerate the organizational decision-making and learning cycle.

Team collaboration

In many organizations, the way in which teams interact and communicate about performance is not geared up to enable organizational learning at scale. Hierarchical decision-making structures, and a command-and-control style of management, have led to team conversations that are dominated by directives, competition and finger-pointing, rather than learning-oriented reflection and dialogue. In these situations, leaders may be able to make a big difference by promoting very simple disciplines and common practices, such as:

- **Freeing up time for team reflection and dialogue:** Leaders need to create the space for regular team reflection and dialogue. When operating in an environment with an accelerating rate of change, it is important for individuals and teams to make time to step back and reflect. New complex developments or unexpected changes require thoughtful analysis and the revisiting of ways of thinking and working. Taking time to observe and review performance outcomes to make sense of what is really happening and why, through unrushed reflection and dialogue, individually and as a team, is essential but rarely practised. Encouraging teams to use agile delivery methodology, which includes standard practices such as 'retrospective ceremony', is a useful way to get started.

- **Creating psychological safety:** A team must create a culture of trust and psychological safety. This is the heart of a good team – often regarded as the elusive magic or x-factor that separates some teams from others. The absence of psychological safety can result in problems and conflict being hidden and going unreported, as team members don't feel that they can speak up. It is an important responsibility for leaders to create a safe environment for open and learning-oriented dialogue to take place. Harvard professor Amy Edmundson has highlighted the importance of psychological safety for teamwork and team performance. According to Edmondson, psychological safety 'describes perceptions of the consequences of taking interpersonal risks in a particular context such as a workplace'.[25] Many companies and business leaders support this perspective based on their own practical experiences. Google's Project Aristotle provides some of the most compelling evidence for the importance of psychological safety within a team. Despite combing 'through every conceivable aspect of how teams worked together — how they were led, how frequently they met outside work, the personality types of the team members', the only significant pattern that Project Aristotle could discern was a correlation between team members feeling psychologically safe and team performance.[26]

- **Embracing conflicts:** While 'conflict' may sound like something to avoid in a team conversation, it plays an essential role in enabling better decision-making and in accelerated team learning – if handled properly. Rather than shying away from conflicts, leaders and teams must seek and appreciate diverse and potentially conflicting perspectives to enhance the performance dialogue. The development of simple communication skills and practices, such as active listening or presenting different views in an effort to facilitate decision-making, is essential – especially for finance leaders and teams.

For some, these steps may come across as straightforward generalizations, but in practice, they reflect another important leverage point of a generative performance management system, especially for feeding back and leveraging key learnings between the strategic and operational performance dialogues. The impact that even small changes can make are significant, and well illustrated by the former Chairman and CEO of P&G, AG Lafley. In his book, *Playing to Win*, Lafley describes how he, together with his long-time CFO Clayton Daley, managed to systematically transform P&G's performance dialogue by creating the time and environment that allowed leaders to engage in fact-based enquiry and learning-oriented, deep dialogue.[27] To manifest this approach in practice, they first refined the *concept* for performance review meetings, promoting open dialogue and team reflection. Second, they changed the meeting *format* by shifting from formal presentation to dialogue. Third, they encouraged and trained teams to use more *questions* in shaping the performance dialogue. While the effects of this approach did not happen overnight, they were able to make a significant influence on the performance culture of the company – a key subject that we will explore further in the next chapter.

Notes

1 Martin, R (2009) *The Design of Business: Why design thinking is the next competitive advantage*, p 30, Harvard Business Review Press, Boston, MA

2 Inspired by: Goddard, J and Eccles, T (2012) *Uncommon Sense, Common Nonsense*: Why some organisations consistently outperform others, p 114, Profile Books, London

3 Martin, TJ (1995) Jack Welch lets fly on budgets, bonuses, and buddy boards, *Fortune* (archive), 29 May, money.cnn.com/magazines/fortune/fortune_archive/1995/05/29/203152/index.htm (archived at https://perma.cc/49BF-4CFG)

4 Horton, R, Searles, P and Stone, K (2014) Integrated Performance Management: Plan. Budget. Forecast., Deloitte, www2.deloitte.com/content/dam/Deloitte/uk/Documents/finance/deloitte-uk-integrated-performance-management-plan-budget-forecast.pdf (archived at https://perma.cc/P2D3-VXMT)

5 Hagel, J III, Brown, JS de Maar, A and Wooll, M (2018) Frame a powerful question, *Deloitte Insights*, www2.deloitte.com/us/en/insights/topics/talent/business-performance-improvement/framing-powerful-questions.html (archived at https://perma.cc/NL6R-Y4AL)

6 Sniderman, B and Brown, JS (2019) Strategic planning: Why you should zoom out and zoom in, Deloitte, May, www2.deloitte.com/us/en/pages/finance/articles/strategic-insights-zoom-out-zoom-in.html (archived at https://perma.cc/49CT-T38C)

7 Malaska, P and Virtanen, I (*2005)* Theory of futuribles, p 12, Finnish Future Society, *Futura*, 2–3

8 Horwath, R (2006) Scenario planning: No crystal ball required, *Strategic Thinker*, www.strategyskills.com/Articles/Documents/ST-Scenario_Planning.pdf (archived at https://perma.cc/DR38-AEWZ)

9 Malaska, P and Virtanen, I (*2005)* Theory of futuribles, p 12, Finnish Future Society, *Futura*, 2–3

10 Meadows, DH (2017) *Thinking in Systems: A primer*, p 183, Chelsea Green Publishing, London

11 Wilkinson, A and Kupers, R (2013) Living in the Futures, *Harvard Business Review*, hbr.org/2013/05/living-in-the-futures (archived at https://perma.cc/PM49-YJPP)

12 Drucker, P (1994) *Managing in Turbulent Times*, p 42, Routledge, Abingdon

13 James, M (2011) Google's CFO on growth, capital structure, and leadership, McKinsey & Company, 1 August, www.mckinsey.com/business-functions/strategy-and-corporate-finance/our-insights/googles-cfo-on-growth-capital-structure-and-leadership (archived at https://perma.cc/5EY4-E7T8)

14 Mankins, M (2017) Great companies obsess over productivity, not efficiency, *Harvard Business Review*, hbr.org/2017/03/great-companies-obsess-over-productivity-not-efficiency (archived at https://perma.cc/T3SD-R36S)

15 Yuval, A (2016) How nimble resource allocation can double your company's value, McKinsey & Company, 30 August, www.mckinsey.com/business-functions/strategy-and-corporate-finance/our-insights/how-nimble-resource-allocation-can-double-your-companys-value (archived at https://perma.cc/Y8ZU-DT67)

16 Gulati, R, Nohria, N and Wohlgezogen, F (2010) Roaring out of recession, *Harvard Business Review*, hbr.org/2010/03/roaring-out-of-recession (archived at https://perma.cc/WGX7-3VLR)

17 Caplan, J (2006) Google's chief looks ahead, *TIME*, content.time.com/time/business/article/0,8599,1541446,00.html (archived at https://perma.cc/ZTG4-AZR6)

18 CIO Journal (2019) Forecasting in a digital world, *The Wall Street Journal*, 8 August, deloitte.wsj.com/cio/2019/08/08/forecasting-in-a-digital-world/ (archived at https://perma.cc/Q8CX-J5MD)

19 Davenport, TH (2009) Make better decisions, *Harvard Business Review*, November, hbr.org/2009/11/make-better-decisions-2 (archived at https://perma.cc/AN33-2FHT)

20 Metcalfe, A (2009) Dialogue and team teaching, Higher Education Research & Development, **28**, pp 45–57, doi.org/10.1080/07294360802444354 (archived at https://perma.cc/46TF-LYVG)

21 Bohm, D (1985) *Unfolding Meaning*, Routledge, London

22 Kane, GC (2019) *The Technology Fallacy: How people are the real key to digital transformation*, p 184, MIT Press, Cambridge, MA

23 Guszcza, J and Schwartz, J (2019) Superminds: How humans and machines can work together, *Deloitte Review*, Issue 24, www2.deloitte.com/content/dam/insights/us/articles/4947_Superminds/DI_DR24_Superminds.pdf (archived at https://perma.cc/2ZZY-5HWK)

24 Hawkeye (2015) Crowdsourcing sales forecasts: How Henkel leverages the collective wisdom of its employees, Harvard Business School, digit.hbs.org/submission/crowdsourcing-sales-forecasts-how-henkel-leverages-the-collective-wisdom-of-its-employees/ (archived at https://perma.cc/JYW2-756K)

25 Edmondson, AC and Lei, Z (2014) Psychological safety: The history, renaissance, and future of an interpersonal construct, *Annual Review of Organizational Psychology and Organizational Behavior*, **1**, pp 23–43, www.annualreviews.org/doi/full/10.1146/annurev-orgpsych-031413-091305 (archived at https://perma.cc/U4B6-GBQN)

26 Satell, G (2018) 4 ways to build an innovative team, *Harvard Business Review*, hbr.org/2018/02/4-ways-to-build-an-innovative-team (archived at https://perma.cc/FK33-PNLD)

27 Lafley, AG and Martin, RL (2013) *Playing to Win*, pp 130–42, Harvard Business Review Press, Boston, MA

09

Performance culture

Culture can be designed

Performance culture is the last but, of course, not least important element and leverage point to be considered in shaping the performance management system. A performance culture creates, expresses and promotes the core organizational values and beliefs that help guide people's behaviours and ways of working during the strategic and operational performance dialogue. Most CFOs feel very comfortable creating and shaping 'concrete' performance management processes, practices and solutions, but may at times perceive culture as elusive – perhaps because much of it is anchored in less 'concrete', often unspoken qualities.

Some CFOs may even neglect it, or let it go unmanaged while trying to transform other aspects of performance management – only to find the transformation of their performance management system confounded by culture. In fact, an executive study conducted by *MIT Sloan Management Review* and Deloitte in 2018 identified culture as one of the major obstacles to digital transformation and business change – a very common, but often neglected finding in research and executive interviews.[1] Why?

The lack of leadership focus and attention on developing a performance culture may be a reflection of a skewed definition of what 'culture' is. In many organizations, the word 'culture' is used to describe 'the way things get done around here', thereby creating an impression that culture is something that cannot be explained and analysed, not to mention designed. But, of course, that is not true. Rather than looking at it as something of a given, CFOs should view performance culture as another important and powerful leverage point that can be designed to enable and drive sustainable change. While leaders may not always be able to articulate exactly what culture is, they acknowledge its importance. According to Deloitte's Global Human Capital Trends Report 2016, 86 per cent of business executives surveyed rated culture as 'very important' or 'important', and 82 per cent said that culture is a potential competitive advantage.[2] However, that report also found that only 19 per cent of respondents believed that their organizations are driving the cultural changes needed to face the new opportunities and challenges of the fast-changing business environment.

Transforming a company's performance culture not only requires a lot of focus, time and effort, but also a systematic approach and strong leadership from CFOs and other executives. Driving cultural change does not mean that executives should sit down with a blank piece of paper to design their new performance culture; rather it means creating increased awareness of the unique strengths and weaknesses of the existing culture. Based on this, leaders will be able to identify potential cultural barriers that may need to be addressed over time. Most importantly, however, leaders will become more consciously aware of the key organizational strengths to build on – especially the behaviours that differentiate an organization and that can thereby support the company's performance ambitions. Behaviours are specific, enduring ways of acting that tend to be easier to define, describe and observe than the less tangible concept of culture.

Within this context, we will use this chapter to introduce two 'variations' of performance culture that can be found in high-performing organizations, and discuss some of the levers that CFOs can consider in driving cultural change.

Experiencing a high-performance culture

Many companies claim to have a high-performance culture, but the reality is that very few do. In fact, not many leaders have ever experienced such an environment, especially those coming from a traditional command-and-control organization. But the difference between the culture of a successful company and a genuine high-performance culture can come as quite a shock. As one executive describes:

> I ran a billion-dollar business for one of the world's most respected companies, but even that experience didn't fully prepare me for the intensity of a true high-performance culture. What I subsequently discovered is that a year in a good company is like a month in my current company.[3]

According to research led by Egon Zehnder, the global executive search firm, high-performance cultures share several common characteristics, such as a highly ambitious performance ethic, an almost manic focus on continuous performance improvement and an unusual level of focus and attention on developing future leaders.[4]

Performance ethic

High-performance cultures flourish on a performance ethic that, according to the Egon Zehnder study, 'combines the ambition to do the unthinkable and the confidence and discipline to deliver the nearly impossible'. This ethic is centred on a deep organizational desire to pursue and excel in highly ambitious performance goals, which tends to be based on a belief system that promotes strong confidence, courage, focused and disciplined execution, and the ability to make decisions and act independently and quickly.

Companies with a strong performance ethic believe that high performance is not dependent on external factors but on internal capabilities, especially in relation to outstanding leadership skills and talent. They consciously aim higher than their peers and execute with a level of confidence and discipline that others may find intimidating. They also know that aiming high is futile in the absence of operational excellence and continuous focus on improvement, and hence work hard to free their people to deliver maximum performance, which, if achieved, tends to be rewarded with far above-average performance bonuses and career trajectories.

Based on multiple conversations with CFOs and other business leaders, it appears that high-performance organizations do not think in 12-month or quarterly performance cycles, but tend to perceive performance improvement as a 'daily way of life', even when they are tied to external investor and reporting obligations. CFOs in these companies make active use of the leverage points that we covered in previous chapters to promote their performance ethic, especially when creating an ambitious and inspiring performance goal, clear accountabilities and a focus on delivering outcomes.

Passion for renewal

While a strong performance ethic is essential for creating a high-performance culture, it needs to be complemented by true passion for relentless renewal. John Hagel, co-chairman of the Deloitte Center for the Edge, believes that leaders need to ignite the 'passion of the explorer' in their workforce to drive scalable learning and accelerated performance improvement. Yet, according to a number of studies, reported by Deloitte in 2014, this passion is sorely lacking in most companies.[5] Even when employees demonstrate passion for their work, it tends to be viewed with an element of suspicion and scepticism, something that occurs most often in cultures that are risk-averse. Yet regardless of how it is perceived, passion is essential to a high-performance culture. As Hagel said:

> Passion and true passion is actually very unpredictable. It heads in unexpected directions because it's constantly seeking out new challenges. But what's really interesting is that passion ultimately is necessary for sustained extreme performance improvement.[6]

According to Hagel, passion either flourishes or disappears when put in certain work environments.[7] Based on his research, there are distinct organizational attributes that are the most predictive of passion: specifically, a work environment that encourages workers to work more cross-functionally, choose projects that they are truly interested in, and connect and interact regularly with clients or peers outside the company. Moreover, in studying various work environments and their impact on performance, the research identified three main goals that companies should work toward in designing their work environment and management practices. First, companies should help workers and teams to focus on the areas of highest business importance and impact, allowing them to make meaningful contributions, as well as offer them new opportunities for continuous learning and personal development. Second, companies should create opportunities for workers to collaborate and connect with other people, both inside and outside the organization. Finally, companies should support their teams to amplify their impact and performance contributions by augmenting their work environment with the right infrastructure.[8] All of these attributes enhance an organization's ability to attract, select, develop and retain the right leadership talent – another core characteristic of a high-performance culture.

Leadership attraction, selection and development

High-performance companies invest a significant amount of time selecting, developing and liberating their leaders to get on with business. They align accountabilities and aim to minimize internal processes and bureaucracy, so their people can focus on what really matters. High-performance cultures tend to be populated with leaders who have the ability, confidence and freedom to make fast decisions, and accelerate execution and learning cycles. Because so few people have experienced and grown up in a high-performance culture, executives tend to invest an unusual amount of senior management time in leadership recruiting and management. Many organizations are famous for employing rigorous, uncompromising assessment to determine whether a candidate will thrive on the intensity, relentlessness and level of expectation required in a high-performance culture. Once the right fit is ascertained, they take risks by giving real responsibility to leaders.

Just consider the culture created at Apple under Steve Jobs. He believed that hiring was the most important thing that he did during his time as Apple's CEO. Indeed, he managed all the hiring for his team – never delegating it. He personally interviewed over 5,000 applicants during his career. Jobs' philosophy of hiring, developing and retaining the best talent is well documented:

> I noticed that the dynamic range between what an average person could accomplish and what the best person could accomplish was 50 or 100 to 1...
> A small team of A+ players can run circles around a giant team of B and C players.[9]

Once Jobs found the right leaders, he was willing to give them a significant amount of freedom, which is reflected by another of his most famous quotes: 'It doesn't make sense to hire smart people and tell them what to do; we hire smart people so they can tell us what to do.'

Based on the same philosophy, high-performance companies tend to invest significantly more in leadership selection and development, specifically by making sure that all executives are culturally ready for bigger responsibilities. At the same time, building a high-performance culture also means dealing with leaders and employees who undermine the culture. As such, it is not uncommon for toxic employees, and leaders or those who are unable to keep pace with the high-performance culture, to be asked to leave. As the CEO of a prominent high-performance company says, 'Accepting non-performance is not fair to those who do perform.' In this regard, high-performance companies are not behaving any differently to leading professional sports teams – a team coach wouldn't hesitate to let go of its stars if they undermined the team spirit.

Pivoting towards a growth-performance culture

A common dilemma that many companies face concerns the growing expectations and pressures on employees. The same forces that are important in creating a high-performance culture can, if further amplified by external change and uncertainty, escalate employee fear and stress levels – often with long-term implications on performance and health. Fortunately, many companies have become more conscious of these implications. After all, creating a culture that is too focused on achieving high performance may not be sustainable in times of unprecedented and accelerating change. For this reason, some companies, while still very much performance-oriented, have shifted the focus to creating a more balanced culture that pays more attention to long-term personal development and well-being; an environment that provides meaning, psychological safety, promotes team collaboration and creates time and space for people to strengthen their mental and physical health.

Cultural aspects and behaviours play an important role. Some of these behaviours include encouraging continuous dialogue and learning, and supporting curiosity and humility. They are fuelled by leaders willing to act as role models and to take responsibility for their shortcomings. A growth-performance culture actively addresses any signs of zero-sum leadership behaviours that are typically evident in a company culture where people are either succeeding or failing, competing instead of collaborating, and where 'true' team players get weeded rapidly. Granted, outcomes and results do matter in growth-performance cultures but in addition to rewarding successes, leaders will proactively and openly treat failures and shortcomings as opportunities for learning and growing. Instead of asking, 'How much energy can be mobilized?' – and receiving a finite answer – leaders in a growth-performance culture should ask, 'How much energy can we liberate?' – to receive an infinite answer.[10]

Microsoft is a good example of a company that has made the successful shift to a growth-performance culture. Following over a decade of nearly flat growth from around 2000 to 2014, the newly appointed CEO in 2014, Satya Nadella, initiated a focused transformation and relatively rapid cultural change journey which, in addition to other transformational steps, resulted in an explosion in growth. In his book, *Hit Refresh*, Nadella describes how he inherited the cultural challenge of a 'fixed mindset'.[11] Employees viewed any failure as an indication of personal defeat, and so avoided the risk-taking that is so badly needed for creative thinking and innovation. Nadella had articulated a bold vision for Microsoft as the chosen platform for technologies of the future, including machine learning, artificial intelligence and cloud computing, but realized that the prevailing culture would hinder rather than support advancement of his strategy. Employee evaluation systems resulted in destructive competition instead of trustful collaboration and cooperation, especially when employees were forced to prove they were among the top performers compared to their colleagues. As a result, people started to avoid working on teams with the highest performers for fear of falling to the bottom. Furthermore, managers of high-performing teams were not incentivized to help manage low performers on other teams. Meetings were formal, scripted and did not provide much opportunity for creativity, risk-taking and innovation.

It was clear to Nadella that a profound change in the culture was required – so he and his senior leadership team decided to focus on encouraging a 'growth mindset', relentlessly embedding the new philosophy in every facet of the organization, from ways of working to leadership hiring and development. Over time, Nadella managed to move away from an extremely internally competitive culture to a growth-performance culture that was much more focused on cooperation, collaboration, listening, learning, empathy and harnessing individual passions and talents. The results speak for themselves: Microsoft's share price grew from US $45 when Nadella took over to more than US $185 in January 2020, outperforming the S&P 500 Index by over 80 per cent during his tenure.[12]

The role of culture in 'pulling' transformational business change

In addition to driving business performance and growth, culture plays an important role in driving transformational business change, and specifically also in developing digital maturity. Culture, as it turns out, can significantly accelerate or inhibit digital business transformation. If a company can lay the groundwork by cultivating a culture that is, amongst other aspects, more adaptable to change, and more open to experiment and take risks, then a more structural, technology-enabled transformation of the business and operating model can proceed more smoothly. Those are among the key findings of the previously mentioned survey of more than 16,000 executives, conducted by the *MIT Sloan Management Review* and Deloitte, and further interpreted and explained in book *The Technology Fallacy* in 2019.[13]

The research revealed that companies at different stages of digital maturity – low, medium and high – are approaching digital transformation very differently. While companies with low and medium maturity are more likely to push digital transformation through managerial directive or by technology implementation, high-maturing companies are inclined to pull transformational change by cultivating a culture that embraces collaboration, agility, experimentation and continuous learning, and thereby create the condition for sustainable business transformation to occur. The findings suggest that cultural change is not something that just happens because of technology-enabled transformation, but rather something that should be addressed upfront to let technology-enabled transformation follow – an approach that is fundamentally different to what most companies choose to do when they start their digital transformation journey.

The CFO's role in driving cultural change

From a CFO's perspective, it is important to pay (more) attention to 'cultural design' as a key leverage point and driver for business transformation, performance and growth. As Peter Drucker allegedly stated: 'Culture eats strategy for breakfast.'[14]

The intention of this chapter, however, is *not* to recommend a certain culture or specific behaviours but to illustrate that culture can play a critical role, not just in driving performance but also in enabling organizational agility and entrepreneurship. A strong performance culture that can positively influence behaviours at all levels of the organization allows companies to become far less reliant on formal control mechanisms such as close supervision, rigid hierarchies and reporting lines, rules and complicated internal procedures. Employees will start to feel encouraged and empowered to interact, contribute, communicate and collaborate, which enhances the organizational ability to accelerate learning and performance improvement.

Within this context, CFOs should take the following aspects into account. First, whatever the chosen approach, it is clear that when culture is aligned with the performance ambitions, goals and management system, very positive results can follow. Second, in a dynamic and uncertain environment in which organizations need to find the agility and energy to adapt and transform themselves on an ongoing basis, and rapidly, a self-driven and learning-oriented culture will become more and more important. Finally, cultural change means that leadership styles need to evolve. While most companies have put in place digital leadership training and coaching programmes, the proportion of companies that believe that they have strong digital leaders in place remains surprisingly low, according to Deloitte's Annual Human Capital Trends Report in 2019.[15] Companies need strong and inspiring leaders who are willing to learn and explore new opportunities, challenges and ways of working – even if they are new to it themselves.

While the model of effective leadership historically was somebody who had all the answers, leadership in the future is about being able to frame the right questions and, most of all, create a secure and trustful working environment. Leaders who are able to build a culture of trust can make a meaningful difference to business performance. Research has found that employees in high-trust organizations are more productive, have more energy at work, collaborate better with their colleagues, are more receptive to engage in experimentation, innovation and change and stay with their employers longer than people working at low-trust companies – critical factors that can fuel strong, sustainable performance improvement in a connected world.[16]

Notes

1 Kane, GC, Palmer, D, Phillips, AN, Kiron, D and Buckley, N (2018) Coming of age digitally: Learning, leadership, and legacy, *MIT Sloan Management Review*, sloanreview.mit.edu/projects/coming-of-age-digitally/ (archived at https://perma.cc/PD29-JHBD)

2 Deloitte (2016) Global Human Capital Trends 2016, The new organization: Different by design, Deloitte University Press, www2.deloitte.com/content/dam/Deloitte/global/Documents/HumanCapital/gx-dup-global-human-capital-trends-2016.pdf (archived at https://perma.cc/6HUR-WXXT)

3 Tveit, M and Olli, L (2015) How exceptional companies create a high-performance culture, EgonZehnder, 10 May, www.egonzehnder.com/what-we-do/ceo-search-succession/insights/how-exceptional-companies-create-a-high-performance-culture (archived at https://perma.cc/4U39-6XHM)

4 Tveit, M and Olli, L (2015) How exceptional companies create a high-performance culture, EgonZehnder, 10 May, www.egonzehnder.com/what-we-do/ceo-search-succession/insights/how-exceptional-companies-create-a-high-performance-culture (archived at https://perma.cc/VU9M-R5KX)

5 Hagel, J III, Brown, JS, Ranjan, A and Byler, D (2014) Passion at Work: Cultivating worker passion as a cornerstone of talent development, *Deloitte Insights*, 7 October, www2.deloitte.com/us/en/insights/topics/talent/worker-passion-employee-behavior.html (archived at https://perma.cc/2SCC-YDAQ)

6 Hagel, J III (2009) Pursuing Passion: Edge Perspectives with John Hagel, 14 November, edgeperspectives.typepad.com/edge_perspectives/2009/11/pursuing-passion.html (archived at https://perma.cc/3MLH-GZPJ)

7 Hagel, J III, Brown, JS, Ranjan, A and Byler, D (2014) *Passion at Work: Cultivating worker passion as a cornerstone of talent development*, Deloitte University Press, www2.deloitte.com/content/dam/Deloitte/co/Documents/human-capital/Passion%20at%20work.pdf (archived at https://perma.cc/XQX5-M4KX)

8 Hagel, J III, Brown, JS and Samoylova, T (2013) *Work Environment Redesign: Accelerating talent development and performance improvement*, Deloitte University Press, 3 June, dupress.com/articles/work-environment-redesign/ (archived at https://perma.cc/5WTP-Z94L)

9 Elliot, J (2012) *Leading Apple with Steve Jobs*, John Wiley, Chichester

10 Schwartz, T (2018) Create a growth culture, not a performance-obsessed one, *Harvard Business Review*, 7 March, hbr.org/2018/03/create-a-growth-culture-not-a-performance-obsessed-one?referral=03759&cm_vc=rr_item_page. bottom (archived at https://perma.cc/FA2L-FBCA)

11 Nadella, S, Shaw, G and Nichols, JT (2019) *Hit Refresh: The quest to rediscover Microsoft's soul and imagine a better future for everyone*, HarperBusiness, London

12 Schwartz, T (2018) Create a growth culture, not a performance-obsessed one, *Harvard Business Review*, 7 March, hbr.org/2018/03/create-a-growth-culture-not-a-performance-obsessed-one?referral=03759&cm_vc=rr_item_page. bottom (archived at https://perma.cc/V2N8-9GLF)

13 Kane, GC (2019) *The Technology Fallacy: How people are the real key to digital transformation*, p 155, MIT Press, Cambridge, MA

14 Engel, JM (2018) Why does culture 'eat strategy for breakfast'? *Forbes*, www.forbes.com/sites/forbescoachescouncil/2018/11/20/why-does-culture-eat-strategy-for-breakfast/?sh=733f694e1e09 (archived at https://perma.cc/K95T-GNHW)

15 Deloitte (2019) Global Human Capital Trends 2019, Deloitte, www2.deloitte.com/content/dam/Deloitte/uk/Documents/human-capital/deloitte-uk-human-capital-trends-2019-updated-latest.pdf (archived at https://perma.cc/BJE8-8F9K)

16 Zak, PJ (2017) The neuroscience of trust, *Harvard Business Review*, hbr.org/2017/01/the-neuroscience-of-trust (archived at https://perma.cc/QL2V-6EJ4)

10

The entrepreneur perspective

Summary

Key insight

One of the most remarkable characteristics of any complex adaptive system, be it a human or an organization, is the ability to adapt, change and protect itself. In systems thinking, this characteristic is called *self-organization*. Building on the observations of Donella Meadows, self-organization should be regarded as the strongest form of systems performance and resilience.[1] In fact, a system that can evolve and protect itself can survive almost any external change, by changing itself. Just think about the human organism, and the systemic mechanism that we developed to evolve (such as the elasticity of our brains to learn, imagine and create) and protect ourselves (such as the ability of our immune systems to develop antibodies for a new disease). As Meadows highlighted, the power of self-organization is so wondrous that we tend to regard it as 'mysterious' or indeed 'divine'. However, she continues that 'further investigation of self-organizing systems reveals that the divine creator, if there is one, does not have to produce evolutionary miracles. He, she or it just has to write marvellously clever rules of self-organization.'[2]

According to systems thinking, any complex adaptive system – biological, social or economic – that gets so 'encrusted' that it loses its intrinsic drive or autonomy to self-evolve or self-protect, and that faces structural boundaries that are too rigid to enable systematic evolution, experimentation and learning, will not be able to thrive and survive in a volatile environment in the long term. While the systems created by nature have self-regulating mechanisms 'built in', the systems created by humans, be they technical or social or mixed, must be actively designed and organized to develop a self-regulating mechanism.

From a systems-thinking perspective, these insights clarify the key inter-vention points for CFOs: encouragement and empowerment of organizational self-activation, self-development and self-organization, and – as far as appropriate – self-control, supported by clearly set boundaries and proac-tive risk management.

This way of thinking is not new but tends to be neglected when compa-nies are faced with growing performance pressures – often resulting in a self-affirming cycle and bias towards reliability-based performance manage-ment practices. Contemporary CFOs are very aware of this risk and are taking conscious steps to reinforce the development of new practices that allow people to participate in a more interactive, collaborative and learning-oriented performance dialogue.

Key findings

- **Growing expectation on performance improvements:** For all the efforts of transforming business operations, companies are often only capturing a fraction of the value offered by modern technology – in many cases because the approach to performance management has remained focused on achieving incremental efficiency improvements only. What might have been a recipe for success in the past is not enough to meet the constantly growing performance pressure of a fast-evolving, connected world.

- **Traditional performance management systems as a barrier for change:** The performance management system found in many established compa-nies has evolved gradually over many decades, reflecting the evolution of the business and operating model, changing leadership styles and perfor-mance cultures. Most of these systems were built on the assumption that the future is predictable, and that financial performance can be planned, targeted and controlled like clockwork – an assumption that no longer holds true. The transformation of these performance management systems presents a complex challenge, but it is an essential one to address, in order to balance stability and agility in a large corporation.

- **A dialogue- and learning-oriented approach to performance management:** A more dialogue- and learning-oriented approach to business perfor-mance management can be essential to enable organizational agility and entrepreneurship. The art of systems thinking can help CFOs identify and address the key leverage points needed to rebalance the strategic and operational performance dialogue in ways that can accelerate organizational learning and performance improvement.

- **The strategic performance dialogue drives organizational alignment and learning at scale:** The strategic performance dialogue encourages the leadership team to engage in ongoing dialogue about the strategic direction and performance ambition of the company, while also focusing on the continuous discipline of reflection and adoption of the performance management system itself. There are five key leverage points for CFOs to consider: the performance goal, the growth model, the management information system (MIS), the accountability model and proactive risk management.

- **The operational performance dialogue balances reliability- and validity-based practices:** For the strategic performance dialogue to be effective operationally, it must be linked to the operational performance dialogue. When both dialogues are aligned, the wheels of organizational learning and performance improvement can start to accelerate. The operational performance dialogue enables CFOs to rebalance validity- and reliability-oriented practices – especially by taking the following key leverage points into consideration: generative planning and budgeting, dynamic resource allocation, fact-based decision-making and team learning.

- **A strong culture is essential to enable agility and entrepreneurship:** A high-performance culture is rare, and only few leaders will have experienced it. It is based on key beliefs and behaviours, which include an almost intimidating passion to achieve the highest possible performance ambitions. Driven by the ever-increasing pressure and pace of change, companies are paying more attention to well-being and personal development – as well as behaviours that 'pull change', such as experimentation, collaboration, dialogue and continuous learning. The development of a strong culture is not only to drive performance but also to replace formal structures and make room for organizational agility and entrepreneurship.

Guiding questions for practical application and further exploration

- **Performance management systems:**
  - o Which management approach does your current performance management system reflect and support – for example, is the system more oriented towards planning and control, or more towards experimentation and learning?

o   To what extent is the system leaning on organizational structures and hierarchies?

o   To what degree is the system amenable to change?

- **Strategic performance dialogue:**

  o   What are the key aspects of strategic performance management in your company – to what extent do they support an ongoing, learning-oriented leadership dialogue?

  o   Is there a clearly defined performance ambition in place that is commonly understood, accepted and supported?

  o   How do you drive long-term growth?

  o   How do you balance accountability and autonomy in your company?

  o   Do you have a centralized or decentralized decision-making culture?

  o   How do you enable people to collaborate effectively across business units and functions?

  o   How do you motivate them to use their full potential to grow and contribute to your organization's success?

- **Operational performance dialogue:**

  o   What are the key aspects of operational performance management in your company – are they more oriented towards providing validity, or reliability?

  o   What opportunities do you see to create more flexibility, and to accelerate the decision-making and learning process?

  o   Is your current approach to budgeting, planning and forecasting dynamic and flexible enough to deal with change and enhance organizational agility?

  o   To what extent do you leverage data analytics and algorithms in your forecasting and decision-making process?

  o   Do you leave time for teams to reflect on their performance, promoting open dialogue and learning as a team?

- **Performance culture:**

  o   What is your performance culture like – what kind of behaviours does your current culture promote?

  o   How would you describe the performance ethic in your organization?

  o   Do people feel passionate about performance, growth and renewal?

- How do you select and develop the next generation of senior leaders?
- How important is personal growth and well-being?
- Are you pushing digital transformation on your organization, either through mandating adoption or by providing technology?
- Or, are you pulling transformation by cultivating the conditions that will elicit the types of change you desire?

HOW TO GET STARTED

Mobilize a cross-functional team with the task to:

1 Assess the current state of your performance management system, considering the key building blocks and leverage points that were discussed in Part Two, as well as the relevant enablers covered in Part One (as indicated in Figure 10.1).

2 Identify key gaps, needs and opportunities to enhance, or if necessary, to transform, the performance management systems accordingly. Develop a transformation strategy and roadmap by paying particular attention to the key interdependencies between each of the building blocks and leverage points.

FIGURE 10.1   Key building blocks of a performance management system (schematic)

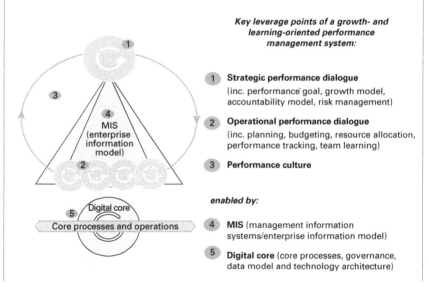

Key leverage points of a growth- and learning-oriented performance management system:

1 Strategic performance dialogue
(inc. performance goal, growth model, accountability model, risk management)

2 Operational performance dialogue
(inc. planning, budgeting, resource allocation, performance tracking, team learning)

3 Performance culture

enabled by:

4 MIS (management information systems/enterprise information model)

5 Digital core (core processes, governance, data model and technology architecture)

Recommended sources for further exploration

- *Deloitte Insights* (2019) Beyond process: How to get better, faster as 'exceptions' become the rule.[3]
- *Deloitte Insights* (2018) Zoom-out/Zoom-in: An alternative approach to strategy in a world that defies prediction.[4]
- Deloitte (2011) Babies, bathwater and best practices: Rethinking planning, budgeting and forecasting.[5]
- *Deloitte Insights* (2020) Building the peloton: High-performance team-building in the future of work.[6]

Notes

1   Meadows, D (2017) *Thinking in Systems: A primer*, p 76, Earthscan Ltd, Abingdon

2   Meadows, D (nd) Leverage points: Places to intervene in a system, The Donella Meadows Project, donellameadows.org/archives/leverage-points-places-to-intervene-in-a-system/ (archived at https://perma.cc/HY8X-M55Y)

3   Deloitte (2019) Beyond process, How to get better, faster as 'exceptions' become the rule, *Deloitte Insights*, www2.deloitte.com/content/dam/insights/us/articles/4158_Business-process-redesign/beyond-process.pdf (archived at https://perma.cc/H4UD-WCW3)

4   Deloitte (2018) Zoom out/zoom in: An alternative approach to strategy in a world that defies prediction, *Deloitte Insights,* www2.deloitte.com/content/dam/insights/us/articles/4615_Zoom-out-zoom-in/DI_Zoom-out-zoom-in.pdf (archived at https://perma.cc/VZF6-B6NU)

5   Deloitte (2011) Babies, bathwater and best practices: Rethinking planning, budgeting, and forecasting, www2.deloitte.com/content/dam/Deloitte/in/Documents/strategy/In-strategy-rethinking-planning-budgeting-and-forecasting-noexp.pdf (archived at https://perma.cc/9FF8-32NM)

6   Watson, J, Evans-Greenwood, P, Peck, A and Williams, P (2020) Building the peloton, Deloitte, www2.deloitte.com/us/en/insights/focus/technology-and-the-future-of-work/high-performance-team-building.html (archived at https://perma.cc/6F8N-PBZK)

PART THREE

The economist perspective (and the art of network thinking)

11

Introduction

The emergence of new digital business models

In *The General Theory of Employment, Interest and Money*, John Maynard Keynes wrote that 'the ideas of economists and political philosophers, both when they are right and when they are wrong, are more powerful than is commonly understood. Indeed, the world is ruled by little else.'[1] Without a doubt, our economic ideas and theories have shaped human history. As long as most of us can remember, there have been shifts within the fields of economics. The majority of these shifts are relatively minor or temporary; for example, triggered by political or regulatory changes, market bubbles that grow and burst, or unexpected events such as political conflicts. In contrast, the most fundamental economic shifts are triggered by significant technological and industrial breakthroughs – which is why we tend to call them 'industrial revolutions'.

What we are experiencing at the time of writing, the early 2020s, and what is commonly referred to as the 'Fourth Industrial Revolution', or perhaps more accurately the 'Digital Revolution', marks one of these historical turning points in economic history. It is a major shift in the intellectual current of the world and will have a substantial impact on our lives and the lives of generations to come – across all aspects of our society. Most economists and business leaders believe that what we are experiencing now is only just the beginning. The digital revolution is driven by the emergence of new digital business models that are transforming our economy at the most fundamental level. In a few short years, the ranking of most valuable companies by market capitalization has become dominated by two new digital business models: digital business platforms and digital business ecosystems.

Examining over 40 years of data from the S&P 500, we can see that the business models that companies have chosen to create value broadly fall into one of four main categories: Asset Builders, Service Providers, Technology Creators and so-called Network Orchestrators.[2] Asset builders emerged from the Industrial Revolution and created most of their value from manufacturing. They were followed by service providers, who emerged in the mid-1970s and early 1980s, and dominated the S&P between 1970 and 1990. Technology creators profited from the information revolution before and around the turn of the millennium, and were followed by network orchestrators, who achieved unprecedented market success and valuation by embracing technological innovation to create digital platforms and ecosystems.

The data shows that technology creators or network orchestrators outperform the other two business models in areas such as return on capital employed (ROCE), return on assets (ROA) and earnings before interest and taxes (EBIT) in both the short and long term, and as such receive valuations two to four times higher than asset builders or service providers. Far more surprisingly, apart from digital giants like Microsoft, Apple, Amazon or Alibaba, very few companies appear to be capturing the extra value created by digital business models – even though these new models are available to all organizations, regardless of their sector.

The transformative power of networks

Regardless of company type and sector, digital business models are designed to leverage a common transformative force within the connected world: network effects. Network effects are changing our understanding about how the connected economy works, thereby challenging the most founda-tional principles of financial management, which is still applied in most companies. Take the law of diminishing returns, for instance. Henry Ford enjoyed significant profits right up until the Dodge Brothers, Walter Chrysler and other automobile companies entered the market, then profit margins started to shrink rapidly for everyone involved.[3]

In the 1990s, however, the economist Brian Arthur noticed something that would challenge the concept of diminishing returns forever. When stud-ying the balance sheets of Infotech firms, he discovered that some companies were seeing increasing, rather than diminishing, returns as the high-tech market matured. Arthur said:

Increasing returns generate no equilibrium but instability: if a product or a company or a technology – one of many competing in a market – gets ahead by chance or clever strategy, increasing returns can magnify this advantage, and the product or company or technology can go on to lock in the market.[4]

Digital business platforms and ecosystems have been designed to leverage network effects and increasing returns to create very powerful demand-side economies at scale, allowing them to grow much faster than anyone else in the market. As they continue to acquire new consumers and partners, even more powerful network effects are created. And it doesn't end there: add artificial intelligence, and the advantage of large networks can extend even further by creating economies of learning – for example, by capturing and sharing enhanced data flows and new consumer insights across an ecosystem.

Seeing and thinking in networks

Networks are all around us. Yet in order to see them we have to change our perspective. We can do this by learning the *art of network thinking*.

Being able to see and think in networks changes our perception of the connected world, and our place in it, by focusing our attention on the relationships between entities, rather than on the entities themselves. Think about humanity. Traditional perspectives and descriptions of humanity are often dominated by analysing the differences of the human race across geographies, nationalities and cultural norms. From a network perspective, however, we can see how humans are inventing and using technology to create a global community where everyone is connected to everyone else with a minimum degree of separation. Or think about the economy. Conventionally, economists have viewed companies as self-interested and autonomous actors that *use* the marketplace to compete with one another. From a network perspective, however, we can see how companies are forming a dense network of connections, relationships and communities that *create* their markets. The reason that some digital pioneers are growing so fast is less about making better deals, or winning a share of existing markets, and more about their ability to create network-driven ecosystems and markets.

Networks are an essential ingredient in any complex adaptable system. Without connections, there would be no system. In biology, for example, molecules connect to create cells, connecting cells create an organism, and organisms connect to create an ecosystem. In an economy, we encounter the same pattern. People connect to create companies, companies connect to create markets, and markets connect to create the economy. Both the biological and economic (as well as the social) world are created by hierarchies of networks. Yet despite the importance of networks in creating our organizations and the economy, their characteristics are rarely understood or considered in day-to-day decision-making.

Moreover, networks cannot only change our *perception* but also the *nature* of systems. Network scientists call these changes 'phase transitions', indicating transformational shifts of the system whenever it passes certain thresholds of connectivity.[5] You can draw an analogy from the physical world. For example, if you take steam and lower the temperature, the steam first transforms into liquid water at 100°C, and then to ice at 0°C. From a network perspective, similar transitions happen when the ratio between network nodes and connections change – in fact, whenever the average number of connections rises above the number of nodes, or vice versa. These effects can be witnessed when smaller groups of nodes and networks start to blend into larger ones – imagine multiple national telephone networks melding into one supra-national network. One moment you have a drinkable liquid, the next moment you have solid ice cubes. One month, you have a few infected people in one part of a city, the next you are facing a global pandemic. One quarter, you have a few people connecting on a new application, the next an explosion of connections to form a new social platform.

Such network transitions, in which 'more' means 'different', appear often and everywhere and illustrate the enormous power that can emerge from networks. In the business world, most of these transitions are enabled through technology innovation. The internet might be the best known example. For around 20 years it was only used by the military and academics, but in the 1990s its use suddenly exploded, triggered by better and cheaper connectivity and accessibility that pushed the connectivity–user ratio to create exponential growth. Moreover, the continued expansion of use of the internet, combined with new digital technology innovation, are driving the connection of people, companies and economies introducing genuinely new, and often highly disruptive, dynamics to our social and economic world. These dynamics have significant influence on how we can interact with each other, and also where we belong. One corollary of being able to connect with everything and everyone is that we are increasingly exposed to a fast-evolving, network-driven economic and societal system.

Such systems not only possess the power to change our economic and social environment but also create a significant cost of being *not* connected, or cut out, of social or economic networks. As such their role is hugely important. What is already the reality for our connected devices can also become true for our organizations and ourselves: we are what we are connected to.[6]

Network thinking is the ability to see, understand and potentially influence how systems change through the influence of connecting networks. Whether we are managing a large company or creating a new community, the art of network thinking is becoming an increasingly important skill to learn and adopt. Understanding how networks emerge, what they look like, how they grow and evolve and which forces they can unleash, is essential for business and finance leaders. Here are some selected features that appear to be the most interesting and relevant for the following chapters.

NETWORK GROWTH[7]

Networks, like systems, share one essential feature: intrinsically driven, accelerated growth. Starting with a few nodes, and the connections forming between them, networks accelerate growth by continuously adding new nodes. They add one node at a time, but because each node can have several connections, the number of connections will grow exponentially, reaching significant scale in a relatively short period of time. The world wide web, for example, grew from the very first website to an exabyte (that's a 1 with 18 zeros) of information within a decade.

NETWORK HUBS

Modelling network growth is relatively easy. Starting from a first node, we keep adding new nodes, one after another. Assuming we have a few connected nodes and would like to add another one, which node should we be connecting to? Network theory tells us that, on average, we tend to prefer the most connected node. For example, when you ask a group of internet users to link to one of two websites, one which has twice as many links as the other, about twice as many users will link to the more connected site (over time).[8] While individual choices are highly unpredictable, a group tends to follow this pattern. In network theory, this behavioural pattern is called *preferential attachment*. It results in what is commonly known as the *rich-get-richer* phenomenon, which explains why well-established nodes attract a disproportionately large number of new connections at the expense of others – and thus form powerful *network hubs* over time.

NETWORK RESILIENCE[9]

An important characteristic of networks is their resilience. More specifically, the deletion of random nodes and connections rarely impacts the nature of large and complex networks. For example, even if a large number of computers or websites were removed from the internet, it would still function well. However, resilience comes at a price: if one or more of the main networks hubs is removed, the network may quickly break down or cease to function properly (just imagine what might happen if your children's favourite social media sites stopped working for a week).

NETWORK COMPETITION

These features, however, do not mean that the most established and senior node, ie the 'first-comer', automatically becomes the most powerful. Take Google, for example, which launched their search engine only in 1997.[10] Despite being a 'late-comer' to the internet, it quickly became the most popular search engine. Why? Because in competitive networks (eg a network of companies competing for consumers), the *fittest* node will win. In network thinking, *fitness* describes the ability to attract and develop relationships relative to everybody else in the network.

NETWORK STANDARDS

Forming digital networks is about enabling organizations and people to interact, communicate and collaborate with each other, enabled by digital technology. The basis for digitally-enabled, seamless interaction, communication and collaboration is *interoperability*, or in other words, establishing network standards.[11] Only systems that can share information seamlessly, based on commonly agreed standards, will form a network. Network standards can be created, owned and controlled by a group of aligned bodies (eg a company that has created a closed operating system), or they can be owned by groups of unaligned bodies (eg an open network such as the world wide web).

DIGITAL (BOOLEAN) NETWORKS

Networks of nodes that can be in a state of 0 or 1, ie digital networks that use the standard language of computer processors, are called Boolean networks, named after the English mathematician and philosopher George Boole (1815–64). The most interesting property of these digital networks is that the number of states the network can be in scales exponentially. A network with two nodes can have four (ie 2^2) states: 00, 10, 01 and 11.

A network with three nodes can have eight (ie 2^3) states, and so on. If we have a network with just 1,000 nodes, the world's fastest computer will need hundreds of millions of years to explore all the possible states. This exponential growth creates a new form of economies of scale. Traditional economists have thought about economies of scale as a function of cost and volume only; but as digital networks form and grow, there is another kind of economy of scale, the potential for novelty, or in other words, the potential for learning, innovation and ultimately knowledge, that increases exponentially and can create enormous economic value and wealth.[12]

NETWORK VALUE

In a connected economy, companies communicate and collaborate across an increasingly wide range of digitally-connected networks of organizations to combine data, insights, ideas and capabilities to innovate new products and services for customers. In this economy, the boundaries of companies are blurring, and value is increasingly created by the network, not the company. The formation, positioning and management within networks, and the ability to extract and monetize a fair share of network-created value for the company, is starting to play a significant role.

Moreover, as explored in Chapter 3, the emergence of new digital technologies is giving rise to the modularization of core processes and operations. We are used to thinking of a company as a set of closed core business processes, but in a networked economy, these core business processes are turning into data flows that extend far beyond the boundaries of any single organization. In fact, companies operating in a digital business ecosystem may contribute just one part of the core business process, and orchestrate the rest across their network.

Thus, in the connected world, where value is increasingly created across organizational boundaries by collaborating and interacting seamlessly across customers, suppliers, and other contributing partners, business leaders have no other choice but to collaborate with others in every aspect of the business – from product development to sales and marketing, to planning and performance management. Those who try to manage their companies as a self-sufficient island will put the survival of their organization at risk.

NETWORK RISK

Just because it is essential for leaders to think and act in new ways, does not mean it is easy. Senior leaders should be prepared to face a new set of unseen business challenges and risk that arise from collaborating in digital networks.

Participating in digital business ecosystems, for example, means that previously confidential information has to be made transparent, and that intellectual property can be exposed.[13] It re-emphasizes the urgent need for companies to build a technological infrastructure that allows them to integrate their systems with that of customers and network partners, and to create new capabilities to protect them from cyber risks. Moreover, leaders must be prepared for the likelihood that their corporate reputation and brands can be impacted, both positively and negatively, by the fortunes of their network partners. Finally, collaborating with other firms to create value does not mean that it is easy to agree how that value can be monetized and shared in a fair and strategically effective manner.

NETWORK COMPLEXITY

The complexity of networks grows with the number of connections between nodes. If the number of connections is greater than the number of nodes, then complexity grows exponentially. The implication of this growth is what network thinkers call a 'complexity catastrophe'.[14] It explains why densely connected networks, such as large organizations, can quickly become very complex and less adaptable. Network thinning brings us back to the two, well-known, opposing forces at work: the economies of learning and exploration, versus the diseconomies of complexity and execution. As an organization or ecosystem grows, its opportunities to share information, learn and innovate increase exponentially, yet its complexity, and hence its ability to drive cross-organizational alignment and execution, collapses exponentially as well. So, forming digital networks, within and across organizations, is not a one-way street to success – but an art that requires careful consideration and design to find the right balance.

Applying network thinking to business and financial management

Applying the concepts of network thinking to the business world can provide us with new perspectives and a deeper level of understanding of the connected world. We realize that in a connected economy networks have started to influence and reshape almost every aspect of business – and that, most likely, we are only just at the very beginning of this transformational development, at the time of writing. Put differently, when we are able to see and think in networks, we realize that in order to survive and thrive, our companies must focus on creating digitally-enabled business connections and collaborative ecosystems with customers, suppliers and other key stakeholders. In doing so, some additional features of network thinking play a role.

From a CFO's perspective, the unique features of networks are increasingly important to understand and consider in all aspects of finance, performance and risk management. Operating in an economy that is increasingly defined by digital networks means that they are no longer able to plan and control the drivers of value creation, and that in order to drive business performance and growth, they need to shift their attention beyond both, traditional finance functional and business organizational boundaries. CFOs must accept that for their company to succeed, the network within which their company operates must succeed, too. And unless CFOs provide the leadership for that to happen, their company is likely to become the subject of powerful, network-driven forces, rather than the one that proactively shapes them.

The art of network thinking is, necessarily but very slowly, starting to change the way we think about business and financial management at the most fundamental level and across all sectors, and as such has key implications for the company's approach to digital business transformation, growth and performance management. Part Three will explore three important aspects for CFOs (Figure 11.1): the fast emergence of powerful new business models, such as digital business platforms (Chapter 12) and the digital business ecosystems (Chapter 13) that are reshaping every aspect of our economy, as well as the need to rethink the concept of 'value creation', specifically the need to focus on long-term multi-stakeholder value creation (Chapter 14).

FIGURE 11.1   Introduction to Part Three

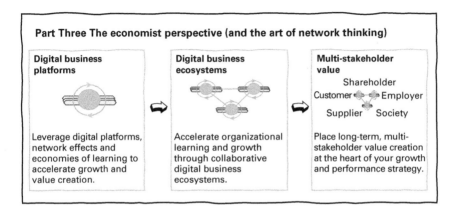

Part Three The economist perspective (and the art of network thinking)

Digital business platforms	Digital business ecosystems	Multi-stakeholder value
Leverage digital platforms, network effects and economies of learning to accelerate growth and value creation.	Accelerate organizational learning and growth through collaborative digital business ecosystems.	Place long-term, multi-stakeholder value creation at the heart of your growth and performance strategy.

Notes

1   Keynes, JM (1936) *The General Theory of Employment, Interest and Money,* p 383, Macmillan, London

2   Kambil, A (nd) The value shift: Why CFOs should lead the charge in the Digital Age, Deloitte, www2.deloitte.com/us/en/pages/finance/articles/cfo-insights-digital-age-business-model-innovation-value.html (archived at https://perma.cc/NL6Z-YZWE)

3   Remo, JC (2016) *The Seventh Sense*: Power, fortune and survival in the Age of Networks, p 239, Little, Brown & Co, London

4   Arthur, WB (1996) Increasing returns and the new world of business, *Harvard Business Review*, July–August, hbr.org/1996/07/increasing-returns-and-the-new-world-of-business (archived at https://perma.cc/DFQ8-LZBX)

5   Solé, RV, Manrubia, SC, Luque, B, Delgado, J and Bascompte, J (1996) Phase transitions and complex systems: Simple, nonlinear models capture complex systems at the edge of chaos, *Complexity*, 1, pp 13–26, doi.org/10.1002/cplx.6130010405 (archived at https://perma.cc/72BS-CBZZ)

6   Remo, JC (2016) *The Seventh Sense*: Power, fortune and survival in the Age of Networks, p 35, Little, Brown & Co, London

7   Barabasi, AL (2003) *Linked: How everything is connected to everything else and what it means for business, science, and everyday life,* p 83, Perseus Books, New York City

8   Barabasi, AL (2003) *Linked: How everything is connected to everything else and what it means for business, science, and everyday life,* p 86, Perseus Books, New York City

9   Mitchell, M (2011) *Complexity: A guided tour,* p 245, Oxford University Press, Oxford

10 Barabasi, AL (2003) *Linked: How everything is connected to everything else and what it means for business, science, and everyday life,* p 96, Perseus Books, New York City

11 Dawson, R (2008) *Living Networks: Leading your company, customers, and partners in the hyperconnected economy*, p 20, Lulu.com (archived at https://perma.cc/RNN7-LW3H)

12 Beinhocker, E (2007) *The Origin of Wealth; Evolution, complexity, and the radical remaking of economics*, p 149, Random House Business, London

13 Dawson, R (2008) *Living Networks: Leading your company, customers, and partners in the hyperconnected economy*, p 44, Lulu.com (archived at https://perma.cc/RNN7-LW3H)

14 Beinhocker, E (2007) *The Origin of Wealth; Evolution, complexity, and the radical remaking of economics*, p 151, Random House Business, London

12

Digital business platforms

In 1997, Apple was fighting a tough battle against a wide range of competitors selling personal computers.[1] Under tremendous pressure, Apple pivoted to focus on the opportunities presented by the rapidly evolving internet. Within just a few years it had created iTunes, a digital marketplace which offered users the chance to choose single songs without buying the entire album. The iPod soon followed, with sales of almost 30 million by 2005. Thanks to its platform-based digital business model, Apple reshaped the entire music industry and redefined the way in which people purchased music.

Apple is not the only platform-based business to start a revolution. Time and time again, digital business platforms have experienced exponential growth and captured significant market share from established firms. In 2020, 7 out of 10 of the most valuable global companies were platform-based companies, including Apple, Google, Microsoft, Amazon, Facebook and Alibaba. While these digital giants are big and powerful enough to transform industries, economies and societies, they do not have a monopoly on creating digital platforms. Practically any company and industry whose product or service is information- or data-related, and where that information is considered valuable, is a candidate for a platform-based model. This is why the companies driving this trend are so diverse: from start-ups to digital giants to traditional firms.

A market study conducted and published by McKinsey in 2019 showed how incumbents and digital-native companies design their strategies to harness the power of platforms.[2] Almost 1,600 C-suite executives were surveyed in companies across different sectors and key geographies. The study found that platforms are no longer the sole domain of digital natives.

Established companies are also driving this trend by establishing platform-based business models as they gain higher levels of digital maturity. The report also indicated not only that platforms are spreading in many digital markets, but that successful platforms built by incumbent companies can significantly improve performance.

In fact, the study found that any type of platform – whether company-owned, third-party, or either cooperating or competing with a global platform – has the potential to increase overall earnings above the benchmark level. Platform businesses do not behave like traditional product and service businesses. They tend to operate with far fewer employees but, at the same time, innovate and grow faster, achieving market valuations that are significantly higher than their direct competitors, often by an order of magnitude. These businesses play by new economic rules that pose challenges to traditional firms that still operate by old rules. According to McKinsey research, more than 30 per cent of global economic activity was projected to be led by platform-based companies by 2025.

A new path to growth

Digital business platforms are designed to leverage network effects. Network effects, as mentioned in the Introduction to Part Three, are a powerful economic force in the connected world. While the leading global companies of the 20th-century industrial age – and as such the majority of today's established companies – were created by leveraging supply-side economies of scale, the giant companies shaping our economies today are created by demand-side economies of scale. Whereas supply-side economies of scale were driven by efficiencies and reduced unit costs by production at scale, demand-side economies are based on efficiencies in social networks, demand aggregation, data-driven insight and learning, app development and other aspects that help make networks bigger and more attractive to participants.

Within the connected world, demand-side economies of scale are fast becoming the primary driver of economic value. This does not mean that supply-side economies of scale are no longer relevant. They continue to be important, especially for established companies, but a digital platform-based business that is able to create demand-side economies of scale and thereby positive network effects can create market size, market advantages and market power that are very difficult for competitors to overcome.

We can use systems thinking to illustrate how demand-side economies of scale can create positive (or negative) network effects. For instance, ride-hailing companies such as Uber, Didi, Lyft or Grab form a classic type of platform business, which performs a matching service helping riders find drivers and vice versa. The growth model depicted in Figure 12.1 illustrates how these platform leverage positive feedback loops (as introduced in Chapter 8) to create network effects that help accelerate growth: drivers are more motivated by demand; the more drivers there are, the wider the coverage, which means faster pick-ups and lower prices.

The figure is a classic example of the so-called 'demand-side economies of scale' of platforms, which occur when an increased number of users have a significant impact on the value of goods or services. These demand-side economies of scale can create positive network effects when they provide real value for each user, but also demonstrate negative network effects when the value is reduced for their users. Negative network effects can occur when the system is not balanced. For instance, when a ride-hailing platform attracts more drivers than passengers, the rate of driver downtime will go up. Conversely, if a platform attracts too many passengers for the number of available drivers, passenger waiting time will increase.

The example highlights several fundamental differences between a traditional, product- or service-producing business and a digital platform business. Traditional businesses operate like a value-creation pipeline – a linear arrangement of value contributions, with producers at one end and consumers at the

FIGURE 12.1   High-level growth model of a ride-hailing platform (schematic)

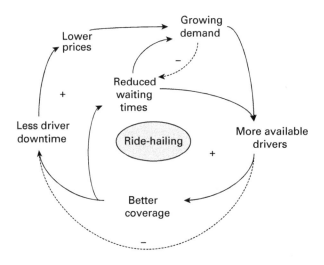

other. In contrast, platforms bring together different types of producers and consumers (some of which are both consumers and producers) to exchange, consume and create value in a variety of ways, made possible by the interactions that the platforms facilitate.

The differences and implications of shifting from a linear value chain of the pipeline business to the more complex value matrix of a digital platform business are significant, and important for CFOs to understand, in particular:

- **Platforms can scale extremely quickly:** Digital business platforms can scale at speed by amplifying networks' effects with digital rather than physical goods. The transfer of digital goods through a network is free, perfect and instant.[3] Once something has been digitized, it can be replicated and shared instantly, as often as desired, from anywhere to everywhere, and at zero marginal costs. By leveraging these economics, digital platforms become almost impossible to compete against.

- **Platforms can leverage assets and resources they don't own:** Uber does not own its cars. Airbnb does not own its rooms. Facebook does not produce its own content. Digital business platforms shift the sourcing and production process from inside to outside, for both digital and physical goods. This provides them with a number of significant advantages. First, it allows them to scale much faster than traditional businesses. With only marginal costs for assets, resources and production, digital platforms can scale as fast as they can add partners. Second, digital business platforms are hard to imitate given that the assets and resources are owned and distributed by a complex network of producers and consumers. Third, digital business platforms can thrive with a limited internal workforce by harnessing platform users as producers, representing an external labour force. By doing this, platforms create opportunities for all participants to focus on what they do best while allocating unwanted tasks to other parties that they connect with on the same platform.

- **Platforms can accelerate learning at scale:** Platforms can use data analytics and artificial intelligence at scale to track and optimize customer interactions and services continuously. Not only do digital business platforms learn for themselves, but they help all participants to learn from each other; for example, by sharing consumer data and insights to accelerate innovations. As Peter Schwartz, senior vice president for strategic planning at Salesforce.com, explains: 'We take this model seriously, not just by building our own platform and applications but by opening our platform to millions of partners, developers and customers, allowing them to customize and layer on top of it.'[4]

- **Platforms invert the organization:** A digital business platform that sources assets and resources externally and drives value creation and learning through a community of users rather than internally, inverts the traditional business model. Moreover, digital business platforms tend to turn 'inside out', for example: by shifting the focus on consumer engagement in marketing and sales from push to pull; by shifting the focus on supply from managing inventory and factories to orchestrating assets that the company does not own; and by shifting the focus of strategy development from creating competitive advantages and overcoming barriers, to orchestrating innovation communities. As such, digital business platforms do not merely create value themselves, they orchestrate value creation by outsiders – and that triggers significant changes for finance, as well as to the approach to business transformation, growth and performance management.

Moving from a pipeline to a platform model

Established companies that intend to transition their business, or a part thereof, from a pipeline to a platform model will have to fundamentally change the way in which they create and capture value by transforming their front office, back office and their approach to value monetization.

From a value-creation perspective, most companies will need to move from an *exclusive* value proposition (ie a value-creation strategy that focuses on addressing specific customer needs through singular products or services) to an *inclusive* value proposition (ie a value-creation strategy that addresses broader customer needs through the coordination and orchestration of various products and services). Developing a new, comprehensive, sustainable value proposition is difficult. It requires a deep understanding of unmet customer needs along the customer journey – from awareness to purchase to after-sales support. If done right, the upside potential for the business can be significant – but if the value proposition does not markedly improve customers' status quo, then the digital transformation and platform will be unsuccessful.[5] Most companies will initiate this transformational shift by transforming their front end with a focus on developing enhanced costumer experience, engagement and retention-focused capabilities.

Building on a newly defined value proposition, companies have to decide whether to build or buy their own delivery capabilities, or whether it makes more sense to create a partnership with an established digital platform business. Implicit in this decision is the identification of the preferred platform interaction and delivery mechanism, ie the way in which target customers and partners will be able to interact with the platform. Establishing a platform delivery mechanism that facilitates seamless, digitally-enabled interactions across customers and a wide network of partners and contributors is critical. As companies move from a pipeline to a platform model, their business success becomes less dependent on the ability to innovate and optimize its own product or service range, and more on their ability to establish an infrastructure and standards as a shared foundation to integrate diverse offerings across a wide network of partners and contributors.

From a value capturing perspective, corresponding changes will be required, ranging from the implementation of new revenue models and billing systems to new approaches to business performance management. The most critical change for established companies is to shift their focus from single customer sales to the creation and optimization of recurring revenue streams. To do this, companies will have to introduce new pricing and monetization mechanisms (for example, a subscription-based, consumption-based or outcome-based payment model). To support this transition, most companies will require new financial transaction systems, new reporting processes and enhanced controls – for example a billing system that is able to cope with high-volume, low-value, transactions.

Finally, and most importantly, delivering all these changes successfully requires business and finance leaders to shift from traditional proprietary thinking to network thinking. Business performance and growth is no longer a zero-sum game but becomes dependent on the ability to attract participants, coordinate and collaborate across a wide network of diverse partners and contributors, in some cases even competitors. Attracting others to collaborate and invest in a platform-based business requires, most of all, the creation of trust. This means, for instance, that management must learn to share business strategies, plans and performance-related information with others. This can be a difficult cultural change, and should not be underestimated. Large established companies are very experienced in coordinating a large number of *providers* within a vertically integrated pipeline model – however, engaging and nurturing a network of *partners* within a horizontally-integrated platforms model is a different challenge.

Managing performance of digital business platforms

Because digital business platforms leverage demand-side economies of scale, rather than supply-side economies of scale, their key value drivers are far less focused on improving operational efficiencies than on driving user interaction. Arguably, the reason that WhatsApp sold for nearly US $20 billion was less related to the leanness of the management and operational teams and more to do with the thriving community of its users. Financial accounting might not factor the value of interaction, and the associated emergence of network effects, but markets do. In fact, from an investor perspective, digital platforms can generate extraordinary market value. Consequently, and in contrast to traditional businesses, the focus of performance management activities must shift from managing internal resources to orchestrating external resources. Disregarding these differences, for example by focusing on standard traditional performance metrics, is a common reason that platforms fail. For most organizations, the management of digital platforms is still a new skill to develop, and one that increasingly requires the attention and support from CFOs and finance.

Traditional pipeline businesses with linear value chains have for a long time been managed with a common and highly familiar set of standard performance reports and metrics. A consumer products company, for example, creates value by turning raw materials and labour into goods and services valued by consumers. It does this by following the largely linear and sequential steps of their core manufacturing and supporting operational processes. In order to optimize performance, therefore, the company must focus primarily on the optimization of their core end-to-end processes, for example through the redesign and digitization of core processes, as discussed in Part One. This business model has shaped the standards of financial accounting and performance management, including the use of common performance metrics such as turnover, cash flow, working capital and operating costs – all of which feel very familiar to us, but are primarily focused on optimizing 'pipeline throughput' by removing bottlenecks and inefficiencies.

These traditional performance metrics are not appropriate for tracking and managing the complex, multi-directional value flows and dynamic network effects in digital platforms. Digital platforms create value through positive network effects by facilitating interactions across a variety of external stakeholder groups and communities. On an operational level, the key performance indicators of digital platforms tend to focus on tracking successful, repeatable and scalable user interactions. Equally, on a strategic level, the performance metrics of platforms tend to centre more on long-term revenue growth driven by continued customer engagement and satisfaction, such as renewal rates or compound growth rates, than on the calculation of total customer lifetime value for key customers.

For a digital platform, the operational and strategic performance tracking and adaptation mechanism should happen continuously and in real time, ideally supported by digital technologies such as machine learning and artificial intelligence. The main goal of this performance management process is the amplification of positive network effects and the resulting acceleration of growth and value creation. Managing digital platforms also involves ensuring that all parties, including producing and consuming platform users, are benefiting from it. A digital platform can only remain healthy as long as the entire community continues to thrive.

A critical success factor and starting point for CFOs in adopting the performance management system for new digital business models is the definition of a performance management system that is in harmony with the company's digital strategy and business operating model. The importance of this step cannot be overstated, especially for established companies, for without a comprehensive overhaul of traditional steering mechanisms, the management of new business models is doomed to fail. Take the example of an automotive original equipment manufacturer (OEM) which is exploring new digital business models as a mobility service provider.[6] If the company transitions from manufacturing and selling capital-intensive products to providing services paid for according to usage, the number of transactions will significantly increase in volume, but fall in value; at the same time, the company will experience a significant increase in intangible assets, while variable costs will decrease.

This new pattern of revenue and profitability requires a very different approach to core business and financial performance management: for example, in managing the fast-growing number of customer transactions through customer-centric value drivers and measures such as daily active users, average revenue per user and conversion rates; and/or, more platform-related KPIs like downtime and utilization. But other aspects of financial management also need to be adopted. The effect on the balance sheet, for instance, is significant, as intangible assets now play a much bigger role. Equally, digital models tend to have a completely different cost profile than traditional business models. Both people- and IT-related costs, for example, play different roles than just contributing to general overhead costs.

Moreover, finance leaders should be aware that the steering mechanisms, including financial statements and metrics, may need to change over the life cycle of the digital business platform. It is critical to identify points at which business model transitions occur, and adjust metrics accordingly. During the platform start-up phase, for example, it is important to focus more on key aspects of platform and interaction design – the pull of users, facilitation of successful interactions and feedback, matching of demand and supply, curation of contents and the creation of user trust in the digital platform. Traditional metrics such as revenue and cash flow are usually not appropriate in evaluating the performance of a digital platform at this stage.

Once a digital business platform has reached scale and created network effects, the focus can shift more towards customer segmentation, transaction management and monetization, as well as the optimization of cash flows and margins. As a platform matures, management needs to focus increasingly on platform quality improvements and innovation to ensure user satisfaction, retention and attraction. At this stage it is critical to monitor user and consumer engagement patterns carefully, especially threats created by competing platforms that may draw user attention away.

From a performance management perspective, these operational and maturity-stage specific measures should over time be balanced with measures that, as far as possible and appropriate, provide a longer-term perspective on the quality and value-creation potential of customer relationships. These may range from customer satisfaction and loyalty indices to renewal and compound growth rates, as well as dynamic customer profitability analytics (for example by adopting commonly concepts such as Customer Lifetime Value).[7]

Finally, for finance leaders, it is becoming increasingly important and insightful to look beyond internal cost structures to consider the cost drivers and structures across the entire economic value chain. The disruptive impact of new digital business models is often explained by superior technology platforms, customer insights and experience only – which are of course important – but this tends to neglect the additional, often significant cost advantage that these new business models can achieve because they are able to manage costs across wider ecosystems, rather than just for themselves.[8]

Smart performance management

The fast evolution of data-rich digital business models, combined with advancements in artificial intelligence, have started a trend, which is the approach of 'smart performance management', which may influence strategic and operational performance management and decision-making in the future. Leading digital platforms have begun to use advanced analytics and artificial intelligence to turn their digital business platforms into self-organizing, smart businesses.

Ming Zeng, chairman of the Academic Council of the Alibaba Group, believes that AI-enabled, smart performance management will become the standard for digital platforms and ecosystems.[9] According to Zeng, being a 'smart business' means learning how to leverage big data and artificial intelligence to continuously and automatically optimize performance, based on a very carefully defined and balanced set of performance indicators and algorithms that react in real time, in line with changing market conditions and customer preferences.

Zeng believes that AI-enabled, smart performance management will not just concentrate on driving operational performance improvement (as discussed in Part One), but will also focus on the refinement of performance goals and metrics itself. For example, when Alibaba launched Taobao, the world's biggest e-commerce website, the performance goal, supported by selected metrics for the management team, was to create *exactly* one million jobs that year. Jack Ma, CEO and founder of Alibaba, advised his management team not just to focus on reaching a very precise revenue-based performance goal and growth ambition, but also told them: 'If you bring in revenues past a certain goal, I will penalize you. Because it means you are trying to make too much money from the site at this point.'[10] Because Ma had set such a meaningful, two-sided goal and metrics threshold, everybody understood what they had to do: to bring in no more and no less than the specified target.

The trend towards 'smart performance management' and AI-enabled decision-making may still sound futuristic for many CFOs in established companies, but will become more relevant as companies transform themselves to create and engage in digital business models. Many questions will have to be answered, many of which will are very difficult to answer. For instance: What are the KPIs that not only reflect past performance to date, but drive our forward-looking, potentially AI-enabled decision-making progress? When predictive analytics suggest a particular course of action, who gets to make the business decision – the data-driven algorithm or the human? How do we deal with conflicting KPIs and trade-offs, especially if decision-making becomes more and more automated? How do organizations define an AI-enabled, appropriately governed decision-making process? How are decision rights allocated between people and machines?

Leading platform-based businesses like Netflix have created cross-functional teams, including finance, to design AI-enabled decision-making and related, scalable learning platforms and mechanisms. Finance may be less focused on making algorithms or enabling digital technology work, but it can still play a key role in defining the right key performance metrics required to guide smart performance management. A 2019 *MIT Sloan Management Review* research report highlighted the re-emerging importance and criticality of selecting the right key performance indicators for corporate leaders – suggesting that in AI-enabled business models, the business strategy will, to a large extent, be influenced and defined by the KPIs that leaders choose to optimize.[11] This means that developing a strategy for AI is not enough; instead, using AI to create strategy will be at the core of algorithmic innovation in smart, data-driven digital businesses.

AI creates what the researchers call 'the big flip' in the role and purpose that KPIs will play. Instead of being used to monitor past performance and outputs to inform human decisions, KPIs are also being utilized as inputs for training machines. In other words, KPIs define the data used to train the algorithms and machines that will run the business. As Michael Schrage, co-author of the *MIT Sloan Management Review* report, explains, the strategic premise is that KPIs and AI are means to strategic ends, not ends in and of themselves – or in other words, KPIs and AI become the key enablers and drivers to achieve desired strategic results. Consequently, asking 'What do we want to achieve and accomplish?' is the better strategic question and challenge than 'What do these data-driven technologies and metrics allow us to do that we couldn't do before?'

The trend towards smart performance management is still in its infancy, and it remains to be seen if and how it can be applied across companies. The conversations about smart performance management highlight the important role that business and finance leaders, not just operational teams, need to play in defining the portfolio of KPIs. As Schrage explains:

> Besides openness to greater data-driven experimentation, the most important leadership skills will revolve around elicitation, facilitation and collaboration for improvement of key performance indicators. Let's call it 'KPI kaizen'.[12]

Strengthening the CFO–CMO–CIO relationship

Running a platform-based business successfully requires strong, cross-functional collaboration. In the past, CFOs may have left the creation and management of digital platforms to the Chief Marketing Officer (CMO) and the Chief Information Officer (CIO) – but as platforms are evolving into business models, a close collaboration between CMOs, CFOs, CIOs and other executives is essential. While CMOs will have to drive the optimization of consumer engagement and interactions, and CIOs lead the creation of underlying data and technology infrastructure, CFOs have a key role to play in shaping the overall performance management system and procedures to convert increased customer interaction and insights into long-term value creation – for example, by analysing key investment choices, shifting appropriate levels of capital and resources from traditional to new business models, and/or communicating the new value strategy to outside investors.

Many marketing teams are making significant transformational efforts towards building new front-office capabilities. For the majority of CMOs, this is a complex undertaking when they are looking for support from CIOs and CFOs. Difficulties range from handling the huge volumes of new data made available from interactions, the creation and cost-effective management of new channels and dealing with sensitive data and information security, to using the new sources of insights effectively for business strategy development and decision-making. A strong collaboration between the CMO, CIO and CFO will help address these challenges more effectively and will position the creation and management of digital business models as a strategic, enterprise-wide transformational effort and priority. Digital business platforms are here to stay and are demanding new capabilities and ways of working, which will take time to develop – a level of change that should not be underestimated by CFOs and other executives.

Notes

1   Hagel, J III, Brown, JS, de Maar, A and Wooll, M (2016) Approaching disruption: Charting a course for new growth and performance at the edge and beyond, *Deloitte Insights*, 5 October, www2.deloitte.com/us/en/insights/focus/ disruptive-strategy-patterns-case-studies/approaching-disruption-for-growth-performance.html (archived at https://perma.cc/3PQU-TL2R)

2   Bughin, J, Catlin, T and Dietz, M (2019) The right digital-platform strategy, *McKinsey Digital*, 7 May, www.mckinsey.com/business-functions/mckinsey-digital/our-insights/the-right-digital-platform-strategy (archived at https://perma.cc/9HJP-ERB2)

3   McAfee, A and Brynjolfsson, E (2018) *Machine, Platform, Crowd: Harnessing our digital future,* p 135, WW Norton & Company, New York, NY

4   Sarrazin, H and Sikes, J (2013) Competing in a digital world: Four lessons from the software industry, *McKinsey Digital*, 1 February, www.mckinsey.com/business-functions/mckinsey-digital/our-insights/competing-in-a-digital-world-four-lessons-from-the-software-industry (archived at https://perma.cc/29DR-438F)

5   Sharma, D, Schroeck, M, Kwan, A and Seshaadri, V (2020) Digital platform as a growth lever, Deloitte, www2.deloitte.com/us/en/insights/focus/industry-4-0/digital-platform-strategy.html (archived at https://perma.cc/8BB4-4LKA)

6   Epstein, R, Witzemann, T and Thomas, M (2020) Shifting gears: How to drive your digital businesses forward with an appropriate steering approach, Deloitte, March, www2.deloitte.com/content/dam/Deloitte/de/Documents/finance-transformation/CFO-Insight-Steering-Digital-Businesses.pdf (archived at https://perma.cc/3Q83-GAV4)

7   Weber, J, Haupt, M, and Erfort, M (2012) Kundenerfolgsrechnung in der Praxis: Wie Sie profitable Kunden identifizieren, p 43, Wiley-VCH

8   Drucker, P (2015) *Management Challenges for the 21st Century*, pp 114–15, Routledge, Abingdon

9   Zeng, M (2018) Alibaba and the future of business, *Harvard Business Review*, September–October, hbr.org/2018/09/alibaba-and-the-future-of-business (archived at https://perma.cc/Z9FT-S9F8)

10 Schrage, M (2019) Don't let metric critics undermine your business, *MIT Sloan Management Review*, 23 October, sloanreview.mit.edu/article/dont-let-metric-critics-undermine-your-business/ (archived at https://perma.cc/8GHD-L6FD)

11 Kiron, D and Shrage, M (2019) Strategy for and with AI, *MIT Sloan Management Review*, 11 June, sloanreview.mit.edu/article/strategy-for-and-with-ai/ (archived at https://perma.cc/3E4W-23NT)

12 MIT IDE (2019) Q&A: How AI can lead corporate strategy, *Medium*, 24 June, medium.com/mit-initiative-on-the-digital-economy/q-a-how-ai-can-lead-corporate-strategy-87c7a7561318 (archived at https://perma.cc/L7ZC-3CL6)

13

Digital business ecosystems

Alibaba has been running a successful e-commerce platform since its inception in 1999.[1] For the first decade it experienced strong growth, but was not considered a major player on a global level until it devised a strategy to develop an ecosystem. After the first decade, Alibaba became a digital giant, surpassing even the most formidable competitors like Walmart to become one of the world's most highly valued companies. How did Alibaba do it?

In the early days, Alibaba simply linked buyers and sellers of goods together. Then when technology became more sophisticated, it moved more and more business functions online, including advertising, marketing, logistics and finance, later adding functions like influencers, product recommenders, and so on. Alibaba's growth story accelerated when the leadership team realized the company could build a digital business ecosystem for a wide community of businesses and consumers of many types, all of which are interacting with one another and the environment on an open, coordinated e-commerce platform. Alibaba's strategic imperative evolved to make sure that the platform does not only facilitate interactions between customers and providers, but that the community itself is able to provide all the resources, or access to the resources, that any online business would need to succeed. Hence it supported the evolution of a highly *productive*, *robust*, *diverse* and *healthy* ecosystem.

As the ecosystem expanded, it continued to create new online businesses in the same way as Amazon, eBay, PayPal and Google have done. In doing so, it has reinvented China's retail sector. Alibaba has become not just an e-commerce or online retail platform. It is a fast-growing, evolving and sprawling data-driven network of sellers, marketers, service providers, logistics companies and manufacturers. As Jack Ma, CEO of Alibaba, explained:

'Our philosophy is that we want to be an ecosystem. Our philosophy is to empower others to sell, empower others to service, making sure the other people are more powerful than us.'[2]

Many of the largest, fastest-growing and most highly valued companies in the world have followed the same path. Most of them have been around barely 20 years. How has so much value and market power emerged so quickly? Because all these companies have taken full advantage of new capabilities in network coordination and data intelligence. The ecosystems they steward are vastly more economically efficient and customer-centric than traditional industries, which is why they are rapidly reshaping industry sectors and economies at scale.

The phenomenon of digital business ecosystems

The word 'ecosystems' has become a buzzword in business, often used synonymously with platforms.[3] While the two are related, it is important to understand and consider the differences. A business ecosystem refers to a group of largely independent organizations collaborating and interacting with each other to pursue a shared goal; whereas a business platform refers to a digitally-enabled business model designed to enable frictionless interactions and transactions between ecosystem members. Core features of a business ecosystem are: the role of each organization within it (eg the ecosystem's orchestrator, participants or complementors); the governance structure of the ecosystem (ie the way these organizations agreed to interact, collaborate to create and share value); and the value propositions of the ecosystem (ie the shared performance goal that these organizations pursue). In this book, we focus narrowly on the *digital business ecosystem*, which is a group of independent organizations that leverage digital technology platforms and solutions to interact and collaborate dynamically.

This new generation of dynamic, digital business ecosystems is rapidly evolving and reshaping our connected economy, sometimes spanning traditionally disconnected industries. Research sponsored by the World Economic Forum estimates that by 2025, emerging digital business ecosystems could account for more than US $60 trillion in revenue.[4] Some of the largest digital business ecosystems are made up of thousands of companies and millions of people. Rather than taking products and services for granted, digital business ecosystems focus on the fast-changing needs of consumers. The most recent digital technologies such as the cloud, the Internet of Things (IoT) and blockchain helps these ecosystems go beyond designing products, services, customer experiences or organizations; it allows them to speedily and continuously redesign whole industries.

In some instances, digital business ecosystems emerge 'naturally' as the digital maturity of organizations increases. Take Microsoft, Apple or Walmart, for example. None of these companies started off with a strategy to create and engage in digital business ecosystems, but this is what they have evolved into and one of the reasons why they have become so successful. By creating products, services and technology platforms for their many ecosystem partners, they have managed to create an environment where everyone can thrive. A large proportion of Walmart's cost advantage in the retail grocery business, for instance, resulted from early, and at the time pioneering, investments in digitally-enabled business ecosystems. Walmart's procurement system provides suppliers with real-time customer information detailing customer demand and preferences, thereby creating a significant information and cost advantage, and attracting other major companies to collaborate, expand and strengthen the ecosystems. Procter & Gamble, for example, has integrated its ERP system with Walmart's, allowing both companies to unlock significant value opportunities in multiple areas.[5]

The growing level of awareness and understanding of how digital business ecosystems work, and the opportunities that they can create has fostered a growing digital maturity of companies. More companies connect and collaborate in digitally-enabled ways, to create products and services that are proving more valuable than any company can achieve in isolation. While the creation of digital business ecosystems is often initiated and orchestrated by the leaders within existing sectors, the ecosystems being created can reach beyond conventional sectors, blurring industry boundaries. A pharmaceutical company, for example, may want to offer a technology-enabled solution rather than a new medication. The digital solution would include real-time monitoring of the patient and adjustment of the treatment, and include a preventative package. This means the organization will have to collaborate beyond its traditional sector boundaries of pharmaceuticals to include integrated, scalable data transmission and processing services.

Core business benefits and risks

Most large organizations already operate within multiple ecosystems; however, the majority of these are traditional, static business ecosystems, primarily designed to aggregate or integrate existing resources or business processes.[6] While these static business ecosystems will continue to have their place, companies are increasingly focused on participating in dynamic, digital network-enabled business ecosystems, allowing organizations to connect and interact with greater agility and speed.[7] To this end, digital business ecosystems are able to create and amplify four core types of benefits:

- First, a business ecosystem can provide fast and flexible access to external capabilities that may be too difficult or too expensive to build internally. This is particularly important in the creation phase. As Bill Joy, co-founder of Sun Microsystems said, 'Not all smart people work for you.'[8] Equally smart but largely independent working talent might be attracted to supporting an inspiring and exciting open ecosystem. Steve Jobs was initially opposed to demonstrating the iPhone to third-party app developers, but when the Apple App Store was established about eight months after the launch of the iPhone, the ecosystem really took off thanks to the explosion of open innovations.[9]

- Second, once launched, digital business ecosystems, like digital platforms, can scale enormously quickly. Since its decision to become a digital business ecosystem orchestrator, Alibaba experienced exponential growth, rapidly becoming the second company to break the magical US $500 billion valuation mark in China.[10]

- Third, digital business ecosystems tend to be more flexible and resilient to the dynamic changes of the connected world. Consider the Windows operating system. Owing to its set-up as a flexible ecosystem, it has managed to remain the dominant operating system for more than three decades, despite enormous changes in this sector.[11]

- Finally, the network and learning effects created by digitally-enabled and highly connected business ecosystems can multiply value creation and capture opportunities for virtually any business across the network – a topic we will come back to shortly.

There are also some challenges to consider. Collaborating effectively across a largely independent and diverse group of organizations can be difficult to manage. Even the ecosystem orchestrators have limited control. A governance framework can help, but must strike a careful balance between setting standards and rules and protecting the freedom to enable open innovation, flexibility, resilience and self-organization. This is why it is so important to design a value-capturing and sharing model that is economically attractive for all participants – another topic we will come back to shortly. In many ways, a business ecosystem has to be a club that others want to join, and it is an equally critical and challenging responsibility for the ecosystem orchestrators to keep the club attractive throughout the business ecosystem life cycle.

Ecosystems need to be willing to accept delayed profitability to expand quickly. Even companies like Alibaba, Amazon and Microsoft had to make significant investments to build their ecosystems before becoming profitable. A study conducted by the BCG Henderson Institute reported the significant risks involved in creating and scaling up a digital business ecosystem, with some organizations experiencing negative profit margins of -60 per cent on average in the first years.[12] Amazon, for example, accumulated more than US $3 billion in losses during its first eight years of operation. Thanks to ongoing investment in its ecosystem, platforms and processes, Amazon managed to establish a strong market position and improve its operating margin from less than 1 per cent in 2013 to 9 per cent in 2018.

While a willingness to accept significant investment and losses early on appears to be necessary, generating a return on these investments is not guaranteed. Even 'successful' ecosystem orchestrators are finding this out the hard way, with growth begetting losses and no end in sight. According to the BCG Henderson study, fewer than 15 per cent of the ecosystems investigated were sustainably successful – and this is probably an optimistic estimate given the impossibility of eliminating survivor bias. The odds of succeeding with ecosystems are therefore no better than for other governance models, and the gains for those organizations that initially succeed may often be temporary. The dynamism and flexibility of ecosystems can cut both ways: the model is evolvable and scalable, but it requires upfront investment, continuous attention and careful management to truly succeed.

A new frontier for established companies

Despite rising awareness of, and enthusiasm for, digital business ecosystems, the management techniques required to run them are still evolving. Many executives are unclear about what it really takes to create, join or manage them effectively. When and where does it make sense to engage in digital business ecosystems, and how should this engagement be designed and governed? How to balance value creation, sharing and protection? Which new capabilities are required to manage operational performance and risk on an ongoing basis? Answering these questions can be difficult – in particular for established companies. Many of them are experienced in managing traditional alliances and partnership models, but handling dynamic, digital business ecosystems is a new frontier.

Many established companies will realize that, in order to engage in a digital business ecosystem, they will have to accelerate the digital business transformation of their current operating model and infrastructure (as discussed in Part One). Research led by the MIT Center for Information Systems Research found that companies that derive more revenues from ecosystems, and that were able to use the ecosystem to gain a deeper understanding of their customers, achieve significantly higher revenue growth and profit margins.[13] The study, however, also found that predominantly smaller companies (with revenues of less than US $1 billion) are becoming more networked, while many of their larger counterparts are struggling to respond, which might reflect the fact that smaller companies are faster at transforming their business and operating model, including their core infrastructure, to participate in digital business networks.

The case studies and stories of established companies that have managed to shift towards an ecosystem-based model consistently emphasize the need for a comprehensive and often radical digital transformation, with fundamental changes from leadership mindset and business strategy to operations and culture. At the Global Peter Drucker Forum in 2018, Zhang Ruimin, the business leader and architect behind the Chinese appliance manufacturer Haier, described the company's conversion to ecosystems thinking and management on two fronts. First, externally facing, as the business gains experience with ecosystems and the Internet of Things, there is a significant change in terms of value-creation opportunities, risks and responsibilities triggered by direct digital connection to consumers, suppliers and other business ecosystem partners. Internally, Haier succeeded due to a radically restructured operating model, the so-called *rendanheyi* model, an intra-organizational ecosystem with hundreds of loosely connected, entrepreneurial micro-enterprises that operate and interact on the organization's platform infrastructure. Even though the *rendanheyi* model may not suit all companies in the same way, Ruimin's key insights seem generally relevant: in order to be successful in developing an ecosystem-based business, a new way of thinking has to be carried through every part of the business and operating model, from product development to performance management. 'This is especially important for the twenty-first century', Zhang stressed. '[The] ecosystem is how we create value.'[14]

HAIER'S TRANSFORMATION INTO A DIGITAL BUSINESS ECOSYSTEM

Based in Qingdao, China, Haier is one of the world's largest appliance makers. In 2018, Haier generated about US $ 35 billion revenue. At that time, Haier employed approximately 75,000 people globally, about 27,000 of them located outside China, many of whom joined Haier when it acquired GE's appliance business in 2016. In the 2010s the gross profits of Haier's traditional core business, appliances, grew by 23 per cent a year. At the same time, the company created more than US $2 billion in market value from new ventures. Despite the significant growth, Haier was able to reduce the number of permanent employees significantly during this period. That said, the company has generated tens of thousands of new jobs in its rapidly expanding business ecosystem.[15]

At first glance, Haier may not appear to be a child of the connected world – but Haier's remarkable performance is the result of a multi-year business transformation from a struggling manufacturer to a thriving, digitally-enabled business ecosystem. One of Haier's key levers that transformed the company was its management philosophy, *rendanheyi*, which places the development and alignment (*heyi*) of employee (*ren*) and user value (*dan*) at the heart of a network-enabled business model. During the first stage of Haier's business transformation, Rendanheyi 1.0, the company created independent (customer-focused) virtual teams with enhanced decision-making rights. The next stage, Rendanheyi 2.0, turned the organization into a conglomerate of so-called micro-enterprises (MEs) – thousands of independently operating, entrepreneurial teams with authority to drive business performance, contracting, budgeting and recruitment decisions on Haier's core industry platform. In 2019, Rendanheyi 3.0 introduced network thinking to create Haier's 'Ecosystem Micro-Enterprise Communities' (EMCs). The EMC model allows MEs to form temporary alliances and micro-ecosystems to address and fulfil specific user needs. According to Haier CEO Zhang Ruimin, Haier aims to become a '3E system: ecosystem organization, ecosystem revenue and ecosystem brand. In an ecosystem organization, it's not the company versus the user, but the company, the user and the supply chain interconnected in an ecosystem.'[16]

To make the EMC model work from a finance and performance management perspective, Haier developed a wide range of new practices, including an approach to track, manage and reward value creation and sharing on an employee level. For example, Haier introduced a performance scorecard called the Win–Win–Value Add (WWVA) statement.[17] The WWVA statement combines a range of financial and non-financial measures to track and manage performance throughout the user journey and life cycle. According to Haier's CFO, Shao Xinzhi, the statement differs from traditional income statements in three ways. First, it accounts for repeatable ecosystem-generated revenues, rather than one-off product-generated revenues. Second, it focuses on the win–win opportunities created through co-creation and cooperation within the wider business ecosystem, trying to prevent the zero-sum game that can result from a traditional focus on individual value maximization. Third, the WWVA is able to account for the value created and shared by individuals, and therefore is people-focused. Haier also introduced a two-dimensional matrix to determine how much each employee will get paid.[18] In this matrix, the horizontal axis represents the company's overall performance using common financial indicators such as revenue, profit, market share, and so on. The vertical axis, however, is measuring *network value* as a function of the network size (ie the number of nodes in the network and the users connected to the network). Haier turns each employee into a node of the company's ecosystem network, and incentivizes them to create both user value (quantitative contributions), and user relationships (qualitative improvements).

Most other aspects of Haier's performance management system have been aligned to the *rendanheyi* model – ranging from target setting to budgeting to performance tracking – and are continuously refined through ongoing experimentation, dialogue and learning as the business model evolves. The *rendanheyi* model has also been deployed outside China, for example at US-based GE Appliances (GEA). According to Haier's CEO Zhang Ruimin, the transformation of GEA was challenging, but ultimately successful, resulting in significant performance improvement.[19]

Key considerations for CFOs

CFOs have an important role to play in assessing and, if appropriate, supporting the creation of and/or participation in digital business ecosystems. For many finance leaders, especially those from established companies, this is a new and challenging role. On the one hand, there are clear economic trends that explain the emergence of digital business ecosystems, and significant value-creation opportunities that arise. On the other hand, there is significant uncertainty and risk that CFOs cannot ignore.

Finance leaders should take the time to understand and evaluate, as far as possible, what these opportunities and risks could mean for their organizations. For some, it may feel like weighing up the risks of 'failing while trying' versus 'failing by not trying'. Most finance leaders, however, will discover that, at the very least, they will have to dedicate considerable (more) time and resources to engage and learn about the companies' opportunities and exposure to digital business ecosystems. Most likely, they will also see the need to accelerate the digital transformation of their core infrastructure. Without new experiences, capabilities and the infrastructure to support it, companies will be unable to participate – and face the risk of being sidelined from the dominant trend that is reshaping our connected economy.

A detailed analysis and exploration of the core financial and business management practices required for digital business ecosystems is urgently needed, but may require some time to be developed as companies start to gain experience in this new domain. The following topics outline a few important aspects that CFOs should reflect on as they embark on this journey.

Value creation

Companies, through their leaders, invest capital and resources in what they believe will create business value. The dominant view on what drives value, and the corresponding capital and resources allocation strategy, is largely influenced by a business's leaders, mental models, their experiences and education. In many companies, however, business leaders have been schooled in an approach in which investments in tangible assets and core operations have taken priority over the cultivation of digital networks, relationships and ecosystems.[20]

A study conducted by MIT Sloan and Deloitte in 2019, examining companies at different levels of digital maturity (as introduced in Part One) found that 80 per cent of digital maturing companies are collaborating with external partners to drive innovation, compared to 33 per cent of companies that are at the earlier stages of their digital transformation and maturity).[21] Most interestingly, however, is the reason for this. It is not because less mature companies fail to recognize the importance of external partnerships (nearly 80 per cent of all respondents stated that these have become vital), but rather because they hesitate to commit the required resources. The study also found that digitally mature companies approach business partnerships very differently – they are much more focused on developing trustful, multidimensional, wide-ranging, capability-building ecosystems that address both short-term and long-term objectives.

Changing the organization's understanding of digital business ecosystems might be the first and one of the most important tasks for CFOs to accomplish. The art of network thinking, as outlined in the introduction to Part Three, can help us understand and articulate underlying dynamics and value drivers of digital business ecosystems, and they can guide us in assessing their relevance and potential for a specific organization and sector. The following core dynamics and drivers of value should be considered:

- **Economies of scale:** Digital business ecosystems can create value not only through *supply-side economies of scale* (for example, the reduction of fixed and variable costs through shared assets, a more flexible and better integrated supply chains, and so on), but also *demand-side economies of scale*. As discussed in earlier chapters, demand-side economies of scale create significant, accelerating growth. From a network thinking perspective, the key reason for this, as discussed earlier, is 'preferential attachment' – a business ecosystem that grows successfully becomes more and more attractive to more participants, and may thereby develop and benefit from 'the-rich-gets-richer' dynamics.

- **Network effects:** Building on these economies of scale, digital business ecosystems can create powerful (direct or indirect) *network effects*, which means that the value of a product or service increases as the number of consumers of these products and services increases. Think about a mobile network – the first owner of a mobile phone gets no benefit, but the value of their phone and network access will start to grow exponentially as more mobile phone owners join the network. Network effects can occur in many industries, such as logistics, utility, hospitality, travel, and so on. There will, however, be relatively low leverage when the communication between network participants is limited – and this is where the opportunity for a digital business ecosystem emerges.

- **Economies of learnings:** Let us assume that, in addition to the growing mobile phone network, the mobile phones and the network connections themselves start to improve – for example, because an ecosystem of companies has formed to work together to improve the quality of the network and mobile phone (for example, in terms of connectivity, functionality, application, user experience, and so on). In this case, not only the value of the products and services for the consumer, but also the knowledge and capabilities of the partnering companies, start to grow faster. In other words, the digital business ecosystem as a whole, and all the individual participants within it, start to get better and better, faster and faster. The ecosystem benefits from second-order increasing returns, which amplify the already exponentially growing value that resulted from the network effects caused by an increasing number of participants.[22] These second-order dynamics are driven by *economies of learning,* ie the exchange and combination of information, and the sharing of knowledge through collaboration, that allow each participant to accelerate their learning and performance improvement process.

Assuming the exchange of information across the ecosystem network has been fully digitized and further enhanced through *self-improving algorithms,* then the learning effects can be compounded, at least until the algorithm cannot be improved any more. So the digital business ecosystem experiences another, higher order of increasing returns – another amplification of the value-creation process. There is a higher level still to economies of learning. Some participants of the mobile phone network may be able to use the data that they collect, and the knowledge they accumulate, to create a new business ecosystem and market – say, a market for connected cars. They may then be able to create and access further levels of collaboration, connections, learnings and value creation.

The combination of economies of scale, network efforts, economies of learning and digitization – all of which are interrelated – create additional dynamics. First, participants benefit from developing wider, long-term, *trust*-based relationships, which provide an incentive to collaborate and learn from each other. Second, the *diversity* of the ecosystem participants, eg in term of sector and geographic origin, can have a positive impact on the ecosystem's ability to learn, improve, innovate and expand. Third, organizations that have taken on a *central position* within the network of a digital business ecosystem, and that are prepared to tap into the network's core data flows, can gain an advantage by extracting valuable insights and learning through enhanced data analytics and artificial intelligence.

Leading digital ecosystem companies, from Google to Alibaba, are ecosystem hubs that are able to leverage accumulated data flows that allow them to create, sustain and grow their competitive advantage – within *and* across multiple sectors. But also established companies can unlock the enormous value potential of digital business ecosystems – be it through participation and positioning within evolving digital business ecosystems (for instance, an evolving IoT system related to their industry sector), the acquisition of networked business (for instance, with a strategy to scale a new digital business model at the edge of the traditional core business) or by creating their own digital business ecosystem (for instance, by launching smart products).

Given the pace at which digital business ecosystems evolve, and the powerful dynamics they generate, it is important for CFOs and their teams to join forces with business and technology teams to conduct a comprehensive analysis of the opportunities, and threats, created by digital business ecosystems, as well as the capabilities that need to be built to engage effectively.

Value capturing and monetization

An important aspect for CFOs to consider and, if necessary, to get involved in, is the design and management of the value-capturing and monetization mechanisms, as well as the value-sharing model. This is a complex task that involves balancing multiple interdependent factors. The value-capturing mechanism, for example, needs to reflect a range of factors, ranging from the specific product and service to the ecosystem's governance and relationship model. The same is true for the design of the monetization mechanisms, which, most of all, needs to balance the desire to monetize and share value with the continued focus on driving ecosystem growth and health (eg when it is useful or necessary to support or subsidize some participants). As digital business ecosystems evolve rapidly, any of the value-capture, monetization and sharing mechanisms need to be monitored and potentially adjusted continuously – not just focusing on the complex dynamics *within* but also *across* ecosystems (eg when ecosystems compete for members, who may decide to shift to another ecosystem if the conditions no longer favour them).[23]

Performance measurement

Another important aspect that CFOs need to think about is business performance management and investor relations. If the company starts to allocate capital and resource to the development of new digital business models, investors and analysts should be involved and informed. For many established companies, this means that not only their narrative for value creation but also their internal and external performance measures and reporting will need to change – in fact, in many cases, the investor and analyst audience itself may have to change.

To receive the benefit of higher valuations from the investor community, CFOs not only have to provide a clear explanation of how network dynamics are being leveraged to drive superior growth and value creation, but they also need to be able to track progress against these promises. With over 80 per cent of valuations being generated by intangibles, standard financials are no longer sufficient. New performance indicators and supporting big data analytics gathered on everything from network growth and ecosystems health, customer interactions and transactions to inventory levels – often in real time, and in quantities previously unimaginable – need to be fused with financial data to constantly measure, monitor and report the results from these new and often unmeasured and unreported sources of value.[24] Just a quick look at the analyst presentations of the leading digital business ecosystems illustrates the change from traditional financial performance reporting. For many CFOs this also means that investments in new commercial and analytical capabilities, and supporting operational infrastructure, are required.

As the example of Haier illustrates, the practices required to track and manage business performance and value creation in digital business ecosystems may deviate significantly from conventional approaches. An income statement that has been developed to manage a 20th-century industrial and asset-based company is unlikely to work for a 21st-century digital business ecosystem – a quick comparison between a ride-hailing and a transport company, a home sharing network versus a hotel chain, an e-commerce platform company and a traditional retailer, illustrates the point. Until new common practices are established and agreed – if they ever are, given the diversity and speed with which new digital business models are evolving – the CFO's creativity, courage and leadership is required to strike a balance between contemporary business management needs and traditional external norms.

Information management

Digital business ecosystems require information management beyond organizational boundaries. If value is generated in digitally-connected and -enabled business ecosystems, a scalable and secure exchange of data between organizations becomes essential – be it to create a more comprehensive view of the customer, or coordinate contributions and activities across a value chain network. Enabling the exchange of data creates significant challenges, especially for large established companies with complex legacy infrastructure. This need is the key driver to transform core operational processes, data and technology platforms, as discussed in Part One.

Companies should pay particular attention to the creation or emergence of common data standards across ecosystems and value chains, and the opportunities and challenges this creates, as discussed in Chapter 3. The trend towards data standard convergence is one of the main drivers of the Fourth Industrial Revolution, and is accelerated by the evolution of digital business ecosystems. Finance leaders do not need to own this domain, but they should pay more attention to it, in collaboration with business and technology teams. As Peter Drucker predicted many years ago, it will not be the technologists and data scientists, but the business and financial leaders who must learn what information they need and exchange to maximize economic value creation.[25]

Ecosystem management

Finance and business leaders have to get used to the fact that, in a connected world, the key value and performance drivers are increasingly located outside the organization. The very notion of creating and participating in a digital business ecosystem challenges the traditional ethos, still held by most traditional businesses, that they are a large self-contained, autonomous-acting business entity that is competing against others in a pre-defined and sector-specific market. This may sound straightforward, but in practice, it can take a very long time for people to realize that cooperation and collaboration, with partners and peers, within and outside industry boundaries, are essential to the success and survival of the organization.

By comparing the life cycle of business and biological ecosystems, Harvard professors Marco Iansiti and Roy Levien have created an analogy that business leaders may find intuitive and useful.[26] They describe how both business and biological ecosystems are characterized by a wide range of factors that are dependent on each other's and the ecosystem's prosperity: if the ecosystem is healthy, individual participants will thrive; if the ecosystem is unhealthy, individual participants will suffer. Or, to cite Ruth Porat, CFO of Alphabet, the parent company of Google, from an interview with BNN Bloomberg in 2020: 'We do well when our partners in the ecosystem do well.'

Many companies operating in business ecosystems are intertwined in multiple, interdependent relationships outside of which they have little meaning. The consequences of these business relationships are often beyond the control of any of the participants. Rather, they result from the overall state of the system, which is subject to continuous change within and outside of the ecosystem network. The analogy with a biological ecosystem is not perfect, of course, but it illustrates a fundamentally important point: to operate successfully in digital business ecosystems, business leaders cannot just participate in finding and closing attractive business deals, but need to make contributions to the long-term health and strength of the ecosystem, and its ability to enable companies to co-evolve and cooperate effectively.

But what do we mean by a healthy business ecosystem? Iansiti and Levien define three key features: productivity, robustness and diversity.[27]

- **Productivity:** The most important parameter indicating a business ecosystem's health and performance is the system's productivity, specifically its ability to consistently convert technology innovations and resources into higher-value goods and services for customers. There are multiple options to consider when monitoring the productivity of ecosystems. A simple but highly effective way could be to monitor the financial, commercial and operational productivity of the most influential, contributing participants – especially in relation to the ecosystem orchestrators and hubs. Take the professional software sector, for example: knowing how companies like Microsoft, SalesForce.Com, SAP or Oracle are performing, and how they are shaping their future, is important for everyone depending on their ecosystems, and usually very transparent. Most of these companies invest a significant amount of resource in arranging annual events for their ecosystem partners to share and shape their business strategy. SAP's partner ecosystem, for instance, brings together a large set of partners that have a nuanced understanding of the needs of local customers.[28] The ability to bring them all together effectively to enhance SAP's product strategy is a critical engine of growth and productivity, not just for SAP but for everyone involved in its digital business ecosystem.

- **Robustness:** Business ecosystems must be robust enough to survive disruptive change and unexpected technological innovation. Companies that engage in a robust business ecosystem have the advantage of being supported by other participants, which can help them navigate times of low demand or unpredictability and protects them against external shocks. Microsoft survived the adoption of the world wide web by embedding itself in an ecosystem made up of independent vendors. There are also cases where key ecosystem players face unexpected difficulties that will put the ecosystem's health and survival at risk – the financial crisis and subsequent breakdown of Lehman Brothers would be one example. Robustness relates to productivity and provides another reason to keep an eye on the commercial, operational and financial strength of key ecosystem players. Depending on the type of business ecosystem, different aspects of robustness can be emphasized. Given that digital business ecosystems are, by nature, dependent on the stability of enabling technologies – for example the Internet of Things – additional, technology-related aspects should be assessed regularly – for example, technology interoperability or connectability. Perhaps most importantly successful business ecosystems drive robustness by creating the ability and culture to continuously expand and renew the ecosystem itself. Even the strongest business ecosystems will encounter market disruption and may lose ground to new competitors at some point. Yet the most robust business ecosystems respond by reinventing themselves constantly, often enabled by the adoption and development of new technology. The rate of renewal is an important indicator, and when monitoring it one should consider both the ecosystem's ability to create technology innovations within the ecosystem (eg Microsoft's development of new cloud platforms and services), and the ability to integrate external capabilities (eg Facebook's fast integration of Instagram and WhatsApp).

• **Diversity:** Although robustness and productivity are essential components of a healthy ecosystem, they do not completely characterize it. Digital business ecosystems thrive on connecting, collaborating, learning and growing together within diverse communities of intensely related partners. They need to protect a healthy, structural balance between platform players, developers, data or technology service providers, and so on. It is this very diversity that allows for the best innovations to emerge. In digital business ecosystems where partners are too similar, there is a greater chance of competition rather than cooperation, which leads to lower levels of innovation. In turn, business ecosystems that bring together a highly diverse set of participants can create significant levels of innovation, even in the most traditional and historically competitive and protective industries. The automotive industry, one of the most competitive sectors, has fought fiercely against emerging niches, such as the entrance of technology and telecommunication players into the OEM-owned domains.[29] As discussed before, it has begun forming highly diverse business ecosystems that turn products for transportation into consumer platforms. Almost all leading manufacturers have created diverse ecosystems to integrate media applications into their cars' built-in control systems, for example. As consumers may eventually adopt self-driving vehicles, this aspect of consumer access alone could be worth hundreds of billions of dollars, shared between automotive manufacturer, technology and network providers, social media and content platforms, insurance and consumer product companies, regulators and other public-sector organizations.

Like a balanced scorecard, companies may consider using the parameters of productivity, robustness and diversity – as well as any other parameters that could reflect core network dynamics, such as structure and centrality – to define a set of additional ecosystem-oriented 'macro performance indicators' to be monitored and discussed regularly. Finance leaders and teams may not be familiar with these types of metrics, but are well placed to facilitate this dialogue, given their core skills and experience in performance and risk management. This would help ensure that ecosystem-related opportunities and risks are clearly defined and monitored, to enhance and protect the value-creation process.

Relationship management

Digital business ecosystems are not just for businesses, but can cover a wide array of relationships with any kind of external organization and people. These may include academic institutions, government entities, NGOs and also competitors (to name a few). As indicated earlier, according to the research conducted by MIT Sloan and Deloitte, the nature of collaboration within a business ecosystem tends to differ depending on the digital maturity of an organization. Digitally mature organizations tend to develop a more diverse set of relationships, with a stronger focus on long-term collaboration.[30] This does not mean that relationships need to be formalized, however. While formal partnerships serve a vital role in driving collaboration, and often create the backbone for forming a wider business ecosystem, the study shows that digitally maturing companies form alliances that tend to involve less formal and less controlled relationships, and that increasingly rely more on relational collaboration and governance than detailed contracts. As the study outlines, strong relationships can have a very positive impact on the cross-pollination of capabilities, which, in turn, enhances innovation, agility and resilience. This means the overall system is less vulnerable in the event of a breakdown of any one part. Increased autonomy for participants does require different forms of governance, especially it requires clear ethical guidelines and boundaries to ensure that the autonomous units serve the ecosystem's overall goals and protect its reputation, an important topic that we will explore further.

Another set of empirical studies shows that the way in which companies prepare and manage their relationships in digital business ecosystems can have significant impact on performance and value creation. Based on research conducted in 2020, scientists at the MIT Sloan School's Center for

Information Systems Research (CISR), have highlighted the importance of *relationship readiness* (eg the development of a distinctive value proposition, and a robust and open infrastructure) and *relationship curation* (eg the development of a joint goal for value sharing and information exchange).[31] The research found that digital business ecosystems in the top quartile of digital readiness had an average market share that was 110 per cent higher than the average market share of the bottom quartile. Ecosystems in the top quartile on curation had an average market share that was 128 per cent higher than the average market share of the bottom quartile.

Governance and risk management

When companies decide to create or participate in digital business ecosystems, their activities become increasingly interconnected, seamlessly spanning across industries and markets globally. As the rate of innovation, collaboration and digitally-enabled interactions rises, the individual organizations, even though formally independent, start to rely more and more on one another. These strengthening connections can create tremendous vitality for the participants, the ecosystem and the economy, but they can also pose significant risks capable of rippling throughout the system. These risks can be external, for example market- or technology-driven; relate to productivity issues experienced by key ecosystems players; or, in many cases, be behaviour-driven. Research by MIT and Deloitte found that some of the main challenges facing business ecosystems are the lack of alignment between participants, a lack of transparency on benefits realization and allocation, the inability to bridge cultural gaps between diverse partners, and insufficient governance to protect the health and trust in the business ecosystem.[32]

Digital pioneers like Alibaba's Ming Zeng warn, 'Never let an MBA near a marketplace that can run itself', but it appears that, at least in the majority of cases, a degree of governance is still required – even though it might not require detailed, bilateral contracts.[33] Most importantly, the type of governance needed will have to create incentives (financially or otherwise, eg social) for participants to join and collaborate, drive alignment of goals, provide fair rules to share value generated by the chosen business and revenue model, monitor risks to protect the integrity and health of the ecosystem, and thereby build trust – rather than seek to control. The main goal of governance is to foster network effects to create and share more value for users and ecosystem participants than they can achieve on their own, or by engaging with other ecosystems. Take the Apple app ecosystem, for instance;[34] there are (some, but limited) contractual obligations and support mechanisms, such as managing who gets to use what data and how they are going to monetize that data, and how revenues will be shared, including the share that Apple gets versus the app developers. The governance of digital business ecosystems is a fast-evolving discipline – and likely to accelerate further as enabling technologies, such as blockchain and smart contracting, mature. Finance may have a key role to play but, in most cases, will need to rapidly develop new skills and capabilities.

Another discipline accelerated by digital ecosystems is the area of risk management – specifically the prevention of *cybercrime*. Every day, Alibaba Cloud blocks 300 million brute force attacks and 20 million web hacking attacks.[35] And that is just one example of the daunting scale of cyber risks everywhere. Already in 2014, Deloitte's quarterly CFO surveys indicated that cyber risks were rapidly becoming the CFO's most worrisome threat, overtaking others like economic volatility, technology disruption and over-regulation.[36] Given the value at risk, CFOs are understandably concerned and focused on identifying potential cyber risks. With a large percentage of CFOs also overseeing IT, they are equally committed to weighing up and determining how and where to invest company resources. Investments in new digital business models and enabling platform technologies such as the cloud and application programming interface (APIs) are essential for companies in the connected world, but can quickly lead to disastrous scenarios if not managed carefully. Facing these 'new truths' is important to institute appropriate levels of governance and risk management models. They may not offer CFOs total security, but with the right governance structures and risk management capabilities in place they may achieve a comfort level that justifies investment in new, innovative, digital business models.

Ethics

Digital business ecosystems do not compete in traditional ways – rather, they change the traditional rules of competition, not just in one sector but across all sectors.[37] Once digital business ecosystems have reached scale, they can leverage their network-based customer connections, relationships and assets in one setting, and then use them to enter another industry and reshape its competitive market structure. The dominating digital business ecosystems and network orchestrators own access to billions of mobile consumers that other product and service providers want to reach, and have created vast networks with partnering businesses and organizations across sectors. Not only can these companies leverage these relationships to accelerate growth in and across their target markets, but they can also influence the flow of information across all these participants. The more users and partners join these networks, the more attractive (and even necessary) it becomes for enterprises to offer their products and services through them.

By driving increasing returns to scale and controlling competitive bottlenecks, these digital superpowers can become even mightier by extracting disproportionate value and tipping the global competitive balance. For instance, by leveraging Alibaba's vast user base, Ant Financial (an affiliate company of the Alibaba Group formerly known as Alipay) was able to attract over half a billion users in less than three years. Founded in 2014, Ant Financial has become the world's highest valued FinTech company in 2018, with a valuation of US $150 billion.[38]

That said, the debate about the regulation of digital business models is ongoing – usually moving between the demands to leave digital business platforms unregulated, and the demands to introduce strict regulations (for example, by breaking up digital ecosystems into smaller companies, or by tightly regulating the services they provide). Those who push for no regulation argue that whatever harm may be done by new digital business models, they are outweighed by the potential of future economic and societal benefits (for example, in terms of accelerated innovation, data and knowledge sharing, collaboration and value creation). Those who push for regulation argue that these digital business models are deliberately designed to challenge economic and social systems and laws (for example, market and competition, territorial and tax-related laws),[39] and that new rules and regulations are required to make sure that users are protected with access to a wide choice of safe products and services online; and that businesses can freely and fairly compete online just as they do offline.[40] It will be interesting to see how the debate continues – most likely it will take more time to analyse, evaluate and navigate the invariable economic and social trade-offs.

Regulated or not, digital business models will continue to challenge established companies and markets across all sectors. They must become a part of the solution by developing responsible strategies and approaches for creating and sharing economic value. The leaders in companies, governments and communities, as well as consumers, should be educated to understand how digital business models operate, and the opportunities and challenges that they create. This will allow them to play an active role in shaping our connected economy, for instance, by making well-considered choices over which ecosystem to join and support – not just based on financial, but also social, environmental and ethical values.

Leaning in to the challenge

CFOs should be prepared to help their companies navigate the fast-evolving world of digital business ecosystems. Some CFOs may, rightfully, highlight the risks of getting involved in digital business ecosystems – but should not ignore the growing risk of doing nothing. Digital business ecosystems are simply becoming too powerful to be ignored, and CFOs need to lean into the change. This does not mean that CFOs should unconditionally support the investment and involvement in ecosystems, but rather develop the different capabilities needed in finance to help assess and potentially manage these new business models effectively.

As the transformation of the connected economy progresses, companies are bound to become part of at least one digital business ecosystem. It is likely that every organization and business leader will have to be prepared to operate effectively in the new world of digital business ecosystems. Furthermore, across all industries and geographies, all ecosystem participants – and particularly the orchestrators and hubs in leading digital business ecosystems – must channel their power for the good of humanity by creating and protecting appropriate standards to sustain our global economical and societal health. In doing so, there may be an exciting opportunity to shift the general perception of digital business ecosystems away from myths and anxieties to one that creates hope to leverage the enormous powers of networks to address some of the world's greatest challenges. This will, however, require a different perspective on what 'shared value' means, or could mean; as well as the recognition that we will need a more sustainable and balanced approach to wealth creation and distribution, in addition to the protection of our natural ecosystems – the focus of the next and final chapter.

Notes

1   Zeng, M (2018) Alibaba and the future of business, *Harvard Business Review*, September–October, hbr.org/2018/09/alibaba-and-the-future-of-business (archived at https://perma.cc/5K64-Y84H)

2 Balakrishnan, A (2017) Jack Ma explains the difference between Alibaba and Amazon: 'Amazon is more like an empire', CNBC, www.cnbc.com/2017/01/18/jack-ma-difference-between-alibaba-and-amazon.html (archived at https://perma.cc/JL9H-KEUC)

3 Jacobides, MG, Sundararajan, A and Van Alstyne, M (2019) Platform and Ecosystems: Enabling the digital economy, World Economic Forum, reports. weforum.org/digital-transformation/wp-content/blogs.dir/94/mp/files/pages/files/digital-platforms-and-ecosystems-february-2019.pdf (archived at https://perma.cc/3MHA-X32X)

4 Jacobides, MG, Sundararajan, A and Van Alstyne, M (2019) Platform and Ecosystems: Enabling the digital economy, World Economic Forum, February, www.weforum.org/whitepapers/platforms-and-ecosystems-enabling-the-digital-economy (archived at https://perma.cc/X4AG-6NMK)

5 Iansiti, M and Levien, R (2004) Strategy as ecology, *Harvard Business Review*, March, hbr.org/2004/03/strategy-as-ecology (archived at https://perma.cc/KQ9C-9ALV)

6 Hagel, J III, Brown, JS and Kulasooriya, D (2012) Performance Ecosystems: A decision framework to take performance to the next level, *Deloitte Insights*, 2 January, www2.deloitte.com/us/en/insights/topics/operations/performance-ecosystems-which-model-is-right-for-you.html (archived at https://perma.cc/E86W-K7CL)

7 Jacobides, MG, Sundararajan, A and Van Alstyne, M (2019) Platform and Ecosystems: Enabling the digital economy, World Economic Forum, February, www.weforum.org/whitepapers/platforms-and-ecosystems-enabling-the-digital-economy (archived at https://perma.cc/X4AG-6NMK)

8 Edstrom, D (2013) MTConnect: To measure is to know, p 19, Virtual Photons Electronics, Ashburn, VA

9 Pudin, U, Reeves, M and Schüssler, M (2019) Do you need a business ecosystem?, BCG, 27 September, www.bcg.com/en-gb/publications/2019/do-you-need-business-ecosystem.aspx (archived at https://perma.cc/XZB8-LNAL)

10 He, L (2018) Alibaba joins Tencent in the exclusive US $500 billion market value club, *South China Morning Post*, 25 January, www.scmp.com/business/companies/article/2130497/alibaba-joins-tencent-exclusive-us500-billion-market-value-club (archived at https://perma.cc/8VYN-V8SV)

11 Nayak, M (2014) Timeline: Microsoft's journey: four decades, three CEOs, Reuters, 4 February, uk.reuters.com/article/us-microsoft-succession-timeline/timeline-microsofts-journey-four-decades-three-ceos-idUSBREA131R720140204 (archived at https://perma.cc/M5PF-2ACK)

12 Reeves, M, Lotan, H, Legrand, J and Jacobides, MG (2019) How business ecosystems rise (and often fall), *MIT Sloan Management Review*, 30 July, sloanreview.mit.edu/article/how-business-ecosystems-rise-and-often-fall/ (archived at https://perma.cc/W4LF-TN8H)

13 Weill, P and Woerner, SL (2015) Thriving in an increasingly digital ecosystem, *MIT Sloan Management Review,* sloanreview.mit.edu/article/thriving-in-an-increasingly-digital-ecosystem/ (archived at https://perma.cc/MZJ2-3Q95)

14 Straub, R (2019) What management needs to become in an era of ecosystems, *Harvard Business Review,* 5 June, hbr.org/2019/06/what-management-needs-to-become-in-an-era-of-ecosystems (archived at https://perma.cc/CU6M-UVSW)

15 Hamel, G and Zanini, M (2018) The end of bureaucracy, *Harvard Business Review*, hbr.org/2018/11/the-end-of-bureaucracy (archived at https://perma.cc/7VA2-RC5Y)

16 Jacobides, MG (2019) Goodbye business as usual, Think at London Business School, www.london.edu/think/goodbye-business-as-usual (archived at https://perma.cc/5XYG-RCD2)

17 Krumwiede, K (2019) Haier's win–win value added approach, *Strategic Finance,* sfmagazine.com/post-entry/february-2019-haiers-win-win-value-added-approach/ (archived at https://perma.cc/5NKR-KSLV)

18 Ruimin, Z (nd) Reflections on managing a multinational corporation in China: Business model innovations of the internet era, *AIB Insights*, documents.aib. msu.edu/publications/insights/v15n2/v15n2_Article1.pdf (archived at https://perma.cc/D2U4-FZ28)

19 Ruimin, Z (nd) Why Haier is reorganizing itself around the Internet of Things, *Strategy-Business,* www.strategy-business.com/article/Why-Haier-Is-Reorganizing-Itself-around-the-Internet-of-Things?gko=cfc69 (archived at https://perma.cc/5ZDT-GHEG)

20 Ajit, K (nd) The value shift: Why CFOs should lead the charge in the digital age, Deloitte, www2.deloitte.com/us/en/pages/finance/articles/cfo-insights-digital-age-business-model-innovation-value.html (archived at https://perma.cc/AL8P-PAS3)

21 Kane, GC, Palmer, D, Phillips, AN, Kiron, D and Buckley, N (2019) Accelerating digital innovation inside and out, *Deloitte Insights*, 4 June, www2.deloitte.com/uk/en/insights/focus/digital-maturity/digital-innovation-ecosystems-organizational-agility.html (archived at https://perma.cc/VN3N-X36R)

22 Hagel, J III, Brown, JS and Kulasooriya, D (2012) Performance ecosystems, Deloitte, www2.deloitte.com/global/en/insights/topics/operations/performance-ecosystems-which-model-is-right-for-you.html (archived at https://perma.cc/7GQU-EAF8)

23 Jacobides, MG, Cennamo, C and Gawer, A (2018) Towards a theory of ecosystems, *Strategic Management Journal*, 39, pp 2255–276, doi.org/10.1002/smj.2904 (archived at https://perma.cc/YV6L-WLLV)

24 Ajit, K (nd) The value shift: Why CFOs should lead the charge in the digital age, Deloitte, www2.deloitte.com/us/en/pages/finance/articles/cfo-insights-digital-age-business-model-innovation-value.html (archived at https://perma.cc/AL8P-PAS3)

25 Drucker, P (2007) *Management Challenges for the 21st Century,* pp 110–15, Routledge, Abingdon

26 Iansiti, M and Levien, R (2004) Strategy as ecology, *Harvard Business Review*, March, hbr.org/2004/03/strategy-as-ecology (archived at https://perma.cc/KQ9C-9ALV)

27 Iansiti, M and Levien, R (2004) Strategy as ecology, *Harvard Business Review*, March, hbr.org/2004/03/strategy-as-ecology (archived at https://perma.cc/KQ9C-9ALV)

28 Casagrande, N (2020) A look back at 12 months of partner enablement, SAP, news.sap.com/2020/08/partner-enablement-steffen-burger-interview/ (archived at https://perma.cc/GD9F-HY8K)

29 Helbig, N, Sandau, J and Heinrich, J (2017) The future of the automotive value chain, 2025 and beyond, Deloitte, www2.deloitte.com/content/dam/Deloitte/us/Documents/consumer-business/us-auto-the-future-of-the-automotive-value-chain.pdf (archived at https://perma.cc/JX3J-4R5A)

30 Kane, GC, Palmer, D, Phillips, AN, Kiron, D and Buckley, N (2019) Accelerating digital innovation inside and out, *MIT Sloan Management Review,* sloanreview.mit.edu/projects/accelerating-digital-innovation-inside-and-out/ (archived at https://perma.cc/KQ9S-SYRB)

31 Sebastian, IM, Weill, P and Woerner, SL (2020) Driving growth in digital ecosystems, *MIT Sloan Management Review*, sloanreview.mit.edu/article/driving-growth-in-digital-ecosystems/ (archived at https://perma.cc/6LEX-53LD)

32 Kane, GC, Palmer, D, Phillips, AN, Kiron, D and Buckley, N (2019) Accelerating digital innovation inside and out, *Deloitte Insights*, 4 June, www2.deloitte.com/uk/en/insights/focus/digital-maturity/digital-innovation-ecosystems-organizational-agility.html (archived at https://perma.cc/VN3N-X36R)

33 Reeves, M (2013) Algorithms can make your organization self-tuning, *Harvard Business Review*, 13 May, hbr.org/2015/05/algorithms-can-make-your-organization-self-tuning (archived at https://perma.cc/ZW8C-VXFH)

34 Van Alstyne, MW, Parker, GG and Choudary, SP (2016) Pipelines, platforms and the news rules of strategy, *Harvard Business Review*, April, hbr.org/2016/04/pipelines-platforms-and-the-new-rules-of-strategy (archived at https://perma.cc/GTV5-DW9S)

35 Gilchrist, K (2019) Alibaba Group thwarts 300 million hack attempts per day, CNBC, 16 October, www.cnbc.com/2019/10/16/jack-ma-alibaba-group-thwarts-300-million-hack-attempts-per-day.html (archived at https://perma.cc/N6TJ-4CSN)

36 Dickinson, G and Kambil, A (2014) What's keeping CFOs up in 2014?, *CFO Insights*, June, www2.deloitte.com/us/en/pages/finance/articles/cfo-insights-concerns-company-performance-pressure.html (archived at https://perma.cc/3YYH-SJHC)

37 Iansiti, M and Lakhani, KL (2017) Managing Our Hub Economy, *Harvard Business Review*, September–October, hbr.org/2017/09/managing-our-hub-economy (archived at https://perma.cc/H9VG-7GTV)

38 Cheng, E (2018) How Ant Financial grew larger than Goldman Sachs, CNBC, www.cnbc.com/2018/06/08/how-ant-financial-grew-larger-than-goldman-sachs.html (archived at https://perma.cc/3ZFD-NBN9)

39 Lobel, O (2016) The law of the platform, *Minnesota Law Review*, www.minnesotalawreview.org/wp-content/uploads/2019/07/Lobel.pdf (archived at https://perma.cc/2BHT-BLWK); Strowel, A and Vergote, W (2016) Digital Platforms: To regulate or not to regulate? European Commission, ec.europa.eu/information_society/newsroom/image/document/2016-7/uclouvain_et_universit_saint_louis_14044.pdf (archived at https://perma.cc/Z7NV-3H35)

40 European Commission (2020) Europe fit for the Digital Age: Commission proposes new rules for digital platforms, ec.europa.eu/commission/presscorner/detail/en/ip_20_2347 (archived at https://perma.cc/Z7LY-4ANK)

14

Multi-stakeholder value

Throughout the book, we have talked about the role of the CFO as a leader of digital business transformation, growth and performance management in the connected world, or in other words as the 'architect of business value'. We have also discussed how the rapid development of our connected world is changing the way our businesses and economy will work, and how CFOs need to amend traditional perspectives and approaches to focus on value creation and protection. However, what we have not done as yet is to step back and reflect on what 'value', or 'value creation', actually means, or could mean.

So, what could have been the first topic to cover in this book will help us conclude our explorative discussion of the evolving role and impact of CFOs in the connected world – allowing us to embed our discoveries and insights covered in previous chapters into a wider economic and societal context.

Long-term multi-stakeholder value creation as a common purpose

In 1970, the Nobel Prize-winning economist Milton Friedman wrote:

> There is one and only one social responsibility of business – to use its resources and engage in activities designed to increase its profits so long as it stays within the rules of the game, which is to say, engages in open and free competition without deception or fraud.[1]

Friedman's perspective strongly influenced the understanding and focus of 'value creation' over the succeeding decades, at least in capitalistic-oriented economies such as the United States and the United Kingdom. The 'primacy of shareholders' or 'shareholder value maximization' became the conventional business wisdom, reflecting the belief that self-interested investors will look to put their capital where it will earn the highest return for the risk involved. Since debt capital is rewarded by a fixed interest rate, while equity returns reflect profitability and future cash flows, shareholders are the best placed to judge whether management is doing a good job at running the business.

In 1997, the influential Business Roundtable (BRT), an association of the CEOs of nearly 200 of the most prominent companies in the United States, enshrined the philosophy of shareholder primacy in a formal, signed statement of corporate purpose. 'The paramount duty of management and of boards of directors is to the corporation's stockholders', the group of executives declared. 'The interests of other stakeholders are relevant as a derivative of the duty to stockholders.'[2] Since 1978, the BRT has periodically issued 'Principles of Corporate Governance'; each statement issued since 1997 has endorsed the principle of shareholder primacy – that corporations exist principally to serve shareholders.

In 2019, the BRT announced the release of a new 'Statement on the Purpose of a Corporation', signed by 181 CEOs, who committed to leading their companies for the benefit of *all* stakeholders – customers, employees, suppliers, communities and shareholders. The new statement supersedes previous statements and thereby marks quite a fundamental shift from shareholder to multi-stakeholder value creation.[3]

What is the reason for this change of direction, and how should businesses react? Business executives feel increasingly challenged to rethink the role of business in society for a number of reasons. Social norms are changing and expectations from employees, customers and even investors are rising fast. Global challenges such as climate change, income inequality, and the exponentially growing power of digital business ecosystems have shaken public confidence in large corporations. More and more public leaders, communities, scientists and politicians are asking for more systemic efforts, global cooperation and regulation, highlighting that individual profit-maximizing businesses alone will not be incentivized or able to tackle these shared global challenges. Even though many executives have rearticulated their individual corporate purpose statements, there is a growing concern that without a more collective effort, we are a long way from being able to address the issues threatening our planet and humanity.

It is not the first time that the system in which value creation takes place has come under fire, not just externally, but also by business leaders themselves. In the early 2000s Jack Welch, former CEO of GE, amongst other US business leaders, declared that focusing on shareholder value as your core strategy was 'the dumbest idea in the world'.[4] Leading companies like Johnson & Johnson held on to their credo to 'put the needs and well-being of the people we serve first' *before* 'stockholders should realize a fair return'.[5] In continental Europe and Japan, legal obligations provided corporate boards and executives with fiduciary duties towards a wider set of stakeholders, including employees (often represented by labour unions), consumers, communities in which the companies operate and the government.

There is a risk that the debate between shareholder- and stakeholder-ism may end up becoming a false dichotomy, while missing the core of the problem.[6] To run a business successfully, executives need to cooperate with a range of key stakeholders. They must generate a decent return on capital to attract investors, develop innovative products and services for customers, provide good working conditions and incentives to interest employees, cooperate with suppliers in a fair manner, and meet legal obligations. Whether profitability is the primary objective, or a necessary constraint to survive, running a successful business is always dependent on cooperating with multiple stakeholder groups. The critical difference, however, lies in how companies operationalize the need to generate profits – specifically the way they balance short- and long-term value creation.

In too many cases, the objectives of shareholder value maximization have turned into an obsession with short-term earnings. To meet quarterly earnings and short-term investor expectations, CFOs have consistently been forced to forego investment in long-term value creation and prosperity for the core business, for other stakeholders and for future generations. For this reason, the final commitment highlighted in the 2019 BRT statement, where executives commit to delivering value 'for the future success of our companies, our communities and our country', is possibly the most critical element.[7]

But what does this mean for CFOs? It means that, while individual companies continue to serve their own corporate purpose, long-term and multi-stakeholder value creation should be regarded as the common 'purpose of corporation' – for the BRT to truly internalize the meaning of their words, companies may require a more holistic perspective and approach to value creation.

Creating shared value

For long-term, multi-stakeholder value creation to become a reality, company leaders, and especially CFOs, need to combine the following value propositions into one coherent and reinforcing approach. While shareholder value dominated the attention of CFOs for several decades, it will continue to play an important role. Finance leaders will – as discussed in previous chapters – need to focus much more on the fast-evolving value drivers for customers (eg customer services-oriented operations), employees (eg accelerated learning) and ecosystems (eg network effects). In addition, CFOs will have to make a much greater effort to reconnect and integrate the positive aspects of capitalism with social progress – an effort that must reach far beyond the standard commitments towards social responsibility or corporate philanthropy (see box on page 214).

A promising, and increasingly recognized and adopted approach, is the concept of 'Creating Shared Value' (CSV), which has been developed by Michael Porter, Professor at Harvard Business School. In a seminal article published in 2011, Michael Porter and Mark Kramer introduced the principles of 'shared value', which 'involves creating economic value in a way that *also* creates value for society by addressing its needs and challenges'. The authors further emphasize that CSV is not about 'social responsibility, philanthropy or sustainability, but a new way for companies to achieve economic success'.[8]

The CSV concept is based on the belief that businesses acting as businesses, rather than charitable donors, can become the most powerful force for addressing major economic and social issues – if they are enabled by a holistic concept of value creation, not just a narrow focus on short-term profit. The core ideas and principles of shared value are not entirely new. Leading global companies have already embarked on many important efforts to create shared value by reconceiving the intersection between customer orientation, society and corporate performance. Their initiatives range from refocused client service and product portfolios to restructured value chains and local ecosystem creation.

Yet awareness of the potential of CSV as an approach to drive and integrate business and social value creation remains limited, and the adoption of its core principles is still very much in its genesis, at the time of writing. Creating shared value requires new management skills and organizational capabilities, particularly by acquiring a far deeper appreciation of our environmental and societal challenges, a much better understanding of how companies can help address these needs at scale while running a financially successful business, and the ability of businesses to collaborate across profit and non-profit boundaries to make a real impact.

More than anything, CSV represents a new mindset that emerges when senior leaders acquire a far deeper appreciation of our environmental and societal challenges, a much better understanding of how companies can help address these needs at scale while maintaining commercial success, and the ability of businesses to collaborate across profit and non-profit boundaries to make a real impact. This thinking can create entirely new and significant opportunities for business transformation, performance and growth in a connected world, at the same time that it benefits society by building businesses to help solve global problems. While opportunities differ by industry, company, geography, and depending on how a company's particular business priorities intersect with social issues, they tend to fall into one of the following three areas:[9]

- Creating shared value from *reconceiving products and markets* involves a focus on enhancing growth, market share and profitability as a result of environmental, social or economic development benefits delivered by a company's products and services. Developing a strategy to unlock these benefits tends to involve the definition of new markets, or market segments, in terms of social ills or unmet needs, which, once clearly defined, can then be served effectively with new service or product innovations. Adidas, for example, has partnered with Nobel Laureate Muhammad Yunus's micro-finance organization, Grameen Bank, to manufacture a low-cost shoe for poor people in Bangladesh. 'The shoes will be cheap and affordable for the poor, besides it will protect people from diseases,' said Yunus.[10]

- Creating shared value from *redefining productivity in the value chain* focuses on improvements in internal business operations; for example, improved cost, quality and productivity through environmental improvements, better resource utilization, investment in employees, supplier capability and other areas. Activities to unlock shared value may require a company (or its suppliers) to increase productivity by addressing environmental and social constraints in its value chains. InterContinental Hotels Group (IHG), the largest hotel company in the world, for example, launched the Green Engage programme to reduce its environmental footprint and energy consumption.[11] The shared value concepts were adopted to identify, prioritize and track opportunities for resource efficiencies and cost reductions across their hotels, using an online tool to update actual shared value returns based on the ever-growing base of programme adopters.

- Creating shared value from *enabling local cluster development* derives from improving the external environment for the company through investments in local communities, suppliers and infrastructure in ways that also enhance business productivity. Novartis, for instance, had for many years been selling medicines in India, focusing on major cities with well-established infrastructure.[12] Yet it recognized that 70 per cent of the country's population live in rural villages, often without being served. In 2007, Novartis began to hire and train hundreds of healthcare educators – usually local women – to raise awareness about basic health-seeking behaviour, and built up a distribution system to 50,000 rural clinics. The company collaborated with doctors, hospitals and NGOs to organize health camps for villagers. By the early 2020s, the programme was providing improved healthcare for 42 million people living in 33,000 villages, having returned a profit within 30 months, and having increased sales 25-fold.

As Porter and Kramer highlighted in 2011, applying the principles of CSV in practice can help companies create value in one area, which then generates new opportunities in others, thereby creating a virtuous circle – creating social value can drive business value, and vice versa.[13] Shared-value thinking is not at all about the redistribution of value already being created, but instead about expanding the total pool of economic, ecological and social value.

When companies embrace the opportunity to create value for business and society in a more integrated way, and when value creation becomes mutually reinforcing, then the business focus can shift from reactive risk avoidance to proactive business development, and from reporting to action. Social value creation is no longer just an 'add-on' compliance requirement or cost that is negatively affecting short-term profit realization, but becomes an important aspect of long-term business value creation, strategy and transformation. This is an important insight and learning, which is worth exploring further, as it allows businesses to generate opportunities for sustainable growth in a connected world, while making greater contributions to tackling major societal challenges – including top priority issues like sustainability and preventing climate change.

CORPORATE SOCIAL RESPONSIBILITY (CSR) AND BEYOND

The roots of *corporate social responsibility* thinking emerged during the Industrial Revolution, when companies started to make strategic investments in corporate philanthropy, which was, in most cases, seen as a necessary 'add-on' expense that companies accepted as a licence to do business.[14] The discussion about the role of business in society enlivened significantly with Friedman's 1970 essay, and was then altered and developed with exponential speed since the 2019 BRT statement. In the half-century between Friedman's essay and the BRT statement, the concept of Corporate Social Responsibility (CSR) became prevalent.

Often used as a catch-all for sustainable, socially conscious business practices, it has offered a recognized route for businesses to be more socially accountable, and to operate in ways that do not negatively affect the wider community, employees, consumers or the environment. While corporate philanthropists had primarily focused on sponsoring non-business-related causes, the CSR movement started to explore opportunities to use the business itself to 'do good' to society and environment. In practice, however, many of these initiatives were approached with an 'offset' mindset, meaning that a company is trying to do good in one field to make up for doing harm in another – as if corporate emissions and pollutions could be offset by social benevolence. Moreover, in most companies, CSR initiatives have played a rather minor role. Small corporate initiatives, volunteering, awareness days and employee perks all fall under the CSR banner, as do recycling policies and dedicated efforts to reduce carbon emissions. The remit of CSR is broad, entirely self-regulated and usually not well coordinated across organizations to reach scale. Not all CSR activities are wrong, of course, but CSR programmes that are no more than cosmetic in order to get a nod on the annual report, or a result of organizations trying to offset their unsustainable practices, may create more harm than value to people and planet, while providing a convenient excuse for corporate short-termism.

That said, the business world has moved on. In 1987, the United Nations World Commission on Environment and Development published a report called *Our Common Future that* launched the idea of sustainable development, and the associated concept of a sustainable business. The commission defined sustainability as 'meeting the needs of the present without compromising the ability of future generations to meet their own needs' – an important, principled statement, yet one that offers little guidance on how a sustainable business might be designed and implemented in practice.[15]

A first step to providing guidance for implementation was the specification of the Millennium Development Goals (MDGs) in 2000, which then led to the definition of the 17 Sustainable Development Goals (SDGs) in 2015 as part of the UN's 2030 Agenda for Sustainable Development. The SDGs address a wide range of interconnected global issues – including those related to poverty, inequality, climate, environmental degradation, prosperity, and peace and justice – highlighting the need for global and cross-sector collaboration to bring together the requisite knowledge, technologies, financial capital and political prowess.

SDGs recognize the critical contributions that businesses have to make in delivering the 2030 Agenda – from contributing finances to providing products and services that address sustainability. A radical reduction of carbon emissions to 'net zero' to prevent global warming, while protecting global economic growth to serve a rapidly expanding global population, and to help lift millions out of poverty, emerges as the defining challenge. Failure to meet the challenge threatens to amplify a wide range of sustainability risks.

Businesses are under increasing pressure to respond – not only in terms of reporting and compliance, but also from a strategic business perspective. The combined reaction of key stakeholder groups – including consumers, employees, regulators and investors – suggest that the momentum toward sustainability is reaching a tipping point.

Consumers

Consumer preferences and purchasing patterns are trending increasingly toward sustainable products and services, especially younger generations. The 2019 Deloitte Global Millennial Survey found that 42 per cent of millennials said they have begun or deepened a business relationship because they perceive a company's products or services to have a positive impact on society and/or the environment.[16] Several studies indicate that more than two-thirds of consumers consider sustainability when making a purchase decision, and are willing to pay more for sustainable products and brands,[17] with Gen Z shoppers leading the way.[18]

Employees

Employees are emerging as an increasingly vocal and powerful stakeholder group that drives a company's business strategy towards sustainability. Companies that fail to meet employees' expectations on sustainability will increasingly face difficulties in attracting, retaining and motivating their current and future talent. The previously mentioned survey conducted by Deloitte found that millennials and Gen Zs show much deeper loyalty to employers that boldly tackle environmental and social issues that resonate with them. One study found that nearly 40 per cent of millennials had chosen a job because of a company's commitment to sustainability,[19] while another reported that over 60 per cent of millennials said that they would not take a job at a company that was not committed to sustainability.[20]

Regulators

National governments and supra-national organizations are increasingly making use of regulatory authorities to urge companies to adopt more sustainable business practices. For instance, in France, regulations approved in 2017 require that multinational companies identify and prevent adverse sustainability impacts resulting from their own activities, as well as the activities of their subcontractors or suppliers.[21]

Investors

Investors are increasingly redirecting capital flows toward sustainable investment funds. At the UN's annual climate conference in 2019, more than 630 investors, collectively managing over US \$37 trillion in assets, signed a statement urging companies to take stronger action to address climate change.[22] In his 2020 annual letter to CEOs, Larry Fink, CEO of BlackRock, the world's largest institutional investor, urged companies to confront the 'new climate reality', indicating that climate risk creates investment risk and that, therefore, organizations should anticipate 'a significant reallocation of capital'.[23] According to Fink, companies that fail to integrate sustainability and climate considerations into their businesses risk being left behind as investors and businesses shift to a low-carbon economy – non-sustainable businesses might be more profitable in the short term, but negative externalities are likely to destroy shareholder value in the long run.

All of these reactions are elevating sustainability as a priority among business executives. The shifting attitudes of key stakeholders do not only reflect business risks but also significant opportunities, making it an imperative for companies to place sustainability at the heart of their strategies.

So how are businesses leaders reacting to this? To get a picture of business leaders' priorities and concerns when it comes to climate change, Deloitte has surveyed executives of leading companies worldwide in 2020 and in 2021.[24] The results of the latest survey were published in March 2021, representing the perspectives of 750 participants. This 2021 survey found that over 80 per cent of all executives are *concerned* about climate change – a similar result found in the 2020 survey. More than a quarter of all executives are *extremely concerned* about climate change. From a geographical perspective, executives in the United States, UK, China and Australia are among the most concerned about climate change (more than 80 per cent of respondents in each of these countries are concerned or very concerned).

Almost 60 per cent of executives see the world at a tipping point for responding to climate change. Despite the gravity of the moment, there is a prevailing sense of hope as 63 per cent agree that immediate action can still limit the worst impacts of climate change. A third of executives believe that the world has hit the point of no return, highlighting a broader sense of urgency to combat climate change before it is too late.

According to the 2021 survey, more than one in four organizations are affected by climate change. The most cited environmental issue is operational impact as climate-related events increasingly disrupt business models and supply networks worldwide. Resource scarcity and resource cost remain leading issue.

Both the 2020 and 2021 survey, however, also indicated that sustainability was still perceived as an 'add-on cost', rather than an integral part of business strategy and transformation.[25] This is surprising, not just because of the stated level of concern, but because 46 per cent of the companies represented in the 2021 survey have stated positive impact on *revenue growth and profitability* as a direct result of their sustainability efforts, as well as a positive impact on *client satisfaction* (49 per cent), *employee recruitment and retention* (47 per cent) and *brand recognition* (38 per cent).

While most executives recognize the value of sustainability efforts, both surveys indicate that they are impeded by short-term thinking – a general trend that was further amplified by the economic impact of the Covid-19 pandemic (the need to focus on the near term emerged as the top obstacle – up to 37 per cent in 2021 from 30 per cent in 2020).[26] When asked which actions are most impactful from an environmental sustainability perspective, executives highlighted the need for collective action and engagement, backed by broader education and the promotion of science-backed climate research.

Pioneering sustainable business transformation

In search of companies that have adopted and applied an integrated approach to value creation, Professor CB Bhattacharya, Chair in Sustainability and

Ethics at the University of Pittsburgh, and founder of the Sustainable Business Round Table, identified several organizations that were able to create significant economic and social value by driving sustainable business transformation.

These companies regard sustainability and social well-being as a business opportunity, rather than a threat or obligation. They are making strategic investments in the development of new business models, new product and service innovations, business networks and ecosystems and business capabilities – all of which will allow them to respond faster and more effectively to the growing demands for sustainable business across multiple stakeholder groups[27] (see box 'Corporate social responsibility and beyond'). As Professor CB Bhattacharya describes in *Small Actions, Big Differences,* his research revealed that many of these companies stand out because their senior leaders have taken full ownership for making sustainability a strategic business priority, and for transforming their companies accordingly.[28] Moreover, these senior business and finance leaders have been able to extend and infuse the feelings of ownership and connection across their organization and to the external world – as the following two examples illustrate.

Example 1: Not all profit is valuable

Francesco Starace, chief executive of Italian multinational energy company Enel Group, still remembers when he first began to rethink why an energy company does what it does, for whom and for what purpose.[29] Starace came to believe that the purpose of an energy business was not to generate short-term profitability by boosting consumers' need for electricity – so, instead, he broadened his view of corporate purpose and responsibility to extend beyond profit, and embarked on an impressive journey that transformed Enel from a traditional electric utility company into a leading global renewable energy powerhouse.

Energy is an important enabler for social and economic development and growth, yet research estimates that there are still over 750 million people globally without access to electricity.[30] While many organizations strive to expand energy access to help meet development goals, doing so with non-renewable technology drives greenhouse gas emissions and propels climate change. Under the leadership of Starace, Enel developed a new business strategy that encompassed and integrated key aspects of business, digital and sustainability transformation – and that tackles the challenge by providing access to affordable, reliable and clean energy, while safeguarding the environment and protecting local communities.

Enel applied the shared value concept and thinking to identify and prioritize initiatives that the company could invest in to accelerate their transformational journey. According to Starace, 'a shared value approach is key to opening new business opportunities by addressing social and environmental challenges in all phases of the value chain'.[31] Enel discovered that a strengthened social purpose, combined with long-term financial interests, could significantly enhance sustainable growth and value creation.[32] Based on this, Enel introduced the concept of sustainability-linked bonds (SLBs). Unlike green bonds, SLBs are not limited to a single project, but structured to pay out a higher coupon if the company meets specified performance indicators linked to the UN's Sustainable Development Goals (SDGs). As Enel CFO Alberto De Paoli explains:

> There is a clear link between sustainability and value creation as, by investing in products that are sustainable from a social and environmental perspective, businesses can maximize products and minimize risk while simultaneously helping to achieve the SDGs.

Parallel to this, Enel decided to make significant investments in the digitization of their core business process and operations, which enables Enel's transformation into a digital business platform and ecosystem that drives efficiency, flexibility and innovation to underpin its operational sustainability.

With Enel's business transformation progressing at pace, Starace's 2030 Vision for Enel, announced in November 2020, included further significant increases in renewable energy investments and the use of sustainable finance tools, aimed at 'boosting further de-carbonization, electrification of consumption and platforms, and creating sustainable shared value for all stakeholders and profitability over the medium and long term'.[33]

Example 2: Not all growth is sustainable

Paul Polman, former CEO of Unilever and a pioneer in shaping and practising multi-stakeholder oriented management thinking, said. 'We need to be part of the solution. Business simply can't be a bystander in a system that gives it life in the first place. We have to take responsibility, and that requires more long-term thinking about our business model.'[34]

Interviewed in 2014, Polman explained how, under his leadership, Unilever explored new ways to balance sustainable and equitable growth while generating long-term financial returns for shareholders.

'The first thing is mindset,' said Polman, who set out to double turnover when he took over the chief executive role in January 2009. Following a 10-year period of no growth, and significant pressure from shareholders, it was critical to recreate the organization's focus on growth. Polman continues: 'The second thing was about the way we should grow. We made it very clear that we needed to think differently about the use of resources and to develop a more inclusive financial growth model.'[35]

In 2010, Unilever created and launched the Unilever Sustainable Living Plan (USLP) as the core business model and strategy for achieving sustainable and equitable growth by serving society and the planet – the company's response to the growing challenges and opportunities of an increasingly resource-constrained and unequal world. The USLP set out to prove that Unilever's growth ambition could be decoupled from its environmental footprint, while having a positive social impact. To operationalize the new strategy, the company implemented a range of clearly defined long-term commitments and targets that reflect the company's economic, environmental and social performance ambition across the value chain.

Unilever's financial growth model, as introduced in 2010, emphasized the commitment to place sustainability at the very heart of the company's long-term value-creation strategy (Figure 14.1). The more popular sustainable brands become, the more the company will grow; the more efficient the company becomes in managing resources, the lower the costs and risks will be, and the more resources can be reinvested in driving sustainable innovation. Yet, as Polman highlighted, and in line with our discussions in previous chapters, a greater focus on long-term growth and value creation does not

FIGURE 14.1   Unilever's sustainability-centred growth model (schematic)[36]

mean focusing less on holding people accountable for progress on operational performance goals, but instead provides a clear reference point from which to drive performance improvement.

'The USLP is our business model. It is not a CSR programme; it is an integrated part of how we operate and it drives a measurable business benefit,' explained Unilever's CFO, Graeme Pitkethly, in an interview in 2016, highlighting key performance drivers, including superior growth of sustainable brands, reduced costs from eliminating operational waste and improving efficiencies, and reduced input risks due to a more integrated supply chain.[37] These have helped Unilever increase trust and employee attraction and motivation significantly.

Just as I started to write this final chapter, in May 2020, Unilever celebrated the tenth and final year of the USLP. Looking back, Unilever's new CEO Alan Jope commented: 'The Unilever Sustainable Living Plan was a game-changer for our business. Some goals we have met, some we have missed, but we are a better business for trying', adding that, while globalization and capitalism are generally good for large companies like Unilever, they must not come at the expense of people and planet.[38]

Sustainability as a key driver for long-term value creation

The achievements and experiences of companies like Enel and Unilever demonstrate that, despite the economic turbulence caused by the banking crisis and Covid-19, a commitment to sustainability can become *the* key driver for long-term growth and value creation. During Polman's tenure, Unilever delivered consistent top- and bottom-line growth that delivered a total shareholder return of 290 per cent (2009–2019);[39] since Starace became the CEO of Enel, the company's share price has roughly doubled (2014–2020).

As both examples illustrate, multi-stakeholder value creation can and should be very different to corporate social responsibility and philanthropy initiatives in that it emphasizes social innovation and well-being as *the source* of economic innovation, and vice versa, which can lead to sustainable economic growth and profitability. Instead of asking companies to compensate for the damage they cause, or to redistribute the profits earned at society's expense, the goal is to earn those profits by benefiting society. While the traditional conception of shareholder value maximization is suggesting that capitalism is a zero-sum game in which a win for companies means a loss for society or vice versa, the principles of shared value creation, or multi-stakeholder value creation in general, are postulating the exact opposite. Multi-stakeholder value creation, as illustrated before, means that everybody must work and win together: companies need healthy customers, employees and societies, and the customers, employees and societies need healthy companies. We are all interconnected and interdependent components of the same economic, ecological and social systems.

Most companies have not approached their businesses in this way, but the stories from Enel and Unilever illustrate that change is not only needed, but also possible. As Porter and Kramer outlined:

> Profits involving a social purpose represent a higher form of capitalism – one that will enable society to advance more rapidly while allowing companies to grow even more. The result is a positive cycle of company and community prosperity, which leads to profits that endure.[40]

Lack of collective progress

Unfortunately, the success stories of Enel and Unilever represent a small minority of pioneers. Just a random look at the annual reports of public companies reveals that only a few companies have fully embraced sustainability as an opportunity for long-term value creation, and have integrated it into their business strategy and transformation journey. This lack of awareness and integration is both a missed business opportunity and a challenge for society.

There may even be a risk that the good progress made in harmonizing performance metrics and reporting standards may result in companies remaining focused on meeting their *own* reporting and compliance requirements, without taking the time to redefine their underlying business strategies, and without considering the wider ecosystems that they operating in.[41] Yet, as systems and network thinking teaches us, in order to drive change with impact, we need to expand our perspective, and our sense of care and responsibility beyond organizational boundaries and time horizons to observe and influence the evolving system as a whole. Then, and only then, will we be able to deliver change with impact. As complex as it may sound, systematic change can only be achieved by addressing a system as a whole through collective responsibility, leadership and action. Limiting our attention to meeting our own needs, and our ambitions to *do no harm*, or relying on a few to make all the difference, is not going to be enough.

Despite the encouraging progress made by a few, we are *collectively* still far away from making enough progress to resolve our most pressing societal challenges, including climate change. According to the 2020 UNEP Emissions Gap Report the world is – despite a dip in greenhouse gas emissions from the Covid-19 economic slowdown – still heading for a catastrophic temperature rise above 3°C this century – far beyond the goals of the Paris Agreement.[42] While there are concrete examples and clear signals that it is possible to make progress, there is yet no evidence that governments and businesses around the world are making a collective effort to bring global emission reductions on track to achieve the 2050 emission and decarbonization targets associated with a 1.5–2.0°C temperature rise.[43] But, what is it that companies can do collectively to drive transformational change?

21st-CENTURY ECONOMIST THINKING

Gaining a better understanding of 21st-century economic thinking is becoming essential for business and finance leaders. Economist Kate Raworth in *Doughnut Economics* highlights many parallels and connection points between the understanding of design, systems and network thinking introduced throughout this book.

The reason we are struggling to balance economic prosperity and sustainability is inherently a design problem, she argues. The dominating business model of established companies follows an industrial design that is degenerative. It is based on the pipeline value chain: we extract natural resource to make products, ship them to consumers, who will consume them and throw the rest away. It progressively depletes the system upon which it depends. While this model has delivered significant economic growth, its design is fundamentally flawed, because it continually weakens a living planet that can only survive by recycling its living building blocks such as carbon, oxygen, water. Our business and economic models have broken the regenerative cycles of our planet – we are 'depleting nature's sources and dumping too much residual waste in her sinks'.[44]

Traditional economics has recognized these 'negative externalities' and introduced policies, quotas and taxes to address them, which can ease the pressure on nature but are not enough to transform our business and economic model. From a systems thinking perspective, such policies offer a weak leverage point. In order to drive transformational change we need to change a system's paradigm, goal, growth strategy and accountabilities, which, according to Kate Raworth, can unlock significant economic and social opportunity.

According to Raworth, when established companies become first aware of the degenerative design of their business and industry, their first-level response is to *do nothing*. As long as environmental taxes are not eroding company's profits, there is no reason to change the business model. The second-level response, *do what pays*, is the most common; it may involve cutting emissions and reducing waste to drive efficiencies, and to pursue the green-branding to attract premium-paying consumers for eco-friendly products. The third-level response of companies is to do their *fair share* by acknowledging the full scale of damage and need for change, yet usually without an intention to transform their pipeline business models. The fourth-level response, *do no harm*, is what is commonly known as 'net zero', and it marks a transformational change and departure from the industrial to a sustainable business strategy and model. Such an approach, however, means that a company would stop short of doing good, of using a new business model to replenish the world by growing the business. Therefore, the fifth-level response, *be generous*, is the most logical and value-adding option, both from an economic and social perspective. It requires a designed transformation from a degenerative to a regenerative business model, allowing the company to flourish by giving back more to nature than was taken out in order to bring society back to the natural ceiling. Put differently, it 'embraces our responsibility to leave the world in a better state then we found it'. When companies are following the mindset and design of a level-five response, the economy starts to transition from a degenerative to a regenerative design, or what has become commonly known as the *circular economy* – an economic model designed to harness renewable resources and energy to continually transform materials into useful products and services.

Driving change at scale and with impact

Driving transformational change at the scale and impact needed to drive systemic improvement around sustainability and climate is not easy – and it is not something that any one organization can achieve on its own. Even the most engaged and leading global organizations are facing significant barriers, including government policies and cultural norms. These barriers are often complex and beyond the level of influence and control for any one company, which is why companies must collaborate more closely across multiple stakeholders and sectors. Consumers, suppliers, peers and competitors, governments, NGOs and communities all have essential roles to play – yet very often, without a common platform or framework, they work in isolation, or perhaps even in opposite directions.

To overcome these barriers, pioneering organizations have started to form alliances and ecosystems, both public and private. Many of these collaborations are in their infancy at the time of writing, but they do create promising opportunities to address the most complex social challenges of our connected world, by creating new business ecosystems to advance a circular economy, or exchanging data in order to address sustainability challenges.

Accelerating the circular economy

In the food sector, for example, Danone has set up a €100 million ecosystem fund to develop and test regenerative business models.[45] Mars Incorporated has increased market access by forming a collaborative ecosystem with micro-entrepreneurs in impoverished urban and rural areas that are difficult to reach through traditional channels.[46] Nestlé, a pioneering proponent of shared value, created the Institute of Packaging Sciences in 2019 to co-develop and test environmentally-friendly packaging materials and systems together with suppliers, research institutions and start-ups with an intention to make its packaging 100 per cent recyclable or reusable by 2025.[47] Together, Danone, Mars, Nestlé and Unilever have established the Sustainable Food Policy Alliance (SFPA), a business ecosystem which aims to shape food-related regulation for key drivers of sustainability, and includes the ambition to shift the industry as whole closer toward a circular economy.[48]

Leveraging digital business ecosystems

Developing innovative business models, products, services and other solutions to tackle sustainability issues requires the sharing and pooling of data from a wide range of public and private sources, as well as the rapid exchange of insight to accelerate learning. The rapid development of Covid-19 vaccines in 2020–2021 is just one recent example that illustrates what is possible when public and private organizations around the world are starting to collaborate and learn in new ways.

In response to the challenge and opportunity of sharing data to drive the sustainability agenda, in 2019 the UN launched Global Pulse, an initiative that works through a global network of digital laboratories to accelerate the discovery, development and responsible use of big data and artificial intelligence innovations and policies for sustainable development.[49]

Companies have an opportunity – and perhaps even an obligation – to create, join, enrich and leverage digital networks and ecosystems to contribute to the data-sharing, learning and collaboration process, and to empower other organizations in their sustainability transition.

Digital business ecosystems, as explored in the previous chapter, are powerful and uniquely positioned to help drive collaboration through shared goals, accelerated learning and other means. They can offer frameworks and governance structures that consolidate sustainability innovations, identify priority areas and leading practices for action, and connect companies with the public and private partners and technology providers. As technologies like AI, the Internet of Things and blockchain proliferate, companies should be prepared to explore and leverage new paths of sustainability-oriented innovations. They should not limit themselves to driving their own digital business transformation and value creation, but also invent business models that can address societal challenges. VeChain, for example, has created a 'Digital Carbon Ecosystem' that leverages a blockchain- and IoT-enabled digital platform and marketplace. As consumers engage in low-carbon actions – for instance by purchasing a low-carbon product – they are able to earn a carbon reduction credit, which can be redeemed for benefits from other ecosystem partners such as retailers or financial services providers.

Redefining the business transformation strategy for a connected world

As the explorations and examples in this chapter illustrate, more and more companies will find that sustainability becomes the major driving force for (digital) business transformation. By viewing sustainability through the lens of value creation, innovation-driven growth and performance improvement, businesses will learn to apply their creativity and capabilities to tackle major societal and environmental challenges, while also creating new business opportunities and accelerating the transformation of their business models and ways of working – including many aspects covered in previous chapters

FIGURE 14.2   Key shifts characterizing transformative approaches to sustainability (examples)[51]

From ...	... To
Risk and compliance-oriented. The company sees sustainability through the lens of risk and compliance only, focusing on preventing sustainability-related threats that could damage the bottom line.	**Opportunity and growth-oriented**. The company sees sustainability through the lens of growth and opportunity, focusing on how sustainability could drive strategic top and bottom line growth.
Profit-driven. The company focuses on driving financial returns for shareholders. Short-term profit maximization drives decision-making.	**Purpose-driven**. The company focuses on long-term multi-stakeholder value. Purpose and sustainability guide strategy and decision-making
Enterprise-focused. The company is internally focused. Interactions with external stakeholders, such as customers, suppliers or communities, are transactional rather than reciprocal.	**Ecosystem-focused**. The company's focus reaches beyond traditional organizational boundaries and involves a collaborative ecosystem, recognizing the company's systemic interdependencies with multiple external stakeholders.
Protective. Companies do not reveal information about their sustainability performance, choosing to shy away from sharing data, networks and ecosystems that could expose company knowledge.	**Transparent**. Companies adopt digital technologies to enable data-sharing and radical transparency to enhance collaboration and collective learning at an ecosystem level.
Linear. The company takes a linear 'take–make–consume–waste' approach to using resources. The raw material is transformed into a product, which is thrown away after it ends its life cycle.	**Circular**. The company strives to adopt a circular model with the aim of preventing waste, aiming to gradually decouple growth from the consumption of raw materials to preserve finite resources.

(see Figure 14.2).[50] In this context, sustainability transformation – technology-enabled or not – becomes a major driver and important aspect of digital maturity, or in other words, an organization's ability to adapt to the fast-evolving environment of the connected world.

The CFO as a catalyst for sustainability transformation

CFOs have a critical role to play in shaping and driving a sustainable business strategy – ensuring that the approach to sustainability is not limited to reporting and compliance requirements, but also becomes a driver for long-term, multi-stakeholder value creation. Investments in sustainability should not be regarded as an 'add-on' cost by finance leaders, but rather as an opportunity to drive business transformation, performance improvement and growth in a connected world. For CFOs, the following steps are essential:

- **New performance paradigm:** The first and most important task for CFOs is – once again – to change existing mental models and underlying assumptions about value creation. Many senior leaders have been schooled in the quest for shareholder value, when sustainability was seen as an externally imposed obligation and a cost. This is a view that is still prevalent in many organizations. This model is changing – perhaps still too slowly but steadily, and increasingly collectively and explicitly, as the BRT's 'Statement on the Purpose of a Corporation' in 2019 demonstrates in addition to the shifting stakeholder demands, and the growing number of examples. CFOs – in close collaboration with other board members and senior leaders – have to review the company's business strategy, investor narrative and capital allocation strategy to reflect the mounting pressures and opportunities created by sustainability.

- **New performance goal:** To shift the organizational focus from short-term shareholder value maximization to long-term multi-stakeholder value creation, CFOs will have to define new, easily understandable, inspiring but achievable performance goals. The introduction of a new approach to value creation might be helped by different language around performance, including both the external performance narrative and the internal performance dialogue. Finance leaders need to be able to explain how social, ecological and economic value creation can be mutually supportive – and ideally, mutually reinforcing.

- **New performance dialogue:** The new, sustainability-oriented performance strategy has to be fully embedded in all aspects of the performance dialogue. With regard to the strategic performance dialogue, this includes the growth model, accountability model (including the formulation of individual and team objectives and incentives), and of course all aspects of proactive risk management. With regard to the operational performance dialogue, CFOs may apply the alternative planning practices introduced in Chapter 8, including zoom-in/zoom-out and scenario planning, to define a set of initiatives that can accelerate the company's journey towards corporate sustainability. The practices of dynamic budget allocation can be used to encourage innovation, experimentation and continuous learning and improvement. All of these steps will need to be supported by an enhanced performance tracking solution, and the capability to monitor and analyse the interrelation between the sustainability-related investment levers, performance drivers, and performance outcomes (as illustrated in Chapter 5), enabling fact-based decision-making and team learning.

- **New business models and capabilities:** CFOs have to pay attention to the structural changes needed to make a sustainable business transformation work. They will have to pay specific attention to new core process (eg embedding sustainability targets and controls across core end-to-end processes), data (eg inclusion of new, non-financial data sets to feed sustainability reporting and analytics) and capability requirements (eg creating organizational awareness and expertise to identify and drive sustainability-oriented value opportunities). It may not always be possible, or desirable, to build all these capabilities in-house, and there might be opportunities to deliver more for less by collaborating with others in a (digital) business ecosystem.

- **New performance culture and leadership:** CFOs have an important role to play in creating a sustainability-embracing performance culture. When asked 'What do you need to get sustainability going?' John Brock, former CEO of Coca-Cola Enterprises (now Coca-Cola Europacific Partners), told Professor CB Bhattacharya: 'Most of all, leaders have to decide what is important to them, and then communicate and act on it, continuously and consistently.' Brock added, 'I don't ever give a speech – and frankly nor do any of my senior team members – without talking about sustainability. It's just a constant pound, pound, pound.'[52] Leaders can drive change by asking questions aimed at defining concrete priorities for a sustainable future, he said. For instance: What and who is driving growth in the future, and what do our customers, employees, suppliers and investors want from the business moving forward? The leadership team should be encouraged to think through what the changing stakeholder demands mean for the business. According to Brock, it is 'this concretizing process and dialogue that gives leaders the chance to bring stakeholder views into the organization, and it allows senior leaders to become more forward-looking'.[53]

An emerging vision for the future

Amid the growing understanding of what sustainability means, or what it could mean, a vision of a long-term, multi-stakeholder and social impact-oriented economy starts to emerge.

In this vision, leading private and public organizations collaborate in business ecosystems to invent new products and services, at a speed and scale that is much greater than any one organization can achieve on its own. These innovations fuel the next wave of economic growth, while addressing major social and ecological challenges in our connected world. Enhanced technology infrastructure allows these business ecosystems to innovate and learn much faster, remain dynamic, and connect and engage more effectively across consumers, communities and with each other – freeing up untapped resources and assets to drive sustainable, equitable and innovation-driven growth.

New practices and norms for financial and performance management emerge. These track and explain the mutually enriching dependencies of sustainability and business value creation, such as the shared value concept, which has become widely accepted and consistently used. Encouraged by a new level of business innovation and transparency, investors reallocate capital to financing sustainable business. Consumers direct a greater share of their spending to social enterprises, thereby spurring every company to measure and pursue impact, and encouraging entrepreneurs to create innovative solutions, thus driving breakthrough increases in scale and productivity.

This economy understands and uses capitalism differently. It establishes a higher form of capitalism and value creation – one in which capital is not going to be prioritized and allocated based on financial returns only, but on a mechanism to select and fund the most promising and impactful innovation that delivers both sustainable economic growth and social impact.

The role of the CFO, as the 'architect of value', the interface between the company and external investors and regulators, and the driver of business transformation in the connected world, continues to evolve and grow. This role will enable future-oriented, systemically thinking leaders who have the imagination and courage to transform business by demonstrating how it can serve society through sustainable economic growth and value creation.

Thinking differently

Albert Einstein taught us that we cannot solve our problems with the same thinking we used when we created them. We have very much followed his advice throughout the book, seeking to challenge conventional paradigms around a linear industrial model; starting with the art of design thinking, then moving on to systems and network thinking. Multi-stakeholder value creation represents another important paradigm shift for business and finance leaders alike.

Multi-stakeholder value creation provides a new framework to integrate the different perspectives and new ways of thinking that we have discussed throughout this book. It is more than just a reframing; there are practical breakthroughs that are made possible. Design thinking, for example, can help us identify new opportunities for value creation by responding to the needs of multiple stakeholder groups, which in combination can give rise to a virtuous cycle of sustainable growth and long-term value creation. Systems thinking can help us navigate the dynamic complexities of the connected world, such as the need to balance our short- and long-term growth ambitions, as well as the need to take a more systemic, circular approach to addressing sustainability. Network thinking can help us identify opportunities to connect and collaborate in new ways that will accelerate the creation of knowledge – the main ingredient for innovation, resource productivity and qualitative growth.

By going back to our definition of digital maturity (as introduced at the very beginning of this book), we have arrived at another important conclusion. The ability of a business to adapt its strategy, structures, capabilities and culture to support a multi-stakeholder model, including all considerations around sustainability and society, represent an increasingly important aspect of digital maturity – and, as such, should also play an increasingly important aspect of any digital business transformation. Put differently – a company that thrives for digital maturity must transform its organization in a way that enhances its ability to respond effectively to the rapidly changing *economic, ecological and social* needs. In a connected world that is increasingly shaped by digital networks, this requires the effective use of digital technologies – for instance, the creation of new digital business models, such as collaborative platforms and ecosystems, to accelerate the rate of data exchange, (sustainable) product innovation and development, (resource) productivity improvements and cross-organizational learning.

The transformational changes needed to implement a digitally-enabled multi-stakeholder model, as schematically depicted in Figure 14.3, is by no means trivial but appears necessary for the survival and success of our companies – and as such also for our interconnected economic, ecological and social ecosystem. CFOs are not expected or able to carry the burden for

FIGURE 14.3   Multi-stakeholder value creation in a connected world (schematic)

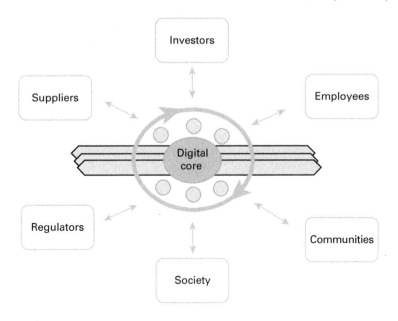

Virtuous cycle of learning, sustainable growth and long-term value creation

Ongoing (digitally-enabled) exchange of data, products and services

Front-line teams 'following multi-stakeholder value'

making these transformational changes happen alone, but – as discussed throughout the book – there are many critically important areas where finance leaders will have to take the lead in driving business transformation, performance and growth in the connected world.

Notes

1 Friedman, M (1970) A Friedman doctrine: The social responsibility of business is to increase its profits, *The New York Times*, 13 September, www.nytimes. com/1970/09/13/archives/a-friedman-doctrine-the-social-responsibility-of-business-is-to.html (archived at https://perma.cc/4BPD-HE9Y)

2 Business Roundtable (nd) Our Commitment, Business Roundtable, opportunity.businessroundtable.org/ourcommitment/ (archived at https://perma.cc/HL6S-6ES2)

3 Business Roundtable (2019) Business Roundtable redefines the purpose of a corporation to promote 'An Economy that Serves all Americans', Business Roundtable, 19 August, www.businessroundtable.org/business-roundtable-redefines-the-purpose-of-a-corporation-to-promote-an-economy-that-serves-all-americans (archived at https://perma.cc/YK7N-8DF6)

4 Denning, S (2017) Making sense of shareholder value: 'The World's Dumbest Idea', *Forbes,* www.forbes.com/sites/stevedenning/2017/07/17/making-sense-of-shareholder-value-the-worlds-dumbest-idea/?sh=5e4547b82a7e (archived at https://perma.cc/8JEF-QBJC)

5 Johnson and Johnson (nd) Our Credo, www.jnj.com/credo/ (archived at https://perma.cc/6YCT-W44H)

6 Winston, A (2019) Is the Business Roundtable statement just empty rhetoric? *Harvard Business Review*, 30 August, hbr.org/2019/08/is-the-business-roundtable-statement-just-empty-rhetoric (archived at https://perma.cc/W5N7-MR9W)

7 Business Roundtable (2019) Business Roundtable redefines the purpose of a corporation to promote 'An Economy that Serves all Americans', Business Roundtable, 19 August, www.businessroundtable.org/business-roundtable-redefines-the-purpose-of-a-corporation-to-promote-an-economy-that-serves-all-americans (archived at https://perma.cc/YK7N-8DF6)

8 Porter, ME and Kramer, M (2011) Creating shared value, *Harvard Business Review,* January–February, hbr.org/2011/01/the-big-idea-creating-shared-value (archived at https://perma.cc/S8K5-SV93)

9 Porter, ME, Hills, G, Pfitzer, M, Sonja Patscheke, S and Hawkins, E (nd) *Measuring Shared Value: How to unlock value by linking social and business results*, Harvard Business School, www.hbs.edu/ris/Publication%20Files/Measuring_Shared_Value_57032487-9e5c-46a1-9bd8-90bd7f1f9cef.pdf (archived at https://perma.cc/D4HH-FRLX)

10 Klein, P (2011) Three great examples of shared value in action, *Forbes,* www.forbes.com/sites/csr/2011/06/14/three-great-examples-of-shared-value-in-action/?sh=5e9b3063595d (archived at https://perma.cc/J894-RX6M)

11 IHG (nd) IHG Green Engage™ system, www.ihg.com/content/gb/en/about/green-engage (archived at https://perma.cc/E2SB-GT5U)

12 Kramer, M (2012) Better ways of doing business: Creating shared value, *The Guardian,* www.theguardian.com/sustainable-business/blog/creating-shared-value-social-progress-profit (archived at https://perma.cc/V73H-S9TT)

13 Porter, ME and Kramer, MR (2011) Creating shared value, *Harvard Business Review,* hbr.org/2011/01/the-big-idea-creating-shared-value (archived at https://perma.cc/S8K5-SV93)

14 Bhattacharya, CB (2019) *Small Actions, Big Difference: Leveraging corporate sustainability to drive business and societal value,* p 121, Routledge, Abingdon

15 United Nations (nd) Report of the World Commission on Environment and Development: Our Common Future, sustainabledevelopment.un.org/content/documents/5987our-common-future.pdf (archived at https://perma.cc/K4HV-CNGK)

16 Deloitte (2019) The Deloitte Global Millennial Survey 2019, www2.deloitte.com/content/dam/Deloitte/global/Documents/About-Deloitte/deloitte-2019-millennial-survey.pdf (archived at https://perma.cc/6VGM-GRC5)

17 Nielsen (2015) Our Story, NielsenIQ, www.nielsen.com/eu/en/press-releases/2015/consumer-goods-brands-that-demonstrate-commitment-to-sustainability-outperform/ (archived at https://perma.cc/QT4G-HUR9)

18 CGS (2019) CGS Survey reveals 'sustainability' is driving demand and customer loyalty, www.cgsinc.com/en/infographics/CGS-Survey-Reveals-Sustainability-Is-Driving-Demand-and-Customer-Loyalty (archived at https://perma.cc/5ESS-X2H3)

19 Peters, A (2019) Most millennials would take a pay cut to work at a environmentally responsible company, *Fast Company,* www.fastcompany.com/90306556/most-millennials-would-take-a-pay-cut-to-work-at-a-sustainable-company (archived at https://perma.cc/X7B2-S8XF)

20 Cone (2016) 2016 Cone Communications Millennial Employee Engagement Study, www.conecomm.com/research-blog/2016-millennial-employee-engagement-study (archived at https://perma.cc/375H-JPTB)

21 Norton Rose Fulbright (2017) A new duty of care for the most significant companies in France, www.nortonrosefulbright.com/en/knowledge/publications/89e03eed/a-new-duty-of-care-for-the-most-significant-companies-in-france (archived at https://perma.cc/6GRZ-UX8C)

22 United Nations (2019) COP25: Global investors urge countries to meet climate action goals, *UN News,* news.un.org/en/story/2019/12/1053081 (archived at https://perma.cc/VQ3Y-DUPU)

23 Fink, L (2021) Larry Fink's 2021 letter to CEOs, www.blackrock.com/corporate/investor-relations/larry-fink-ceo-letter (archived at https://perma.cc/6G6A-MT9D)

24 Deloitte (2021) 2021 Climate Check: Business' views on environmental sustainability, www2.deloitte.com/global/en/pages/risk/articles/2021-climate-check-business-views-on-environmental-sustainability.html?id=gx:2sm:3li:4Exec::6lea:20210324133600::4647947339:5&utm_source=li&utm_campaign=Exec&utm_content=lea&utm_medium=social&linkId=114199146; (archived at https://perma.cc/2P7K-KBDA); Deloitte (nd) Climate check: Business's views on environmental sustainability, www2.deloitte.com/global/en/pages/about-deloitte/articles/covid-19/business-climate-check.html (archived at https://perma.cc/3KP3-GEY2)

25 Deloitte (2021) 2021 Climate Check: Business' views on environmental sustainability, www2.deloitte.com/global/en/pages/risk/articles/2021-climate-check-business-views-on-environmental-sustainability.html?id=gx:2sm:3li:4 Exec::6lea:20210324133600::4647947339:5&utm_source=li& utm_campaign=Exec&utm_content=lea&utm_medium=social&lin kId=114199146; (archived at https://perma.cc/2P7K-KBDA); Deloitte (nd) Climate check: Business's views on environmental sustainability, https://www2.deloitte.com/global/en/pages/about-deloitte/articles/covid-19/business-climate-check.html (archived at https://perma.cc/9WAA-N9G9)

26 Deloitte (2021) 2021 Climate Check: Business' views on environmental sustainability, www2.deloitte.com/global/en/pages/risk/articles/2021-climate-check-business-views-on-environmental-sustainability.html?id=gx:2sm:3li:4 Exec::6lea:20210324133600::4647947339:5&utm_source=li&utm_ campaign=Exec&utm_content=lea&utm_medium=social& linkId=114199146; (archived at https://perma.cc/2P7K-KBDA); Deloitte (nd) Climate check: Business's views on environmental sustainability, https:// www2.deloitte.com/global/en/pages/about-deloitte/articles/covid-19/business-climate-check.html (archived at https://perma.cc/3KP3-GEY2)

27 Kerrigan, S and Kulasooriya, D (2020) The sustainability transformation, Deloitte, www2.deloitte.com/us/en/insights/topics/strategy/sustainable-transformation-in-business.html (archived at https://perma.cc/4EJE-HXLS)

28 Bhattacharya, CB (2019) *Small Actions, Big Difference: Leveraging corporate sustainability to drive business and societal value,* Routledge, Abingdon

29 Bhattacharya, CB (2020) Taking ownership of a sustainable future, *McKinsey Quarterly*, www.mckinsey.com/featured-insights/leadership/taking-ownership-of-a-sustainable-future (archived at https://perma.cc/2F3V-TW8Q)

30 IEA (2020) SDG7: Data and Projections: Access to electricity, www.iea.org/ reports/sdg7-data-and-projections/access-to-electricity (archived at https:// perma.cc/HP65-GX9M)

31 Hurst, G (2016) Enel: Redefining the value chain. Shared value initiative, sharedvalue.org.au/wp-content/uploads/2019/08/Enel-Case-Study_December-2016.pdf (archived at https://perma.cc/SC6V-4GFN)

32 Bhattacharya, CB (2020) Three CEOs offer lessons on their pursuit of sustainability, *McKinsey Quarterly,* 12 May, www.mckinsey.com/featured-insights/leadership/taking-ownership-of-a-sustainable-future (archived at https://perma.cc/2F3V-TW8Q)

33 Enel (2020) Enel's 2030 vision in 2021–2023 Strategic Plan: A decade of opportunities, www.enel.com/media/explore/search-press-releases/ press/2020/11/enels-2030-vision-in-20212023-strategic-plan-a-decade-of-opportunities - (archived at https://perma.cc/HP3A-7XHS)

34 Polman, P (2014) Business, society, and the future of capitalism, *McKinsey Quarterly*, 1 May, www.mckinsey.com/business-functions/sustainability/our-insights/business-society-and-the-future-of-capitalism (archived at https://perma.cc/EM6W-UDK9)

35 Polman, P (2014) Business, society, and the future of capitalism, *McKinsey Quarterly*, 1 May, www.mckinsey.com/business-functions/sustainability/our-insights/business-society-and-the-future-of-capitalism (archived at https://perma.cc/EM6W-UDK9)

36 Unilever Partner Zone (2013) Unilever's sustainable living plan helps cut cost and drive growth, *The Guardian*, 22 April, www.theguardian.com/sustainable-business/unilever-sustainable-living-plan-growth (archived at https://perma.cc/4LG3-R753)

37 *FDE* (2016) The navigator – CFO Graeme Pitkethly on the future of Unilever, *FDE*, 5 July, www.the-financedirector.com/features/featurethe-navigator-ceo-graeme-pitkethly-on-the-future-of-unilever-4941069/index.html (archived at https://perma.cc/254J-LUEF)

38 Unilever (2020) Unilever celebrates 10 years of the sustainable living plan, Unilever, press release, 6 May, www.unilever.com/news/press-releases/2020/unilever-celebrates-10-years-of-the-sustainable-living-plan.html (archived at https://perma.cc/VKK5-ZPKQ)

39 Unilever (2018) Unilever CEO announcement: Paul Polman to retire; Alan Jope appointed as successor, press release, 29 November, https://www.unilever.com/news/press-releases/2018/unilever-ceo-announcement.html (archived at https://perma.cc/B3RY-T6Y5)

40 Porter, ME and Kramer, M (2011) Creating shared value, *Harvard Business Review*, January–February, hbr.org/2011/01/the-big-idea-creating-shared-value (archived at https://perma.cc/S8K5-SV93)

41 World Economic Forum (2020) Measuring stakeholder capitalism: Towards common metrics and consistent reporting of sustainable value creation, www.weforum.org/reports/measuring-stakeholder-capitalism-towards-common-metrics-and-consistent-reporting-of-sustainable-value-creation (archived at https://perma.cc/ZU8Q-8E88)

42 UNEP, UNEP DTU Partnership (2020) Emissions Gap Report 2020, www.unep.org/emissions-gap-report-2020 (archived at https://perma.cc/JN9B-LXB6)

43 Pielke, R (2019) The world is not going to halve carbon emissions by 2030, so now what?, *Forbes*, www.forbes.com/sites/rogerpielke/2019/10/27/the-world-is-not-going-to-reduce-carbon-dioxide-emissions-by-50-by-2030-now-what/?sh=119fdd493794 (archived at https://perma.cc/R65W-5B8B); Ritchie, H and Roser, M (2017) CO2 and Greenhouse Gas Emissions, ourworldindata.org/co2-and-other-greenhouse-gas-emissions (archived at https://perma.cc/MZ87-YEMV)

44 Raworth, K (2017) *Doughnut Economics: Seven ways to think like a 21st-century economist,* p 182, Random House, London

45 *Financial Times* (2016) Emmanuel Faber, Danone CEO: On the alert for blind spots, www.ft.com/content/4986f600-ec33-11e5-bb79-2303682345c8 (archived at https://perma.cc/ZA38-QYJ3)

46 Economics of Mutuality (2018) Kenyan President expresses support for Project Maua, eom.org/content-hub-blog/kenyan-president-uhuru-kenyatta-expresses-support-for-project-maua (archived at https://perma.cc/H6HT-UZ77)

47 Nestlé (2019) Nestlé inaugurates packaging research institute, first-of-its-kind in the food industry, www.nestle.com/media/pressreleases/allpressreleases/nestle-inaugurates-packaging-research-institute (archived at https://perma.cc/4XY8-DECG)

48 Sustainable Food Policy Alliance (nd) Environmental, foodpolicyalliance.org/issue/environment/ (archived at https://perma.cc/A2T4-U4Y4)

49 UN Global Pulse (nd) Big Data and Artificial Intelligence, www.unglobalpulse.org/ (archived at https://perma.cc/97D6-K5D4)

50 Kerrigan, S and Kulasooriya, D (2020) The sustainability transformation: Look ahead, look inside, and look around, *Deloitte Review*, Issue 27, www2.deloitte.com/content/dam/insights/us/articles/apac63528_the-sustainability-transformation/DI_DR27-Sustainability-transformation.pdf (archived at https://perma.cc/9W7S-LVN3)

51 Kerrigan, S and Kulasooriya, D (2020) The sustainability transformation: Look ahead, look inside, and look around, *Deloitte Review*, Issue 27, www2.deloitte.com/content/dam/insights/us/articles/apac63528_the-sustainability-transformation/DI_DR27-Sustainability-transformation.pdf (archived at https://perma.cc/9W7S-LVN3)

52 Bhattacharya, CB (2020) Taking ownership of a sustainable future, *McKinsey Quarterly*, www.mckinsey.com/featured-insights/leadership/taking-ownership-of-a-sustainable-future (archived at https://perma.cc/2F3V-TW8Q)

53 Bhattacharya, CB (2020) Taking ownership of a sustainable future, *McKinsey Quarterly*, www.mckinsey.com/featured-insights/leadership/taking-ownership-of-a-sustainable-future (archived at https://perma.cc/2F3V-TW8Q)

15

The economist perspective

Summary

Key insight

The economist perspective explored in Part Three encourages finance leaders to look beyond the boundaries of an organization, and to perceive themselves and their companies as an interconnected element of a fast-evolving, highly networked, complex, socioeconomic system that we describe in this book as 'the connected world'.

The art of network thinking helps finance leaders recognize several new aspects that are very relevant to driving business transformation, performance and growth in a connected world. For one, value creation is driven by the network that an organization belongs to, rather than the organization itself. The art of management is about positioning the company to extract that value by participating in the networked economy. Second, network effects are becoming increasingly powerful and have given rise to new digital business models, especially digital business platforms and ecosystems, which are reshaping our economy across different sectors, and which therefore require new management approaches, capabilities and governance models. Third, the digital transformation of established businesses needs to accelerate – new technologies enable the creation of platforms and modular operating models with information and value flows distributed across customers, suppliers, partners and even competitors.

Leading organizations in the connected world require well-developed human capabilities – imagination, empathy, creativity, rationality, morality and – more than anything else – a deep sense of compassion and responsibility for the world we live in.

The significant growth of our physical economy, and the related use of natural resources, as well as the rise of emissions and pollution, have grown beyond sustainable limits, leaving us with three ways to respond.[1] One, we ignore all the signals and continue driving short-term economic growth, hoping that technological innovation will catch up to solve the problem for us – a scenario that most likely will make things worse.[2] Two, we impose new rules and boundaries – a necessary step but one that is not going to eliminate the cause of the problem. Three, we respond by addressing the underlying root cause – the paradigms which define our economic goals, incentives and information flows and that drive systemic behaviours. Paradigms are the source of any systems – our deepest, underlying and unstated assumptions and beliefs about how the world works.

From Johannes Kepler to Albert Einstein, and from the Agricultural to the Industrial Revolution, whenever a paradigm shift occurs, systems can transforms radically and rapidly. Paradigms are harder to change than anything else about a system, but once it happens there is little that can hold up transformational change.[3] All it takes is that enough people start to think and see the world from a new perspective. To help people see the world differently, most of all, we need two things: one, we need to adopt and teach new ways of thinking and seeing; and two, we need to support and promote a generation of leaders who are willing and able to create and execute a renewed vision of a transformed, sustainable economic, ecological and social system.

Key findings

- **The economic system is changing dramatically:** What we are experiencing in the first decades of the 21st century, commonly referred to as the 'Digital Revolution', marks a fundamental economic shift that is having a substantial impact on our society. The Digital Revolution is driven by the emergence of new digital business models that are transforming our economy at the most fundamental level. In a few short years, the ranking of most valuable companies by market capitalization has become dominated by two digital business models: digital business platforms and digital business ecosystems.

- **Digital business models are reshaping the economy:** Companies are creating and adopting digitally-enabled, network-based business models to leverage network effects that enable them to accelerate growth and value creation in a connected economy. These models, including digital business platforms and digital business ecosystems, are no longer the sole domain of digital natives – established companies can adopt these new business model through self-creation, acquisition or collaboration. Spanning traditionally disconnected industries, and across borders, these digital business models are fast reshaping our businesses, economy and potentially our society.

- **The management of digital business models is less developed:** While traditional businesses operate like a value-creation pipeline – a linear arrangement of value contributions, with producers at one end and consumers at the other – digital businesses models bring together different types of producers and consumers to exchange, consume and create value through platforms and ecosystems. Despite the enthusiasm surrounding these new digital business models, the implications for business and financial management are often less developed and understood, leaving executives unclear as to what it takes to create, join or manage an ecosystem successfully and responsibly.

- **Digital business ecosystems create new challenges but also opportunities for society:** Digital business ecosystems are here to stay, and are likely to evolve and expand further, causing significant disruption but also new opportunities for nearly every business, as well as our economy and society as a whole. It is essential for every leader to understand how digital ecosystems work, and to lean into the challenge to ensure the powerful dynamics created by these business models are used with care and responsibility – not just to gain competitive advantage, but to strengthen economic and societal ecosystem health. The power of digital business can be intimidating, but may also offer new opportunities to address major economic and societal issues at scale and with impact.

- **Long-term multi-stakeholder value creation as a common purpose:** Global challenges such as climate change and income inequality have shaken public confidence in business. Even though many executives have rearticulated their individual corporate purpose statements, there is a growing concern that, without a more collective effort, we are a long way from being able to address the issues threatening our planet. A commitment to a *common* purpose centred on long-term multi-stakeholder value creation encourages corporations to balance and integrate the interests of shareholders with those of customers, employees and society. The adoption of new value concepts, such as the concept of Creating Shared Value (CSV), as well as adopting commonly agreed (sustainability-oriented) performance metrics and reporting standards represent important steps towards a collective effort. That said, companies, and CFOs in particular, can go further by exploring sustainability as a source of value creation – and thus as a key aspect of business strategy, (digital) business transformation and ultimately higher digital maturity.

Guiding questions for practical application and further exploration

- **Digital business platforms:**
  - o Where are new digital business platforms and digital business ecosystems emerging in your sector, and how are they affecting the market in which you operate?
  - o How are these digital business models performing in the market, especially in relation to serving new customer needs?
  - o How do they compare with traditional business models?
- **Digital business ecosystems:**
  - o Which part of your business would lend itself to leveraging the connected economy, network effects or related economies of learning by creating or collaborating with a digital business platform or ecosystem?
  - o What would be the key drivers of value creation, and how could a new business of this kind be managed effectively?
  - o What would be the implications from a process, data and technology perspective – and which investments in core capabilities and infrastructure would be required to support the functioning of this model?
  - o How does this align with your key takeaways from Parts One and Two of this book?
  - o Which strategic and operational risks may emerge from adopting (or not adopting) new digital business models?

- **Shared value creation and sustainability:**
  - What is the dominating definition of 'value' in your company?
  - To what extent does this definition reflect the expectations of long-term multi-stakeholder value creation?
  - What is the impact of net-zero and sustainability on your value-creation strategy?
  - Where do you see the major trade-offs and/or new business opportunities to link economic and societal value creation?
  - What opportunities and challenges do you see in leveraging the power of business ecosystems to make a greater economic and societal impact?
  - Are there opportunities to use sustainability as a driver for business transformation?

HOW TO GET STARTED

For digital business platforms and ecosystems:

- Develop a strategic network analysis that evaluates the growth and value-creation potential by analysing network connections, position and development scenarios (with regard to network innovation, growth, supply chain optimization, and so on).

For multi-stakeholder value creation and transformation:

- Assess your current business strategy against a multi-stakeholder model.
- Identify and evaluate strategic business opportunities and risks (for example, by analysing the changing needs, expectations and preferences of each stakeholder group), and develop a response strategy to unlock and protect long-term multi-stakeholder business value (Figure 15.1).

Recommended sources for further exploration

- *Deloitte Insights* (2020) Digital platform as a growth lever.[4]
- Deloitte University Press (2015) *Business ecosystems come of age.*[5]
- *Deloitte Insights* (2020) The sustainability transformation.[6]

FIGURE 15.1   Strategic sustainability assessment framework (schematic)

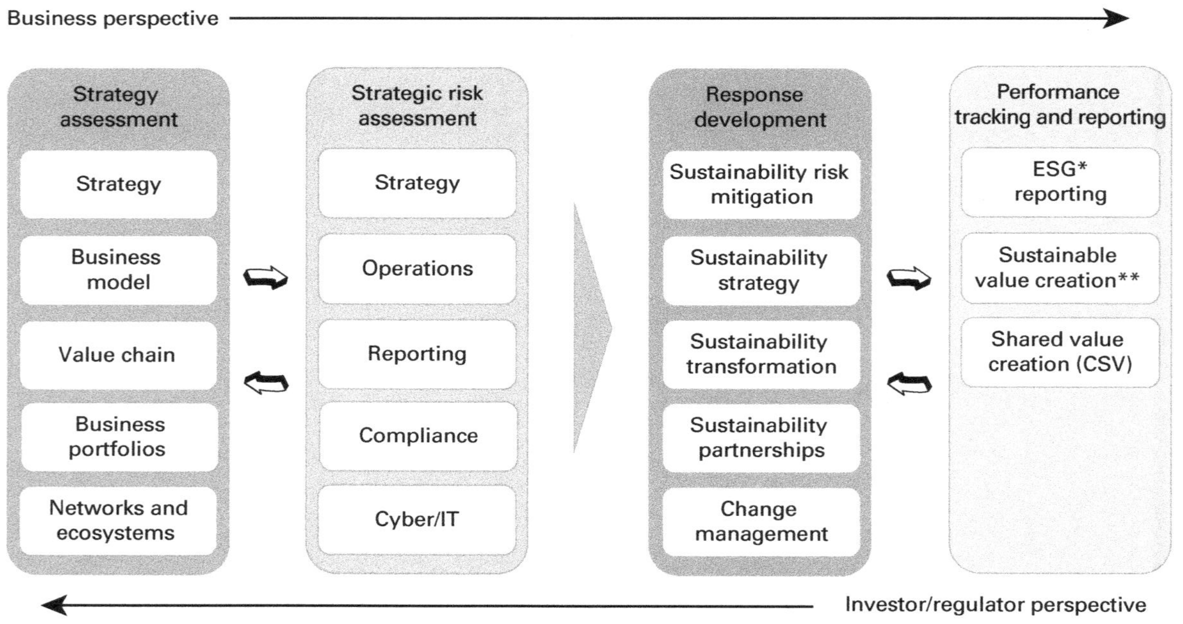

Business perspective

Strategy assessment
- Strategy
- Business model
- Value chain
- Business portfolios
- Networks and ecosystems

Strategic risk assessment
- Strategy
- Operations
- Reporting
- Compliance
- Cyber/IT

Response development
- Sustainability risk mitigation
- Sustainability strategy
- Sustainability transformation
- Sustainability partnerships
- Change management

Performance tracking and reporting
- ESG* reporting
- Sustainable value creation**
- Shared value creation (CSV)

Investor/regulator perspective

* Environmental, social and governance
** eg proposed common metrics and consistent reporting of sustainable value creation (World economic forum, 2020)

Notes

1 Meadows, D, Randers, J and Meadows, D (nd) *Limits to Growth: The 30-year update*, pp 234–36, Chelsea Green Publishing, London

2 Deloitte (nd) Climate scenarios and consumer business: Four futures for a changing sector, www2.deloitte.com/uk/en/pages/consumer-business/articles/climate-scenarios.html (archived at https://perma.cc/N75H-T7J6)

3 Meadows, D (1999) Leverage Points: Places to intervene in a system, Sustainability Institute, donellameadows.org/wp-content/userfiles/Leverage_Points.pdf (archived at https://perma.cc/Q3QZ-YVLG)

4 Sharma, D, Schroeck, M, Kwan, A and Seshaadri, V (2020) Digital platform as a growth lever, *Deloitte Insights*, www2.deloitte.com/content/dam/insights/us/articles/6735_TMT-Digital-transformation-series-No--11--Digital-platform-as-growth-lever/DI_TMT-Digital-transformation-series-No-11-Digital%20platform-as-growth-lever.pdf (archived at https://perma.cc/HMP3-AQ7E)

5 Bruun-Jensen, J and Hagel, J (nd) *Business ecosystems come of age*, Deloitte University Press, www2.deloitte.com/content/dam/Deloitte/co/Documents/strategy/Business%20Transformation.pdf (archived at https://perma.cc/Y7CM-MNMB)

6 Kerrigan, S and Kulasooriya, D (2020) The sustainability transformation, Deloitte, www2.deloitte.com/us/en/insights/topics/strategy/sustainable-transformation-in-business.html (archived at https://perma.cc/4NUP-HGF9)

BIBLIOGRAPHY

Anthony, SD, Viguerie, SP, Schwartz, EI and van Landeghem, J (2018) 2018 Corporate longevity forecast: Creative destruction is accelerating, *Innosight*, February, www.innosight.com/wp-content/uploads/2017/11/Innosight-Corporate-Longevity-2018.pdf (archived at https://perma.cc/4R8M-KV2S)

Arthur, WB (1996) Increasing returns and the new world of business, *Harvard Business Review*, July–August, hbr.org/1996/07/increasing-returns-and-the-new-world-of-business (archived at https://perma.cc/RC62-S3CB)

Atsmon, Y (2016) How nimble resource allocation can double your company's value, McKinsey & Company, 30 August, www.mckinsey.com/business-functions/strategy-and-corporate-finance/our-insights/how-nimble-resource-allocation-can-double-your-companys-value (archived at https://perma.cc/9QUP-JECF)

Bean, R and Davenport, TH (2019) Companies are failing in their efforts to become data-driven, *Harvard Business Review*, 5 February, hbr.org/2019/02/companies-are-failing-in-their-efforts-to-become-data-driven (archived at https://perma.cc/JS2A-8C8T)

Beinhocker, E (2007) *The Origin of Wealth: Evolution, complexity and the radical remaking of economics,* Random House Business, London

Bhattacharya, CB (2020) Three CEOs offer lessons on their pursuit of sustainability, *McKinsey Quarterly*, 12 May, www.mckinsey.com/featured-insights/leadership/taking-ownership-of-a-sustainable-future (archived at https://perma.cc/UW8U-AKHK)

Bughin, J, Catlin, T and Dietz, M (2019) The right digital-platform strategy, *McKinsey Digital*, 7 May, www.mckinsey.com/business-functions/mckinsey-digital/our-insights/the-right-digital-platform-strategy (archived at https://perma.cc/EXT7-NESQ)

Business Roundtable (2019) Business Roundtable redefines the purpose of a corporation to promote 'An Economy that Serves all Americans', Business Roundtable, 19 August, www.businessroundtable.org/business-roundtable-redefines-the-purpose-of-a-corporation-to-promote-an-economy-that-serves-all-americans (archived at https://perma.cc/AE4J-T7LC)

Business Roundtable (nd) Our Commitment, Business Roundtable, opportunity.businessroundtable.org/ourcommitment/ (archived at https://perma.cc/W2RT-WGUN)

CFO Journal (2017) For CFOs, disruption gives rise to new leadership challenges, *The Wall Street Journal,* 25 October, deloitte.wsj.com/cfo/2017/10/25/for-cfos-disruption-gives-rise-to-new-leadership-challenges/ (archived at https://perma.cc/SJ5L-YGLB)

CIO Journal (2019) Forecasting in a digital world, *The Wall Street Journal*, 8 August, deloitte.wsj.com/cio/2019/08/08/forecasting-in-a-digital-world/ (archived at https://perma.cc/3SW6-H2KX)

Clancy, T (2018) Systems thinking: Three system archetypes every manager should know, *IEEE Engineering Management Review,* **46** (2), pp 32–41, 1 second quarter, June 2018, doi:10.1109/EMR.2018.2844377

Collins, J and Porras, J (2005) *Built to Last: Successful habits of visionary companies,* Random House Business, London

Davenport, TH (2009) Make better decisions, *Harvard Business Review*, November, hbr.org/2009/11/make-better-decisions-2 (archived at https://perma.cc/ZWN6-H7UU)

Davenport, TH (2010) *Analytics at Work: Smarter decisions, better results,* Harvard Business Review Press, Boston, MA

Davenport, TH and Ronaki, R (2018) Artificial intelligence for the real world, *Harvard Business Review*, January–February, hbr.org/2018/01/artificial-intelligence-for-the-real-world/ (archived at https://perma.cc/L8J9-GS4T)

Deloitte (2016) Business meets design: Creative changes starts here, Deloitte, June, www2.deloitte.com/content/dam/Deloitte/de/Documents/technology/Whitepaper-business-meets-design-english-long-version.PDF (archived at https://perma.cc/G7KB-S2M6)

Deloitte (2018) Robotic roll-outs reap results: 95% of organisations using RPA say the technology has improved productivity, Deloitte, 10 October, www2.deloitte.com/uk/en/pages/press-releases/articles/robotic-roll-outs-reap-results.html (archived at https://perma.cc/N3M5-K33S)

Deloitte (2018) Special Edition: European CFO Survey, Spring, www2.deloitte.com/content/dam/Deloitte/pt/Documents/finance/180615_CFO-Survey-Report_Digital-Chapter_Interactive.pdf (archived at https://perma.cc/B2G9-E73G)

Deloitte (2019) Global Human Capital Trends 2019, Deloitte, www2.deloitte.com/content/dam/Deloitte/uk/Documents/human-capital/deloitte-uk-human-capital-trends-2019-updated-latest.pdf (archived at https://perma.cc/RU8U-RSEX)

Deloitte (2020) 2020 Global Human Capital Trends Report: The social enterprise at work, Deloitte, www2.deloitte.com/cn/en/pages/human-capital/articles/global-human-capital-trends-2020.html (archived at https://perma.cc/4344-KPTT)

Dickinson, G and Kambil, A (2014) What's keeping CFOs up in 2014?, *CFO Insights*, June, www2.deloitte.com/us/en/pages/finance/articles/cfo-insights-concerns-company-performance-pressure.html (archived at https://perma.cc/EGM3-KCMQ)

Drucker, P (1992) Planning for Uncertainty, *The Wall Street Journal*, July

Drucker, P (2001) *The Management Challenge for the 21st Century*, HarperBusiness, London

Drucker, P (2006) *The Practice of Management*, Reissue edn, HarperBusiness, London

Drucker, P (2007) *Management Challenges for the 21st Century*, Routledge, Abingdon

Dweck, CS (2006) *Mindset: The new psychology of success*, Random House, New York, NY

Ehrenhalt, S (2016) Crunch time: Finance in a digital world, Deloitte, www2.deloitte.com/content/dam/Deloitte/uk/Documents/strategy/deloitte-uk-so-crunch-time.pdf (archived at https://perma.cc/B6M6-5G5J)

Elliot, J (2012) *Leading Apple with Steve Jobs*, John Wiley, Chichester

Epstein, R, Witzemann, T and Thomas, M (2020) Shifting gears: How to drive your digital businesses forward with an appropriate steering approach, Deloitte, March, www2.deloitte.com/content/dam/Deloitte/de/Documents/finance-transformation/CFO-Insight-Steering-Digital-Businesses.pdf (archived at https://perma.cc/Y963-6H9W)

Experience Ford (nd) www.ford.co.uk/experience-ford/history-and-heritage#assemblyline (archived at https://perma.cc/3YBJ-N89D)

FDE (2016) The navigator: CFO Graeme Pitkethly on the future of Unilever, *FDE*, 5 July, www.the-financedirector.com/features/featurethe-navigator-ceo-graeme-pitkethly-on-the-future-of-unilever-4941069/index.html (archived at https://perma.cc/5QQU-8RLB)

Friedman, F (2014) Why CFOs should 'own' analytics, *CFO*, 29 October, ww2.cfo.com/analytics/2014/10/cfos-analytics/ (archived at https://perma.cc/9XL4-3AJW)

Friedman, M (1970) A Friedman doctrine: The social responsibility of business is to increase its profits, *The New York Times*, 13 September, www.nytimes.com/1970/09/13/archives/a-friedman-doctrine-the-social-responsibility-of-business-is-to.html (archived at https://perma.cc/BS3T-HABC)

Gilchrist, K (2019) Alibaba Group thwarts 300 million hack attempts per day, CNBC, 16 October, www.cnbc.com/2019/10/16/jack-ma-alibaba-group-thwarts-300-million-hack-attempts-per-day.html (archived at https://perma.cc/8PS7-NP3R)

Gurumurthy, R and Schatsky, D (2019) Pivoting to digital maturity: Seven capabilities central to digital transformation, *Deloitte Insights*, 13 March, www2.deloitte.com/us/en/insights/focus/digital-maturity/digital-maturity-pivot-model.html (archived at https://perma.cc/DC54-GZPF)

Hagel, J III (2009) Pursuing passion, Edge Perspectives with John Hagel, 14 November, edgeperspectives.typepad.com/edge_perspectives/2009/11/pursuing-passion.html (archived at https://perma.cc/WHW4-3ZYP)

Hagel, J III and Wooll, M (2019) What is work? *Deloitte Insights*, 28 January, www2.deloitte.com/us/en/insights/focus/technology-and-the-future-of-work/what-is-work.html (archived at https://perma.cc/9JYU-FTSA)

Hagel, J III, Brown, JS and Kulasooriya, D (2012) Performance ecosystems: A decision framework to take performance to the next level, *Deloitte Insights*, 2 January, www2.deloitte.com/us/en/insights/topics/operations/performance-ecosystems-which-model-is-right-for-you.html (archived at https://perma.cc/MAV4-6J3L)

Hagel, J III, Brown, JS, de Maar, A and Wooll, M (2016) Approaching disruption: Charting a course for new growth and performance at the edge and beyond, *Deloitte Insights*, 5 October, www2.deloitte.com/us/en/insights/focus/disruptive-strategy-patterns-case-studies/approaching-disruption-for-growth-performance.html (archived at https://perma.cc/W67M-234R)

Hagel, J III, Brown, JS, de Maar, A and Wooll, M (2018) Moving from best to better to better, *Deloitte Insights*, 31 January, www2.deloitte.com/insights/us/en/topics/talent/business-performance-improvement/process-redesign.html (archived at https://perma.cc/DUZ5-PQ7Q)

Hagel, J III, Brown, JS, Ranjan, A and Byler, D (2014) Passion at work: Cultivating worker passion as a cornerstone of talent development, *Deloitte Insights*, 7 October, www2.deloitte.com/us/en/insights/topics/talent/worker-passion-employee-behavior.html (archived at https://perma.cc/K7UR-VAYP)

Hagel, J III, Wooll, M and Brown, JS (2019) Skills change, but capabilities endure: Why fostering human capabilities first might be more important than reskilling in the future of work, *Deloitte Insights*, 30 August, www2.deloitte.com/us/en/insights/focus/technology-and-the-future-of-work/future-of-work-human-capabilities.html (archived at https://perma.cc/BUR3-5WWC)

Harvard Business Review Analytic Services (2011) Risk Management at a time of global uncertainty, *Harvard Business Review*, hbr.org/resources/pdfs/tools/17036_HBR_Zurich_Report_final_Dec2011.pdf (archived at https://perma.cc/LTV3-R3SZ)

He, L (2018) Alibaba joins Tencent in the exclusive US$ 500 billion market value club, *South China Morning Post*, 25 January, www.scmp.com/business/companies/article/2130497/alibaba-joins-tencent-exclusive-us500-billion-market-value-club (archived at https://perma.cc/P3S8-NUMW)

Holley, C (nd) What CEOs want – and need – from their CFOs, Deloitte, www2.deloitte.com/us/en/pages/finance/articles/what-ceos-want-and-need-from-their-cfos.html (archived at https://perma.cc/53FM-J7BU)

Homburg C, Stephan, J and Haupt, M (2005) Risikomanagement unter Nutzung der 'Balanced Scorecard', *Der Betrieb*, 58 (20), pp 1069–075

Horton, R (2014–16) Finance Business Partnering: less than the sum of its parts, Deloitte, www2.deloitte.com/content/dam/Deloitte/uk/Documents/finance/deloitte-uk-finance-less-than-the-sum-of-the-parts.pdf (archived at https://perma.cc/HP3G-23QK)

Horton, R, Searles, P and Stone, K (2014) Integrated Performance Management: Plan. Budget. Forecast, Deloitte, www2.deloitte.com/content/dam/Deloitte/uk/Documents/finance/deloitte-uk-integrated-performance-management-plan-budget-forecast.pdf (archived at https://perma.cc/AXN4-TUQG)

Iansiti, M and Lakhani, KR (2017) Managing our hub economy, *Harvard Business Review*, September–October, hbr.org/2017/09/managing-our-hub-economy (archived at https://perma.cc/GY28-NH2D)

Iansiti, M and Lakhani, KR (2020) Competing in the age of AI, *Harvard Business Review*, January–February, hbr.org/2020/01/competing-in-the-age-of-ai (archived at https://perma.cc/398J-X4TU)

Iansiti, M and Levien, R (2004) Strategy as ecology, *Harvard Business Review*, March, hbr.org/2004/03/strategy-as-ecology (archived at https://perma.cc/3YKR-RD45)

Inside Big Data (2017) The exponential growth of data, *Inside Big Data*, 16 February, insidebigdata.com/2017/02/16/the-exponential-growth-of-data/ (archived at https://perma.cc/6AZW-63Q3)

Jacobides, MG, Sundararajan, A and Van Alstyne, M (2019) Platforms and ecosystems: Enabling the digital economy, World Economic Forum, February, www.weforum.org/whitepapers/platforms-and-ecosystems-enabling-the-digital-economy (archived at https://perma.cc/7QLL-GDTT)

Kahneman, D (2012) *Thinking Fast and Slow,* Penguin, London

Kambil, A (nd) The value shift: Why CFOs should lead the charge in the digital age, Deloitte, www2.deloitte.com/us/en/pages/finance/articles/cfo-insights-digital-age-business-model-innovation-value.html (archived at https://perma.cc/RV2D-J4EA)

Kane, GC, Palmer, D, Phillips, AN, Kiron, D and Buckley, N (2017) Achieving digital maturity: Adapting your company to a changing world, *MIT Sloan Management Review*, 13 July, sloanreview.mit.edu/projects/achieving-digital-maturity/ (archived at https://perma.cc/9CVB-7RWZ)

Kane, GC, Palmer, D, Phillips, AN, Kiron, D and Buckley, N (2018) Coming of age digitally: Learning, leadership, and legacy, *MIT Sloan Management Review*, sloanreview.mit.edu/projects/coming-of-age-digitally/ (archived at https://perma.cc/9PK9-QHAV)

Kane, GC, Palmer, D, Phillips, AN, Kiron, D and Buckley, N (2019) Accelerating digital innovation inside and out, *Deloitte Insights,* 4 June, www2.deloitte.com/uk/en/insights/focus/digital-maturity/digital-innovation-ecosystems-organizational-agility.html (archived at https://perma.cc/P55V-52RH)

Kane, GC, Palmer, D, Phillips, AN, Kiron, D and Buckley, N (2019) Innovation inside and out: Agile teams, ecosystems, and ethics, *MIT Sloan Management Review*, 4 June, sloanreview.mit.edu/projects/accelerating-digital-innovation-inside-and-out/ (archived at https://perma.cc/SG9R-URT9)

Kiron, D and Shrage, M (2019) Strategy for and with AI, *MIT Sloan Management Review*, 11 June, sloanreview.mit.edu/article/strategy-for-and-with-ai/ (archived at https://perma.cc/G9HU-SHY2)

Kurzweil, R (2001) The law of accelerating returns, Kurzweil Accelerating Intelligence, 7 March, www.kurzweilai.net/the-law-of-accelerating-returns (archived at https://perma.cc/A4NN-LPQY)

Lafley, AG and Martin, RL (2013) *Playing to Win*, Harvard Business Review Press, Boston, MA

Levy, F (2005) *The New Division of Labor: How computers are creating the next job market*, new edn, Princeton University Press, NJ

Loughrey, C (2017) Minority Report: 6 predictions that came true, 15 years on, *The Independent*, 25 June, www.independent.co.uk/arts-entertainment/films/features/minority-report-15th-anniversary-predictive-policing-gesture-based-computing-facial-and-optical-a7807666.html (archived at https://perma.cc/UY2Y-3W45)

Manyika, J (2011) Google's CFO on growth, capital structure, and leadership, McKinsey & Company, 1 August, www.mckinsey.com/business-functions/strategy-and-corporate-finance/our-insights/googles-cfo-on-growth-capital-structure-and-leadership (archived at https://perma.cc/9GTA-JE3N)

Martin, R (2009) *The Design of Business: Why design thinking is the next competitive advantage*, Harvard Business Review Press, Boston, MA

Martin, RL (2013) Rethinking the decision factory, *Harvard Business Review*, October, hbr.org/2013/10/rethinking-the-decision-factory (archived at https://perma.cc/3ST5-9CYB)

Martin, TJ (1995) Jack Welch lets fly on budgets, bonuses, and buddy boards, *Fortune* (archive), 29 May, money.cnn.com/magazines/fortune/fortune_archive/1995/05/29/203152/index.htm (archived at https://perma.cc/DM7P-3YN9)

McAfee, A and Brynjolfsson, E (2018) *Machine, Platform, Crowd: Harnessing our digital future*, WW Norton & Company, New York, NY

Meadows, DH (2009) *Thinking in Systems: A primer*, Earthscan Ltd, Abingdon

Meejia, J (2018) This simple method is used by Bill Gates, Larry Page and even Bono to tackle their biggest goals, CNBC, 14 August, www.cnbc.com/2018/08/14/this-goal-setting-method-is-used-by-bill-gates-larry-page-and-bono.html (archived at https://perma.cc/LA78-67FF)

MIT IDE (2019) Q&A: How AI can lead corporate strategy, *Medium*, 24 June, medium.com/mit-initiative-on-the-digital-economy/q-a-how-ai-can-lead-corporate-strategy-87c7a7561318 (archived at https://perma.cc/XKZ5-NYGK)

Munger, M (nd) Division of Labor, The Library of Economics and Liberty, www.econlib.org/library/Enc/DivisionofLabor.html (archived at https://perma.cc/V7TV-MHSX)

Nadella, S, Shaw, G and Nichols, JT (2019) *Hit Refresh: The quest to rediscover Microsoft's soul and imagine a better future for everyone*, HarperBusiness, London

Nayak, M (2014) Timeline: Microsoft's journey: four decades, three CEOs, Reuters, 4 February, uk.reuters.com/article/us-microsoft-succession-timeline/timeline-microsofts-journey-four-decades-three-ceos-idUSBREA131R720140204 (archived at https://perma.cc/XJB8-2CV2)

NPR (2012) 'Signal' and 'Noise': Prediction as art and science, *NPR*, 10 October, n.pr/UPXRS4 (archived at https://perma.cc/B5FZ-L4DQ)

Parker, GG, Van Alstyne, MW and Choudary, SG (2016) *The Platform Revolution*, WW Norton & Company, London

Pink, DH (2005) *A Whole New Mind: Why right-brainers will rule the future*, Riverhead Books, New York, NY

Polman, P (2014) Business, society, and the future of capitalism, *McKinsey Quarterly*, 1 May, www.mckinsey.com/business-functions/sustainability/our-insights/business-society-and-the-future-of-capitalism (archived at https://perma.cc/BP5B-M2CQ)

Porter, ME and Kramer, M (2011) Creating shared value, *Harvard Business Review*, January–February, hbr.org/2011/01/the-big-idea-creating-shared-value (archived at https://perma.cc/2DFW-A35M)

Pudin, U, Reeves, M and Schüssler, M (2019) Do you need a business ecosystem?, *BCG*, 27 September, www.bcg.com/en-gb/publications/2019/do-you-need-business-ecosystem.aspx (archived at https://perma.cc/SX5Z-LAY6)

Puiu, T (2020) Your smartphone is millions of times more powerful than the Apollo 11 guidance computers, *ZME Science*, 11 February, www.zmescience.com/science/news-science/smartphone-power-compared-to-apollo-432/ (archived at https://perma.cc/FDM9-MAFM)

Rae, J (2015) 2014 Design Value Index results and commentary: Good design drives shareholder value, Design Management Institute, May, www.dmi.org/page/DesignDrivesValue (archived at https://perma.cc/26B2-NHZE)

Redman, TC (2016) Bad data costs the U.S. $3 trillion per year, *Harvard Business Review*, 22 September, hbr.org/2016/09/bad-data-costs-the-u-s-3-trillion-per-year (archived at https://perma.cc/KH29-MQUG)

Reeves, M (2013) Algorithms can make your organization self-tuning, *Harvard Business Review*, 13 May, hbr.org/2015/05/algorithms-can-make-your-organization-self-tuning (archived at https://perma.cc/TM4T-8BDV)

Reeves, M, Lotan, H, Legrand, J and Jacobides, MG (2019) How business ecosystems rise (and often fall), *MIT Sloan Management Review*, 30 July, sloanreview.mit.edu/article/how-business-ecosystems-rise-and-often-fall/ (archived at https://perma.cc/QBL7-H6XD)

Sarrazin, H and Sikes, J (2013) Competing in a digital world: Four lessons from the software industry, *McKinsey Digital*, 1 February, www.mckinsey.com/business-functions/mckinsey-digital/our-insights/competing-in-a-digital-world-four-lessons-from-the-software-industry (archived at https://perma.cc/2GQX-7XG4)

Schmiedgen, J, Rhinow, H, Köppen, E and Meinel, C (2015) Parts without a whole? The current state of design thinking practice in organizations, Study Report No. 97, Hasso-Plattner-Institut für Softwaresystemtechnik an der Universität Potsdam, thisisdesignthinking.net/why-this-site/the-study/ (archived at https://perma.cc/K2CD-2CJJ)

Schrage, M (2019) Don't let metric critics undermine your business, *MIT Sloan Management Review*, 23 October, sloanreview.mit.edu/article/dont-let-metric-critics-undermine-your-business/ (archived at https://perma.cc/N7FT-RG6M)

Schwartz, T (2018) Create a growth culture, not a performance-obsessed one, *Harvard Business Review*, 7 March, hbr.org/2018/03/create-a-growth-culture-not-a-performance-obsessed-one?referral=03759&cm_vc=rr_item_page.bottom (archived at https://perma.cc/83VR-69G8)

Senge, PM (1990) *The Fifth Discipline: The art and practice of the learning organization*, Doubleday/Currency, New York, NY

Shaywitz, D (2019) Novartis CEO who wanted to bring tech into pharma now explains why it's so hard, *Forbes*, 16 January, www.forbes.com/sites/davidshaywitz/2019/01/16/novartis-ceo-who-wanted-to-bring-tech-into-pharma-now-explains-why-its-so-hard/amp/ (archived at https://perma.cc/76U7-ST7C)

Sheppard, B, London, S and Yeon, H (2018) Tapping into the business value of design, *McKinsey Quarterly*, 21 December (podcast), www.mckinsey.com/business-functions/mckinsey-design/our-insights/tapping-into-the-business-value-of-design # (archived at https://perma.cc/YD56-22KR)

Smith, T, Stiller, B, Guszcza, J and Davenport, T (2019) Analytics and AI-driven enterprises thrive in the Age of With, *Deloitte Insights*, www2.deloitte.com/content/dam/Deloitte/ec/Documents/technology-media-telecommunications/DI_Becoming-an-Insight-Driven-organization%20(2).pdf (archived at https://perma.cc/3UPV-G98M)

Sniderman, B and Brown, JS (2019) Strategic planning: Why you should zoom out and zoom in, Deloitte, May, www2.deloitte.com/us/en/pages/finance/articles/strategic-insights-zoom-out-zoom-in.html (archived at https://perma.cc/JV83-GF6J)

Straub, R (2019) What management needs to become in an era of ecosystems, *Harvard Business Review*, 5 June, hbr.org/2019/06/what-management-needs-to-become-in-an-era-of-ecosystems (archived at https://perma.cc/XZW5-VYWS)

Thier, J (2020) 2020 trends: Rise of the CFO-COO, *CFO Dive*, 26 January, www.cfodive.com/news/2020-trend-cfo-coo/571060/ (archived at https://perma.cc/D2EP-25QZ)

Tveit, M and Olli, L (2015) How exceptional companies create a high-performance culture, EgonZehnder, 10 May, www.egonzehnder.com/what-we-do/ceo-search-succession/insights/how-exceptional-companies-create-a-high-performance-culture (archived at https://perma.cc/785Y-7Y2V)

Unilever (2020) Unilever celebrates 10 years of the sustainable living plan, Unilever, 6 May, www.unilever.com/news/press-releases/2020/unilever-celebrates-10-years-of-the-sustainable-living-plan.html (archived at https://perma.cc/983W-5T8U)

Unilever Partner Zone (2013) Unilever's sustainable living plan helps cut cost and drive growth, *The Guardian*, 22 April, www.theguardian.com/sustainable-business/unilever-sustainable-living-plan-growth (archived at https://perma.cc/HF6L-YHDX)

INDEX

The main index is filed in alphabetical, word-by-word order. Acronyms are filed as presented. Numbers are filed as spelt out, with exception of rendanheyi series, which are filed in chronological order. Locators in italics denote information within a figure.

CPSIA information can be obtained
at www.ICGtesting.com
Printed in the USA
LVHW071115251121
704387LV00001B/1